Horizons of Assent

ALAN WILDE

HORIZONS OF ASSENT

 Modernism, Postmodernism,
and the Ironic Imagination

UNIVERSITY OF PENNSYLVANIA PRESS

PHILADELPHIA

First published in 1981 by The Johns Hopkins University Press
with the generous assistance of the
Andrew W. Mellon Foundation.

Library of Congress Cataloguing-in-Publication Data

Wilde, Alan.
    Horizons of assent.

    Bibliography: p.
    Includes index.
    1. Irony in literature.   2. Literature, Modern—20th
century—History and criticism.   3. Literature—
Aesthetics.   I. Title.
PN56.I65W54 1987   809'.91   87-6042
ISBN 0-8122-1248-7

for Ellen and Phil Kimbel
and for Bill Kirby

 CONTENTS

PREFACE TO THE PAPERBACK EDITION

Wordsworth notwithstanding, the five years since *Horizons of Assent* was first published seem to have passed with remarkable speed, which may explain why, if I were writing the book today, I would (for better or for worse) make few substantial changes. On the other hand, I would certainly adjust some of its emphases, beginning with the relation between the two major subjects it engages: irony and the dominant literary movements of the twentieth century. I noted at the time that in speaking about irony I meant my classifications and designations to be seen as expendable, as means to a larger end. No doubt partly because of my focus on irony in the book's introduction and partly because of my Adamic penchant for supplying names to describe its various forms and subforms, many critics fastened on this taxonomic aspect of the book and overlooked my intended use of irony as a heuristic tool in an examination of this century's literature. In saying this I don't mean at all to disclaim an interest in irony and the ironic, I mean even less to abandon my claim that irony needs to be understood not merely as a technique in the service of satire but, particularly in the last hundred years or more, as a vision in its own right: a special way of apprehending a world perceived, in one way or another, to lack unity and cohesion. What I do want to suggest is that, given the chance, I would want to put in the foreground questions about modernism and postmodernism; to these questions, I still think, transformations in the ironic imagination provide the most useful keys.

As for the literary historical and the critical concerns of the book, if I were reconsidering these, I would most likely leave as they are my discussions of early and late modernism but would attempt to recontextualize some of my conclusions about postmodernism—as I have, in fact, in a more recent work called *Middle Grounds: Studies in Contemporary American Fiction.* Here again, it seems to me that what is at issue are matters of emphasis. In the intervening years postmodernism has, as I see it, not so much changed its nature as established its claims. It has, in other words, and despite some critics who continue to regard it as a wrinkle in the larger fabric of modernism, attained the status and respectability of an independent movement (as independent as any movement can be). Indeed, as several recent studies indicate (I am thinking of books like Jean-François Lyotard's *The Postmodern Condition: A Report on Knowledge,* Hal Foster's collection *The Anti-Aesthetic: Essays on Postmodern Culture,* and, to a degree, Charles Newman's *The Post-Modern Aura),* the term has been stretched to include painting, sculpture, architecture, feminism, communications, and even, according to one speaker at the 1986 MLA convention, medicine. In short, critics both here and abroad have embraced the word postmodernism as their preferred way of designating various, perhaps most, of today's innovative attitudes, arts, artifacts, and technologies. Whether as a result it has lost some of its edge, or whether it will come in time to have some of modernism's amplitude and resonance, remains to be seen.

In any case, as a way of characterizing literature and, particularly, fiction, the term seems at last to have won out over several competing and plausible designations, among them fabulation, post-contemporary fiction, postrealist fiction, and surfiction—it seems even, for some critics, to have become a synonym for "contemporary." But to find the word useful and usable is not to deny that, to a remarkable degree, it remains overdetermined. And for good reasons. The problem of "canon formation" currently concerns critics of all centuries, periods, and movements. That concern becomes crucial when the subject is contemporary literature, where writers (and their critics) are intent not on maintaining but on establishing claims both of inclusion and of relative eminence. (I recall the outrage of one critic who objected to my choice of Barthelme instead of Pynchon as my representative postmodern figure and of another who, having announced that he would never again read Barthelme or Coover, invoked the name of the Sicilian novelist Sciascia as his own preferred alternative. Pynchon and others, but not Sciascia, figure prominently in *Middle Grounds.*) I suppose that most teachers of courses in postmodern fiction would regard as "canonical" works by Barth, Barthelme, and Pynchon, and would include some works (which ones is less clear) by each, but even that is not absolutely certain; one would, in any case, be hard put to predict the further selections that went to make up this or that syllabus.

The point I'm arguing can perhaps be best made by attending to the writers who are central to three recent and impressive critical works that devote themselves to postmodern or, at any rate, to nonrealistic contemporary fiction. Charles Caramello's *Silverless Mirrors* has chapters on Gass, Barth, Federman, and Gangemi; Larry McCaffery's *The Metafictional Muse* focuses on Coover, Barthelme, and Gass; and Patrick O'Donnell's *Passionate Doubts* considers Barth, Nabokov, Elkin, O'Connor, Hawkes, and Pynchon. The fact of two overlapping figures (Gass and Barth) pales beside the variety of figures who appear in only one of these books. And one could easily go on: Gass makes no appearance in John W. Aldridge's *The American Novel and the Way We Live Now;* Barth is absent from Richard Pearce's *The Novel in Motion;*

both (and everyone else so far mentioned, except for Barthelme) find no place in Jack Hicks's *In The Singer's Temple.*

My purpose in mentioning these various studies is not to quarrel with them but simply to draw the obvious conclusion that, in the absence of a fixed canon, critics of contemporary fiction inevitably lay claim to creating one by their choice of the authors they examine. Furthermore, in these choices (and exclusions) they establish as well their sense of the literary landscape: of how works cluster, or can be made to cluster, and of how they fall, or can be made to fall, into different or opposing camps. The conventional wisdom opposes postmodernism to realism, and, *grosso modo,* the contrast will serve. But as some critics have begun to recognize in the last five years, postmodernism is itself less monolithic—less exclusively metafictional and reflexive, less a literary illustration of poststructuralist theory—than it once seemed to be. My hope is that this book has played, and will continue to play, some role in this process of discrimination, and also, in the identification of those writers who, refusing the methods and assumptions of both self-referential and realistic fiction, seek instead, in and through the acts of definition that literary works comprise, to bring into effective being both themselves and the world they realize for us.

December 1986

 ACKNOWLEDGMENTS

I have found the writing of this book a good deal easier and more pleasant thanks to the encouragement and good counsel of many friends and colleagues; and it is with considerable pleasure that I set ironies of all kinds aside for the moment and acknowledge my debt to those—in particular Charles Altieri, Frederick P. W. McDowell, my colleagues Richard Kennedy, Philip Stevick, George Deaux, and Robert Buttel, and my student Frederick Orensky—who have helped me at one point or another to clarify some of the problems addressed in the following chapters or who have brought to my attention works that might otherwise have gone unnoticed. I am indebted as well to those graduate students who, in recent seminars, have responded so alertly, even passionately, to discussions of irony and ironic texts.

Degrees of gratitude are difficult to calibrate, but there are some friends with whom I have worked more closely still and to whom, at least in degree, I owe still more. I find it impossible to imagine a more intelligent, creative, or flexible reader than Marjorie Perloff. Her always perceptive, imaginative, and painstaking criticisms of my manuscript proved invaluable to me as I set about revising it. Jane Tompkins has been characteristically generous with her time and advice and as characteristically acute in her suggestions; and she has been in various ways instrumental in bringing this study into being. With Daniel O'Hara I have discussed for a number of years the philosophical problems that arise in any study of irony, and I have profited greatly from our conversations. My student and assistant Paul Hiles has helped incalculably and indefatigably with the mechanics involved in the preparation of the manuscript, and with more substantive issues besides. And, finally, my most profound thanks go to Jack Undank, who has read with as much intelligence and sensitivity as patience every word of my text not once but several times, and from whose wise and sympathetic suggestions I have benefited in ways it is hardly possible to acknowledge with any sense of adequacy.

The generous support of Temple University and the unfailing kindness and encouragement of William Sisler and Judith Stivelband of The Johns Hopkins University Press have enabled me to complete this book in the shape and at the time I had hoped for.

Of the chapters that appeared in various journals, all have been revised, and some of them, notably chapters 2, 3, and 6, have been substantially rewritten in part or in whole. I want to express my gratitude to the following journals (and to their editors) for permission to reprint the essays first published in their pages. Chapters 1 and 3 derive from "Modernism and the Aesthetics of Crisis," *Contemporary Literature*, Vol. 20, No. 1 (copyright 1979 by the Board of Regents of the University of Wisconsin System), pp. 13-50, and from "Language and Surface: Isherwood and The Thirties," *Contemporary Literature*, Vol. 16, No. 4 (copyright 1975 by the Board of Regents of the University of Wisconsin System), pp. 478-91. Substantial parts of chapter 2 appeared as "Depths and Surfaces: Dimensions of Forsterian Irony" in *English Literature in Transition*, Vol. 16, No. 4 (1973), pp. 257-74, and as "Desire and Consciousness: The 'Anironic' Forster" in *Novel: A Forum on Fiction*, Vol. 9, No. 2 (Winter 1976), pp. 114-29 (copyright Novel Corporation, 1976). I have, in addition, incorporated into the chapter small portions of an essay called "The Naturalisation of Eden," which first appeared in *E. M. Forster: A Human Exploration*, ed. G. K. Das and John Beer (London: Macmillan Press, 1979) (copyright Alan Wilde, 1979). Two chapters were published in *boundary 2* under the following titles (copyright *boundary 2*, 1976, 1980): "Barthelme Unfair to Kierkegaard: Some Thoughts on Modern and Postmodern Irony," Vol. 5, No. 1 (Fall 1976), pp. 45-70; "Surfacings: Reflections on the Epistemology of Late Modernism," Vol. 8, No. 2 (Winter, 1980), pp. 209-27.

 ABBREVIATIONS

Since the works from which I have quoted are, in general, after their first citation in the footnotes, referred to subsequently and parenthetically in the text, and since it has proved convenient to employ abbreviations for many of them, readers may find it helpful to have those abbreviations assembled in one place. I have indicated in parentheses the chapters and footnotes in which the works are initially cited and in which the reader will find bibliographical information about the editions used in this study.

Am   Donald Barthelme, *Amateurs* (5:22)
AN   E. M. Forster, *Aspects of the Novel* (2:4)
CB   Donald Barthelme, *Come Back, Dr. Caligari* (6:3)
CL   Donald Barthelme, *City Life* (6:3)
Dog   W. H. Auden and Christopher Isherwood, *The Dog Beneath the Skin* (3:15)
EA   Edward Mendelson, ed., *The English Auden: Poems, Essays and Dramatic Writings, 1927-1939* (Introduction:18)
G   Christopher Isherwood, *Goodbye to Berlin* (3:11)
GD   Donald Barthelme, *Great Days* (5:11)
GP   Donald Barthelme, *Guilty Pleasures* (6:3)
HE   E. M. Forster, *Howards End* (2:4)
I   D. C. Muecke, *Irony* (Introduction:7)
IPS   Cleanth Brooks, "Irony as a Principle of Structure" (1:10)
MPT   Cleanth Brooks, *Modern Poetry and the Tradition* (1:5)
N   Christopher Isherwood, *The Last of Mr. Norris* (3:11)
NAP   Murray Krieger, *The New Apologists for Poetry* (1:12)
OBB   William Gass, *On Being Blue* (4:21)
PhP   Maurice Merleau-Ponty, *Phenomenology of Perception* (1:21)
PI   E. M. Forster, *A Passage to India* (1:13)
PP   Maurice Merleau-Ponty, *The Primacy of Perception* (1:20)
S   Donald Barthelme, *Sadness* (6:3)
SW   Donald Barthelme, *Snow White* (6:3)
TC   E. M. Forster, *Two Cheers for Democracy* (1:15)
TD   Ronald Sukenick, "Thirteen Digressions" (Introduction:1)
TDF   Donald Barthelme, *The Dead Father* (1:1)
TGP   W. H. Auden and Christopher Isherwood, *Two Great Plays* (1:40)

TNF Joe David Bellamy, ed., *The New Fiction: Interviews with Innovative American Writers* (6:6)
TPF P. N. Furbank, "The Personality of E. M. Forster" (2:3)
UP Donald Barthelme, *Unspeakable Practices, Unnatural Acts* (6:3)
WWU Cleanth Brooks, *The Well Wrought Urn* (1:10)
WWW William Gass, *The World Within the Word* (5:25)

Horizons of Assent

 INTRODUCTION

The 1954 Fall Term had begun. . . . Again in the margins of library
books earnest freshmen inscribed such helpful glosses as "Description of Nature" or "Irony."
   —Vladimir Nabokov, *Pnin*

Irony has taken some hard knocks from critics lately, a victim in
particular of its association with modernist strategies and theories. The
reaction is understandable enough, given the urgent desire in recent years
to proclaim the emergence of a new sensibility—understandable even
when one recognizes that much of this animus originates with writers
who are themselves, however one defines the term, essentially ironic in
their attitudes and techniques.[1] When the mood is for manifestos and
declarations of independence, oedipal impulses typically direct themselves
against the central assumptions of the previous generation or, alternately,
thrust forward claims of radical historical discontinuity. But anyone
surveying recent literature (and, increasingly, criticism of it as well) is
unlikely to find reasons for either celebrating or mourning the death of
irony. Whether or not one agrees with Geoffrey Thurley, for example,
that "a preoccupation with irony and self-knowledge has secured a dis-
location of sensibility exactly the reverse of the synthesis Richards, Eliot
and Leavis intended to guarantee,"[2] the fact is that his argument works to
discredit not irony in general but what particular writers did with it. Of
course, irony has undergone significant transformations since Thurley's
"intellectualist critics" annexed it, but that is precisely the point. Somehow
irony manages again and again to escape its association with this or that
school and to recast itself constantly into new and unpredictable modes.
With all the resilience and tenacity of some allotropic element, it contrives
both to declare its flexibility, its openness to change, and to retain its
essential identity as a characteristic response to the polysemic world we
inhabit. This being the case, what we require today are not recriminations
against ancestral specters—the apparently still potent ghosts of irony

1

past—but, in this respect at least, a more neutral discrimination of ironies: a taxonomy of specific (but not rigidly exclusive) forms, which, even as they proliferate and continue to coexist in various states of imbalance, assert at some level their family resemblance.

These sketchy remarks on the problematics of irony and the methodological problems involved in undertaking an examination of its various shapes are obviously not offered, except in the most general way, as a description of the book's subject or as an anticipation of arguments that need to be conducted in the following chapters. On the other hand, in saying even this much I may already have restricted too narrowly and limited too severely the scope of this study, which, by intention at least, means to explore not simply the question of irony but a number of other and associated questions as well. To be sure, the concern with irony determines the book's perspective—and thus its choice of examples, its organization, and its omissions; but something more, and more ambitious, I want to suggest, is also at issue. And inevitably so; for in attempting to provide a way of understanding irony as a mode of consciousness, a perceptual response to a world without unity or cohesion and, still more, in attempting to specify the evolving forms of the ironic imagination in the twentieth century, one necessarily turns to the embodiment of that imagination in works of art (more specifically and most often, for my purposes, in literary works). And further—assuming that one rejects the notion, Neo-Kantian or structuralist, of irony as always and in all ways the same—to its embodiment in the historical configurations that, however raggedly and imperfectly, those novels, poems, and essays constitute. It follows, then, that to consider the various modes of irony in this century entails no less a consideration of the relations among the principal literary movements of approximately the last hundred years.

To intimate an analogical relation between irony and any of the various arts and movements in which it is manifest is not, however, to answer or even to address the question that lurks in the formulation, namely, where one locates the cause and where the effect of the phenomenon I'm proposing. In fact—and I had better make my position clear straightaway —the question seems to me both illegitimate and, to the degree that it presupposes the primacy either of the constituting imagination or of impersonal, determining factors external to man, misleading. The investigative procedures I have in mind come closer, allowing for a difference in context, to the "to-and-fro voyage" that defines the nature of Leo Spitzer's "philological circle"[3] and to the currently more popular notion of a hermeneutic circle.[4] In short, between the different kinds of irony I plan to examine and the movements that both generate and are generated by these various ironies the relation is, to borrow Robert R. Magliola's handy phrase, one of "mutual implication."[5] And so too between the forms of irony and the striking dimensional shifts—the intertwining, as the titles of the book's three parts suggest, of the concepts of depth and surface—that express in yet another way the perpetual, dynamic re-creations of the ironic imagination. To observe the dominance and, eventually, the undermining of modernism's characteristically vertical orderings of disconnection; to recognize the confused and contradictory allegiance of late modernism to both depth and surface; and to discover, in some exemplary cases at least, postmodernism's reconstitution of a new, horizontal depth: a "surface," as John Ashbery writes, " . . . that is not superficial but a visible core"[6]—to do all this is to become aware of one further analogue to the changes in irony itself and, again, to acknowledge the reciprocal influences among the problems explored in this study. In another sense, then, I'm offering not one but a variety of perspectives, which are intended to be seen as coordinate and mutually reinforcing. But for rhetorical purposes at least, irony remains *primus inter pares*, its morphological transformations serving as the major clue on the one hand to the implications (literary, psychological, and ethical) of the metaphors of depth and surface and, on the other, to the undoubted fact of change in the literary sensibility of the twentieth century and in the nature of the literary works it has produced.

My vocabulary and various of my concepts will already have suggested that my position is—although only roughly and in a totally undoctrinaire way—phenomenological; but of that more in a while. For the moment, I want simply to indicate that in attempting a discrimination of twentieth-century ironies I have tried to eschew the traditional, "objective," and static categories ("Impersonal Irony," "Self-disparaging Irony," "*Ingénu* Irony," "Dramatized Irony," to quote four chapter headings from D. C. Muecke's largely admirable book, *The Compass of Irony*)[7] by means of which critics tend to approach the subject and have attempted instead to arrive at more flexible and considerably fewer categories of my own. I can hardly claim, since the example of Kierkegaard, above all, inevitably casts its shadow, to be the first to treat irony as a mode of consciousness, an all-encompassing vision of life; but the tendency of most critics is still, I believe, to regard irony as little more than a series of techniques and strategies (which, in a secondary, derivative sense, it of course continues to be). The tendency is most apparent perhaps in Wayne C. Booth's *A Rhetoric of Irony*,[8] a book that is in many ways more a defense of civility than a study of irony. But to the degree that it is the latter, its focus is precisely on irony as technique and, in addition, on those ironies that are, as Booth says, stable: that is, intended, covert, and finite. Not surprisingly, the least satisfactory part of the book is the one that, in moving toward the present, attempts to wrestle with but only succeeds in taming what are called "Instabilities." Muecke comes closer in his two books to dealing with irony as a way of imagining the world, though he perpetuates (and no doubt more thoroughly than he intends) the usual opposition between irony as technique and as vision. As I've already suggested, Muecke seems to me to remain too complacently in thrall to many of the standard and by now unhelpful methods of rationalizing the protean and elusive nature of irony, which has perhaps become more obvious, thanks to the burgeoning of postmodern literature and the criticism it has provoked, in the years since the appearance of his books. In any case, the major flaw, the chief limitation, of his work locates itself elsewhere—specifically in his fundamental habit of defining irony essentially as a contrast between reality and appearance: a division that all too easily assumes and perpetuates a separation between consciousness and the world of which it is inevitably part.

So much, at present, for Booth and Muecke, to whom I'll return in a subsequent chapter. For the same reason, I plan to disregard for now both Kierkegaard and Cleanth Brooks, although *The Concept of Irony* "hovers" (to borrow and bend to my own purposes one of the more suggestive of that book's metaphors) over much of what follows, while Brooks's works, which remain an admirably lucid and comprehensive statement of the New Critical position, are considered more appropriately in connection with the larger question of modernism. It is not, in any case, my intention to survey the voluminous critical literature that deals with the subject of irony; but some studies, either because they have contributed to my own formulations (no less valuably if only by provoking negative reactions) or because they epitomize current attitudes, ought to be mentioned. To begin with the least controversial of these works: Norman Knox's *The Word Irony and Its Context, 1500-1755*, a superb historical survey that stops, as its title says, in the middle of the eighteenth century, would seem to be irrelevant to my immediate purposes. In fact, Knox's conclusion that throughout the period he deals with, irony is "most often a tool of satire or ridicule"[9] provides (the interval of a century and a half notwithstanding) the basis for defining the first of the ironic modes I want shortly to propose—the point being that, just as the more recent ironies that are the major subject of this study can be seen to rise in the eighteenth and to gather force in the nineteenth century,[10] so satire, however diminished or attentuated its impact, continues on, in the face of the collapse of widespread norms, certainly into the early years of the twentieth century and even to the present, thereby establishing the standard form, so to speak, from which later ironies are, as one likes, a development or a deviation.

For Thurley, as the comment I quoted earlier indicates, they are clearly a deviation; and *The Ironic Harvest*, a brilliant and provocative book in its own (unmistakably English and oddly parochial) way, is intent primarily on reestablishing what he takes to be the true tradition of English poetry. Hayden White's concerns are very different ones, and *Metahistory* is a far more ambitious and compendious undertaking; but the book yields nothing to Thurley's in its anti-ironic asperities. Indeed, and perhaps because irony is at the moment both more prevalent and more innovative on this side of the Atlantic—as it is, in different ways, on the other side of the Channel—White's indictments are, if anything, more comprehensive and more all-encompassing still. But before coming directly to these indictments, it should probably be noted that *Metahistory*, as White freely acknowledges, is heavily indebted to Northrop Frye's *Anatomy of Criticism* and particularly to Frye's cyclical theory of modes, archetypes, and so on. On the other hand, if *Metahistory* is fully as schematic as Frye's *Anatomy*, it is by no means as disinterested in its application of the theory—a fact that, ironically enough, appears to undermine Frye's belief that since "our five modes evidently go around in a circle," irony was, even as he elaborated his position in 1957, moving "steadily towards myth."[11] In other words, the nature and development of postmodern irony both belie Frye's deterministic theory and explain White's more rancorous attempt, in his "value neutral and purely Formalist" study, to bring about "a rejection of Irony itself."[*][12] Irony, in short, is alive though hardly, in White's view, well, since its mode is purely and simply *"negational"* (p. 34).

Metahistory manifests, then, despite its putative allegiance to cyclical theories, both a less sanguine belief in the necessary supersession of irony and a more active desire to set history, historiography, and, in a broader sense, culture in general on their proper path. Frye's *"sparagmos, or the sense that heroism and effective action are absent, disorganized or fore-doomed to defeat, and that confusion and anarchy reign over the world"* (p. 192; the passage is one that White quotes) becomes, one feels, less "the archetypal theme of irony and satire" than, as White sees it, an accurate description of things as they currently are; and it is difficult not to detect in his tirades a troubled awareness of recent, as well as of older, developments in linguistic philosophy. So, in one of the central statements of his position, he maintains that "the trope of Irony . . . provides a linguistic paradigm of a mode of thought which is radically self-critical with respect not only to a given characterization of the world of experience but also to the very effort to capture adequately the truth of things in language. It is, in short, a model of the linguistic protocol in

---

*It is only fair to note that White himself acknowledges and attempts to justify this inconsistency: "I do not deny that the Formalism of my approach to the history of historical thought itself reflects the Ironic condition from within which most of modern academic historiography is generated. But I maintain that the recognition of this Ironic perspective provides the grounds for a transcèndence of it" (p. 434).

which skepticism in thought and relativism in ethics are conventionally expressed" (pp. 37-38). And what follows soon thereafter is even more to the point: "In its apprehension of the essential folly or absurdity of the human condition, [Irony] tends to engender belief in the 'madness' of civilization itself and to inspire a Mandarin-like disdain for those seeking to grasp the nature of social reality in either science or art" (p. 38).

The suggestiveness of White's remarks can be judged by the examples (not necessarily the ones White himself would supply) they inevitably and immediately conjure up, which seem to validate the substance of his argument. The reflexiveness of so much recent literature, the critical quarrels over mimesis and referentiality, the arbitrariness of signs, and the by-now depressingly familiar prison-house of language—to choose instances almost at random—all serve to confirm the magisterial gloominess of his beliefs. And if I have dwelt at such length on *Metahistory*, it is because the book's arguments seem to me to describe accurately the condition of much contemporary irony. But not of *all*. My quarrel with White, of which the rejection of his (and Frye's) cyclical theories is part, centers on what seems to me the unshaded absoluteness of his position: the inability to recognize the potential for affirmation within even the most self-conscious of ironies and to see that, in this respect as in others, the disunities of irony suggest not only the world's absurdity but, whether through language, action, or gesture, the creative and redemptive forces of consciousness as well. The need may be, then, not to transcend irony but to accept it, while at the same time generating from its sense of fracture a more modest and perhaps more attainable view than White's of both "truth" and "possibility." In short, faced with such overwhelming conceptions of development as those put forth in *Metahistory* and Frye's *Anatomy*, one is tempted to affirm, without either complacency or despair, an ideal of what, for the moment, I want simply to call "the unfinished."

Which is not, however, to embrace uncritically such currently fashionable notions as absence and play, which one associates with the theoretical defenders of irony, who are, perhaps, its most avid practitioners as well. I can hardly attempt here even the most cursory survey of the various approaches that are conflated in the awesome name of Deconstruction, but some note needs to be taken of that "school," most of whose members touch on and sometimes overwhelm the problem of irony, bringing to it various degrees of illumination or obscurity. No doubt, Derrida's is the name most readily associated with the methodologies of Deconstruction, and Daniel O'Hara, in an essay on *Of Grammatology*, has nicely related irony, defined as "the power to entertain widely divergent possible interpretations—to provoke the reader into seeing that there is a radical uncertainty surrounding the processes by which meanings get determined in texts and interpreted by readers," to the entire Derridean enterprise, which is, as O'Hara says, a "method for making problematical the entire question of 'reading'"[13] Nevertheless, I want to focus instead and briefly on what are arguably the still more extreme ideas of Paul de Man, which must do duty here for all the displacements and duplicities, deferrals and "differances," decenterings and aporias hectically swirling around the academic marketplace as I write.[14] Developing Friedrich Schlegel's concept of parabasis ("A sudden revelation of the discontinuity between two rhetorical codes"),[15] de Man offers a definition of irony as "the permanent parabasis of an allegory (of figure)" and then proceeds to the closing statements of *Allegories of Reading*: "Irony is no longer a trope but the undoing of the deconstructive allegory of all tropological cognitions, the systematic undoing, in other words, of understanding. As such, far from closing off the tropological system, irony enforces the repetition of its aberration" (p. 301). No one, I imagine, will accuse this formulation of pandering to a taste for simplicity, and some explanations are clearly in order. To begin with, it is apparently the case that for de Man interruption is encoded in any and all texts. It follows that texts are subversive and the process of reading interruptive; and thus irony becomes the continual explosion of resolution, the undermining of an always promised but never achieved closure. The emphasis on discontinuity (the juxtapositions and successivities that, for de Man, relocate themselves in a landscape or mirage of discourse) is obviously useful as a reechoing of the vision long since articulated by most of the major modernist texts, just as the repeated stress on the lack of closure contributes to an understanding of the quality of postmodern irony. But in the light of White's strictures and de Man's own linguistic emphasis, it is hard to avoid once again the sense, which emanates from so much deconstructive criticism, that writers are being relegated or indeed forced to smother in the folds of language, while their works are scanned and undermined by the ironic—in Derrida's case, playful—surveillance of a relentlessly hygienic philosophical intelligence. Not since the epistemological crises of the eighteenth century—a century that not too paradoxically haunts this intelligence—have so many theoreticians absorbed, displaced, and rewritten a vast cultural anxiety, its symptoms earlier or simultaneously embodied in far messier authors, whose practices fortunately struggle beyond and transform the limits they ought, according to the theoreticians, logically to have observed.

Little is to be gained, I think, by indefinitely prolonging this catalogue of irony's opponents and proponents; but it may be useful to pause over one last book, Jonathan Culler's admirably intelligent *Flaubert: The Uses of Uncertainty*, which seems to me largely to avoid the different dangers exemplified by these two groups of critics. Working from a context that gives special importance to the question of interpretative procedures, Culler manages both to do justice to the linguistic concerns of the deconstructionists and to avoid something of their reflexive, claustrophobic approach. The reader's desire for closure becomes, for example, less a matter of impossibility than a diminishing of the richness of the text: "On the one hand [irony] . . . strikes indirectly at the general process of organizing the world in relation to oneself so as to make sense of it. . . . But on the other hand . . . many of the delights come from the call to interpretation that it issues."[16] Those delights do not, however, if I'm reading the book correctly, exclude the reader's experience of the world (though increasingly in Flaubert's fiction they confound it); and so Culler contrives, more than some of his mentors, to discover in irony both "affirming and negating qualities" (p. 25), even as he makes (far more than Booth, for example) the reading process extraordinarily problematic and self-conscious and irony itself, rightly, I believe, a more complex and indeterminate affair—a matter, for the reader, of "vertiginous uncertainties" (p. 194).

That these uncertainties are neither purely "negational" (White's word) nor limited to the enclosed and enclosing space of the text is exactly what I hope to imply by my approach. If the Revolution of 1848 had never taken place and if, at the very moment of its eruption in Paris, Frédéric Moreau and Rosanette had never visited Fontainebleau or its neighboring towns, forests, and primordial quarries, fleeing political, artistic, and natural realities and illusions, "fuyant le vertige, presque effrayés,"[17] Culler's readers would not have *their* dizzy or hallucinatory delights. The vortices, the circular, spinning figures of Flaubert's texts also provide an allegory of his narrators' and his own self-conscious and premonitory journeys, their *errance* between life and art (or within these) and between negation and affirmation. Neither these analogies nor the specificities of Flaubert's irony would be possible without the "mutual implication" of a particular consciousness and its partly given, partly restructured world—Flaubert's, to begin with, but then, repercussively, his narrators', characters', and readers'. This implication and interanimation give rise to texts and historic movements, as texts and history give rise to further, renewed, and deviant implications.

The phenomenon of negativity is never, in any case, pure and opaque shadow but a result of the obliging, evolving modes and substance of a darkness gathering, taking shape reactively, about a concealed and contrary lambency or effulgence. As far as modernism is concerned, the notion of negation is best registered as a powerful, self-defensive response, a movement of withdrawal from those personal and external disjunctions that an increasing number of contemporary writers, if hardly their critical counterparts, seem intent on reversing. Fifty years after the fact, Auden's "ironic points of light" supply, in their skeptical yet hopeful call for "an affirming flame"[18] a curiously apposite comment on, variously, the larger hopes of modernism, the revealingly divided aims of the decade before the Second World War, and the more restricted or at least more restrained aspirations of our own age. It would appear to be time to examine—not beneath the wide, conjectural sky of human destiny, its clouds merely repetitious or racing with teleological fury, nor within the irresistible, transhistoric waves of language and trope—those forms of irony through which certain writers and movements of this century constitute their specific presence and meanings. To subsume this formulation to the terms of a long-standing debate: structures of mind and art have their definable histories, their *langue* and their *parole*—in this case, their ironies and ironic transformations, whose suggestive, tentative forms history or criticism does better to describe contextually than to overhomogenize and (however disguised the effort may be as a cool epistemological critique of Truth in utterance) polemically to dismantle.

· · ·

The impossibly perfect, that is, the linguistically innocent, book (already a contradiction) devoted to irony would be one without categories—and perhaps without that first, inherited taint, agent, and category, the word *irony* itself. This, I hasten to add, is not that book. But the classifications and designations it employs are, unlike Adam's, expendable: an ad hoc shorthand deliberately "inadequate" in the idealistic, philosophical sense. They are intended to enjoy a strictly performative function as discriminating and temporary instruments of what Bergson called "l'auscultation intellectuelle," a "truly empirical" sounding of the movements and sinuosities within the concrete appearances of single or grouped phenomena. Summarily, then, and in anticipation of later elaboration, I would propose the following divisions, which, once they have done their work, may be allowed either to wither away or, at most, to render in a continuing debate further exploratory service. One: *mediate irony*, which I've already alluded to in my discussion of Knox's book (irony at this stage serves to mediate a fundamentally satiric vision), imagines a world lapsed from a recoverable (and in the twentieth century, generally a primitivist) norm. Man's state is, in the root meaning of the word, and not in Empson's more diffuse application of it, *[19] ambiguous: like Adam and Eve after the Fall—that event to which all students of irony eventually recur to exemplify the world's disunity, the world seen *sub specie ironiae*

---

*Empson defines ambiguity as "any verbal nuance, however slight, which gives room for alternative reactions to the same piece of language" (p. 3). Empson's concern is to reveal complexity, and one recognizes in his work the typically modernist desire to demonstrate the tensions within unity.

—human beings wander about, hoping to regain paradise. ("They hand in hand with wand'ring steps and slow, / Through *Eden* took thir solitary way," as the final lines of *Paradise Lost* announce.) The ideal, in other words, is one of recovery, an ideal of harmony, integration, and coherence. Or, alternatively, as E. M. Forster's Mr. Emerson proclaims, paradise may be seen as "really yet to come"*[20]—a reward for those capable of recognizing and correcting (to choose another word that derives from the sense of wandering) the *error* of their ways. In either case, the possibility of recuperation, of mending the fracture, persists, and with it, the dream—moral, psychological, or interpersonal—of wholeness. Two: by contrast, *disjunctive irony* (the characteristic form of modernism) strives, however reluctantly, toward a condition of paradox. The ironist, far more basically adrift, confronts a world that appears inherently disconnected and fragmented. At its extreme or "absolute" point, that stage of its development which will be my primary concern in what follows, disjunctive irony both recognizes the disconnections and seeks to control them (control being, though not quite as Sukenick defines it, one of the chief imperatives of the modernist imagination); and so the confusions of the world are shaped into an equal poise of opposites: the form of an unresolvable paradox, like that illustrated and enacted by Virginia Woolf's Sasha Latham, when, standing in Clarissa Dalloway's garden and viewing it simultaneously or in rapid succession as irradiated by a "cloud of gold" and as subdued to "prosaic daylight," she asks herself helplessly "which view is the true one?"[21] Inevitably, works of disjunctive and more particularly of absolute irony achieve not resolution but closure—an aesthetic closure that substitutes for the notion of paradise regained an image (Yeats's "Translunar Paradise,"[22] for example) of a paradise fashioned by man himself. Three: finally, *suspensive irony* (which I connect with postmodernism), with its yet more radical vision of multiplicity, randomness, contingency, and even absurdity, abandons the quest for paradise altogether—the world in all its disorder is simply (or not so simply) accepted. "With a true sense of the randomness of life's moments," to quote Jerzy Kosinski, "man is at peace with himself—and that peace is happiness."[23] Ambiguity and paradox give way to quandary, to a low-keyed engagement with a world of perplexities and uncertainties, in which one can hope, at best, to achieve what Forster calls "the smaller pleasures of life" and Stanley Elkin, its "small satisfactions."[24]

*So as to avoid a confusing multiplication of terms in this introduction, I want simply to mention in passing a matter of some importance, reserving fuller discussion for later chapters. Briefly, then, my various references to or suggestions of an ideal that modifies irony or that irony calls into being are meant to imply a category of what I shall speak of as the *anironic*: the complementary vision that accompanies irony in each of its forms and that includes, most notably, the "assent" of my title.

The development is, then, in a manner of speaking, from Forster's passionately uttered "Only connect . . ." to Ashbery's far more casual "connexion," which "connects up, / Not *to* anything, but kind of like / Closing the ranks so as to leave them open."[25] I should say, however, that in tracing this development, my intention has not been to give equal emphasis to each of its stages. Mediate irony, about which much has been written under other names, is essentially a premodernist phenomenon; and though its impact will be felt throughout—as a point of departure, a touchstone, or a presence in the background—it hasn't seemed necessary to me to devote a separate chapter to it. The focus is instead on disjunctive and suspensive irony; and the three parts of this work deal in turn with their defining features and, allowing for the fact that no simple temporal divisions are possible or desirable, with their relation to modernist, late modernist, and postmodern literature.

There are other reasons, besides the desire to show the evolution of specific ironic modes in this century and despite the danger I've noted of appearing too schematic, for my adoption of a tripartite organization. But I can best suggest these by developing a bit further the nature of the book's plan. Each of the sections begins with a comprehensive chapter on the movement in question and is followed by a more particular study of a single author: Forster, Ivy Compton-Burnett, and Donald Barthelme. The choice of these authors is altogether deliberate, although I recognize that the juxtaposition of the three may seem at first sight unusual, if not downright bizarre. But the diversity among them, along with, in each case, their special representativeness, is exactly the point. Forster, whose fiction is, as compared with the work of the other two, certainly the most traditional but whose novels show at the same time the most consistent development, serves as my example in the first section because his career (including the posthumous novel and stories) seems to me to illustrate better than that of any other major modernist the progression through and the interweaving of all the various forms irony assumes in the twentieth century. Compton-Burnett, on the other hand, figures in the second section precisely because her eminently eccentric status helps to sustain my argument about the existence and ethos of late modernism as a genuine, if not completely determinate, interlude or space of transition between its more famous predecessor and successor. And the final section, moving into territory still unexplored or, at any rate, largely uncharted, takes Barthelme as its exemplary figure not because, as in Forster's case, he illustrates sequential stages of twentieth-century irony but because his work holds simultaneously in suspension, as no other contemporary writer's does, the congeries of usually divergent impulses critics tend conveniently and perhaps too facilely to lump together under the label of postmodernism.

In a larger sense, the kinds of decisions at work in my selection of these three authors underlie as well the nature of the more general chapters and, still more broadly, the concatenation of the book's three parts. My aim, in other words, has been not to provide an exhaustive and seamless history of irony or of literary movements but to offer suggestive paradigms and embodiments of their major, shifting, and mutually defining forms. My choices have had their consequences of course and require a few words of explanation. Modernism, to begin there, remains the most significant and international of this century's movements—a judgment that few, I think, would want to dispute—and in selecting figures to illustrate its connection with irony, I have repeatedly faced the need to set limits to the abundant possibilities that inevitably present themselves. Every reader of this book will, I expect, regret or resent the absence of his or her favorite ironist from among the ranks of those discussed. The regret is as comprehensible as it is predictable; and I can only assert my belief that for the purposes of defining disjunctive irony it is, by and large, most useful to concentrate on British literature (as, arguably, the most revelatory of its characteristic features); and, in addition, to focus —so as to catch it at its moment of maximum crisis and achievement, its stage of simultaneous triumph and obsolescence—on what is, admittedly, an already advanced stage of the high (or, as I shall come to call it in the middle section of this book, the early) modernist enterprise.

That decision once made, it seemed natural enough, considering the vexed and peculiar relations between such writers as Eliot and Auden or Forster and Isherwood, to take England in and around the thirties as the locus for a discussion of late modernism: a category or movement whose validity and whose features I want especially to establish and argue for. But the switch in the third part of the book to American literature is bound to appear more problematic. Why at this point, it might legitimately be asked, cut the thread that has so far stitched together writers of a single tradition? There are, in fact, several answers that, given the nature of my intention, follow as a matter of course. First of all and to put the matter baldly, postmodernism is essentially an American affair;[26] and one would be hard put (especially if, as I do, one regards Beckett as a modernist figure) to discover relevant examples in England today, where writers, when they are not, like Thurley, calling for a return to a native tradition or working in traditional forms of realism, seem intent primarily on continuing to work out the lessons of modernism.[27] But there is more to it than that. As it transforms itself yet once again in contemporary America, irony paradoxically continues the inexorable process of change I've insisted upon from the beginning. In any case, it may help to mitigate the apparent precipitousness of my transatlantic leap if I invoke here the shift in the axis of the art world earlier in this century from Paris to New

York. I doubt that many critics, when discussing Jackson Pollock, say, feel the need to summon up the Ashcan School or to apologize for a comparable transatlantic movement of attention from postimpressionism or surrealism to abstract expressionism. And with good reason: as American painters of a generation back looked to Paris, or easily conferred and collaborated with exiled Europeans in their midst, so contemporary American writers turned at the start of their careers to England and the Continent, cutting their literary teeth (in John Barth's recent phrase),[28] that is, defining their positions and innovations not, for the most part, in terms of their immediate national predecessors but with reference to the example of writers like Eliot and Joyce.

The question of influence must be demonstrated later on. For now, and by way of synthesizing the principal themes I've so far been stressing, it is tempting to turn to symbolic account this transgressing of national boundaries simply by noting that what obtains here applies more generally to the nature of irony itself, which—far from describing regular cycles (and unless one regards it in such general or archetypal terms as to deprive it of all its historical and existential specificity: the successive incarnations that make concrete what otherwise remains merely a vague and insubstantial abstraction)—is in every way a violation of fixities: modal, temporal, psychological, and, in this case, geographic. And indeed, the transgressing of limits is as unavoidable as it is unforeseeable, for irony, confounding all attempts to secure its essence in perdurable shapes or patterns, demands to be viewed, not as a reaction to a world that is everywhere and always the same, but as the articulation of man's situation at a particular time and in a particular place. Not, it goes without saying, every man's: I want to avoid suggesting, in an excess of enthusiasm for my subject, that all literature is ironic and all writers ironists. On the other hand, it is certainly the case that in the twentieth century the ironic vision of life so overwhelms the arts that by now we perhaps take for granted its almost ubiquitous presence. How to make vivid that presence in all its variations is, as I see it, the critic's job at present; and to accomplish it what is required is the awareness of the always changing horizon that determines and defines, in its interactivity with consciousness, the nature of man's perception of his world and, through his evasion or confirmation of that perception, his dealings with it.

·   ·   ·

The reference to "horizons" just now and in my title is meant, among other things, to acknowledge a debt to the writings of Maurice Merleau-Ponty and particularly to the belief that, as one of his recent critics puts it, "le monde est inachevé; car le sujet percevant, toujours situé, n'a jamais qu'une vue partielle du monde" and, further, that "l'homme, lui aussi, *est inachevé* tant que l'histoire n'est pas arrivée à son terme."[29] The sense of a fluid and shifting horizon, of a world outside the self that both impinges on consciousness and is in some way determined by it, has, to start with that, helped to confirm my conception of irony neither as a fixed tropological device nor as a static way of apprehending the world but rather as a mode of consciousness variably responsive to changes in man's ongoing, necessarily creative history. My debt, however, here and elsewhere, is more occasional and informal than systematic: a matter of appropriating from Merleau-Ponty's work a scattering of ideas and insights that do not, as I make use of them, pretend to represent a comprehensive and sustained philosophy or methodology. (Readers expecting an orthodox phenomenological study will do well to prepare themselves for any number of impurities, even heresies.) The faith in the primacy of perception, for example, which is manifestly central to the whole of Merleau-Ponty's philosophical undertaking, makes possible and plausible the sense of irony not only as a way of perceiving the word but, more fundamentally, as an instinctive, untutored, and, as it were, a gestural seizing of the world, which simultaneously makes an unavoidable claim on human beings as so many consciousnesses incarnated in it. At the same time, the desire to engender or generate the world, or rather *a* world, implies as well the inevitability of moving beyond the level of perception, since, as Merleau-Ponty writes: "However firm my perceptive grasp of the world may be, it is entirely dependent upon a centrifugal movement which throws me toward the world."[30]

We are *thrown*, then (and it is worth noting, as an index to Merleau-Ponty's thought, the characteristic activity, even violence, of his verbs), toward ever more sophisticated articulations of the original perceptual encounter. The relevance of these beliefs to the understanding of language and works of art is clear enough, since, in these post-New Critical times, we manifestly and increasingly look at a novel or a poem, even a painting, not simply as the resolution of maximal tensions or as a perfection of structure but, instead, as an interwoven and tensive structure of beliefs, which may (but also may not) resolve themselves into an aesthetic whole but which, in any case, reveal the sign of their author's connection with being: the emblem of an intentional relation to the world. It follows that, if one is to understand fully the extent and intensity of irony in this century and to recognize its pervasive, incremental vision of disunity, it becomes necessary to search out beneath the calculated resolutions and, more recently, the no less calculated irresolutions that conceptualize and give aesthetic form to modernist and contemporary works of literature the more radical traces of the originary, preconceptual, prelinguistic encounters—those ineffaceable emblems that persist partly in covert presuppositions (thematized, for example, at the level of character conflict and plot development) or in obsessive images worked into the texture of novels and poems but, still more, and more tellingly perhaps, in the less obvious technical devices that do not so much shape the works in which they appear as betray their gaps and interstices: the silences Merleau-Ponty habitually discovers amid "the prose of the world."

All that I've so far said presupposes a more fundamental indebtedness to Merleau-Ponty's point of departure: the rejection of dualistic thinking that he shares with other phenomenologists and that proposes, to quote Descombes again, not "une synthèse qui réconcilierait les deux points de vue" but "une synthèse 'finie', c'est-à-dire inachevée et précaire" (p. 72). We return here to the concept of the unfinished, the incomplete, and thus to the notion of process and creativity. But more to the immediate point is the light that Merleau-Ponty, along with Husserl, Heidegger, and others, sheds on the crisis point of modernism, namely, the omnipresent separation of self and world, which needs to be seen more accurately as the burden of subjectivity—the idealist tendency, so apparent, for example, in Woolf's stories, which conceives of the world as something to be acted upon, to be transformed (or not, as happens in moments of doubt or fear or exaggerated self-awareness) by consciousness alone. The self, in other words, whether or not intentionally, endows the world with all of its value and meaning; and it is the enormity of the task imposed upon it that accounts for the various modernist evasions and failures—the familiar movement toward a transcendence of phenomenal experience, or the aestheticizing of it, or, again, the paralyzing awareness of life as so many unbridgeable chasms—that lead inexorably to modernism's collapse.

On the other hand, Merleau-Ponty's effort to restore or recover the being of the world* suggests the attempt, ambiguously foreshadowed in late modernism, of some postmodernists at least to exchange for the role of the modernist spectator that of the more active participant. That participation—or the desire to achieve it—leads in turn to the other half of my title: to the idea or ideal of assent†, and to the direction in which I see this study tending. In short, the characteristic movement of ironic art in this century describes a double and seemingly contradictory progression, which, on the one hand, recognizes the increasing disintegration of an already disjunct world and, on the other, not only submits but

---

*Even if, as Descombes holds, the enterprise is to be seen finally as an "idéalisme *réformé*, mais non *surmonté*" (p. 88).

†I have chosen the word *assent* deliberately to suggest a response that partakes of neither the passivity of acquiescence nor, quite, the forcefulness of assertion. Once again, it is helpful to recur to the Latin root of the word. *Sentire* can mean, variously, to feel, to perceive, to experience, and so on. More specifically, *assentari* is a frequentative verb derived from *assentire*: "to join in feeling," which expresses precisely the notion I want to convey.

(again in some cases) assents to it, or to its inherent possibilities. The gesture of assent is, to be sure, considerably more tentative and provisional than those large-scale attempts on the part of the early modernists in particular to resolve and connect the antinomies of their world. But that is the crux of the matter. Twentieth-century irony simultaneously and progressively calls into question the possibilities of order and, coming to accept the inescapability of a world that is necessarily unfinished, achieves at times a kind of accommodation with that world and—since we witness here a rejection of modernism's dualisms—with the self. Assent becomes, then, the creation of value not in place of but *within* the *Lebenswelt*, the world that offers itself not simply as a heap of broken images—the detritus of outworn ages—but, for all its multitudinousness, as the locus of a potential inviting its activation. All of which is not to suggest a meliorative view either of man or of his art or, indeed, of irony over the last hundred years—and still less to intimate the superiority of recent over modernist art—but simply to acknowledge what has always been true: that in the indeterminacy of man's horizon the beginnings of new adjustments of consciousness effloresce.

Between Kierkegaard's image of the hovering ironist, gazing down upon an existence from which he at least supposes himself to have escaped, and Heidegger's *Dasein*, looking outward toward the world he inhabits, there exists a change that is as much axiological as epistemological; and the shift in value, as well as in position, is best defined, for my purposes, in terms of a displacement of the dimensionality (in this case from vertical to horizontal) that determines both the angle and fixity of man's perceptions and of the more complex structures he develops from them. Thus irony, as the typical form, at all levels, of this century's response to the problematics of an increasingly recessive and dissolving self and an increasingly randomized world, strives, by constantly reconstituting itself, to achieve the simultaneous acceptance and creation of a world that is both indeterminate and, at the same time, available to consciousness. My title is meant, therefore, to legitimate the possibility, toward which the whole of this century alternately jolts and glides, of attaining a state of mind that encompasses in that synthesis "inachevée et précaire" both the inevitability of acceptance and the capacity, more active and even at times more joyous, for assent.

PART I

Depths and Surfaces

ONE

Modernism and the Aesthetics of Crisis

Like the Dead Father, that gigantic figure who overwhelms the land-scape of Barthelme's second novel and who serves, among other things, as an emblem of the modernist past, the movement appears at the moment to be *"dead, but still with us, still with us, but dead"* or, alternately, "dead only in a sense."[1] Alive enough, at any rate, to remain a provocation to different factions of the postmodern camp, an incitement to sometimes irascible, sometimes querulous literary and academic violence. The anti-modernist attacks are various of course, as various as the many current systems and ideologies that give rise to them, but in sorting through these ample and heterogeneous indictments, it seems possible to identify, without excessive arbitrariness, two predominant sorts. One centers on the "religio-aesthetic withdrawal [of symbolist modernism] from exis-tential time into the eternal simultaneity of essential art."[2] For those who hold this widespread view, modernism presents itself as a congeries of so many closed, spatial, formally organized works: a series of self-sustaining or organic constructs distantly proclaiming their inherent superiority to the messiness of life. On the other side—and here, roughly speaking, we are dealing with writers of fiction rather than with academic critics—there are those who, like Barthelme, see as they look around them, or rather, hear above and behind them, the persisting echoes of still loud, com-manding voices. So, in her novel *Speedboat* Renata Adler has her narrator reflect, in what is, deliberately, the most unheroic of contexts, on the burden of the modernist past. The section runs, in its entirety, as follows: "'Take off everything but your slip,' the nurse said. 'Doctor will be with you in a moment.' Nobody under forty-five, in twenty years, had worn a slip, but nurses invariably gave this instruction. There they all are, however, the great dead men with their injunctions. Make it new. Only connect."[3]

19

What the two interpretations have in common is, most obviously, the sense of modernism as something monumental, not to say marmoreal: a gallery of timeless heterocosms or imperious speaking heads. Is this what modernism was: a heap of icy aesthetic shapes or a ragbag of detachable moral injunctions? No doubt, there is some evidence for both of these positions, but to assent unequivocally to either is to miss the spirit—the interrogative accent behind the imperative mood—of at least one of the injunctions Adler quotes. Forster's "only connect" expresses desire, not achievement; and it is in the space between the two that modernism, less complacent and smug in its withdrawal than William V. Spanos suggests, reveals the dynamics of its often desperate undertaking.

I'll return later in this chapter to the question of postmodern attitudes and judgments, but before coming directly to modernism itself (early modernism for the most part, as my examples will make clear), it will be helpful to make a short detour in the direction of modernist criticism, past *and* present. If I seem thereby to be in danger of constructing a Chinese box of sorts, I can only say that modernism seems at this point to require a somewhat archaeological approach, an uncovering of sedimented layers of criticism that obscure our view of the thing itself. In fact, it may be to the point to take a further step and suggest that modernist literature is by now virtually inextricable from the shape modernist criticism has impressed upon it. If so, then the next problem lies in the definition of that shape and in the additional recognition that, despite the emergence of so many competing schools and methodologies, the line of modernist criticism remains strong and unbroken. As an illustration of that fact and as a way of getting at the presuppositions in question, I want to refer to an essay by a contemporary critic: F. C. McGrath's "The Plan of *The Waste Land.*" McGrath's aim is to identify "beneath the superficial fragmentation [of the poem] a specific structural plan that is both *consistent* and *coherent* and that provides a means of *resolving* numerous ambiguities in the poem that have plagued its interpreters for over fifty years."[4] The words I have italicized are staples of the New Critical vocabulary, with its emphasis on the unification of the apparently disparate; and in their service McGrath demonstrates skillfully and lucidly that "there is no rebirth in *The Waste Land* . . . and no restoration. The absence of rejuvenation in the modern waste land is the major statement of the poem" (pp. 23-24). In short, the rain does not fall.

But almost forty years ago, Cleanth Brooks, using an approach to which McGrath and more than one generation of critics are heir, argued that the rains do fall. Eliot's "application of the principle of complexity" works to "give the effect of chaotic experience ordered into a new whole."[5] Both critics are right, of course—or, at any rate, there is evidence to support both contentions: the "dry sterile thunder without rain" of line

342 is followed at lines 394-95 by "a damp gust / Bringing rain," which gives way in turn, in the next two lines, to the statement that "Ganga was sunken, and the limp leaves / Waited for rain."[6] How, then, to resolve the contradiction? The answer, which may seem at first glance no more than an evasion of the problem, is that resolution is neither possible nor desirable—and, quite possibly, not intended. One can agree that the poem's vision of disorder, articulated through techniques expressive of fragmentation and discontinuity, is yet, in its totality, a highly ordered structure. Moreover, one can argue—reading the final stanza not as a conclusion but as a telescoping résumé of the poem as a whole—that *The Waste Land* ends with a sense of formal closure. But closure is not resolution, and no amount of exegetical juggling will eliminate the antinomy of despair and fulfillment (personal fulfillment at least) for which the rains, not falling or falling, stand as correlative symbols. Briefly, then, I want to argue that the structure of Eliot's poem—and of many other modernist poems and novels—is based on what I propose to call absolute irony: the conception of equal and opposed possibilities held in a state of total poise, or, more briefly still, the shape of an indestructible, unresolvable paradox.*[7]

In speaking of closure and in addressing myself more generally to the form of *The Waste Land*, I may seem to be edging toward a notion of reflexiveness. But this is not what I'm after, at least not if one defines the term in the usual way, as Maurice Beebe does when he writes: "Modernist art turns back upon itself and is largely concerned with its own creation and composition."[8] To a degree, no doubt, one can read Eliot's poem in this way—specifically as a ratification of the mythic method Eliot describes in his essay on *Ulysses* and thus as an affirmation of art.[9] But it is more to the point to see in the reflexiveness that inevitably follows from nonresolution a reference back not to the artwork—whether as a self-sustaining or as a self-defining creation—but, more intimately, to an informing consciousness in a peculiar state of crisis: that crisis of profound and radical indecision to which "The Hollow Men" speaks so cogently.

The reference to "paralysed force" in the first section of that poem predicts the ubiquitous "Shadow" of the last, which, while it defines the familiar action-impeding mechanism of self-consciousness in twentieth-century literature, maps as well the anterior field of consciousness itself. Which is to say that, if (as phenomenologists hold) consciousness is always consciousness of something, then Eliot's Shadow, relentlessly

---

*De Man uses the phrase "absolute irony," which he derives from Baudelaire's "*comique absolu*," to mean something very different from what I intend. See p. 198 of his essay. As I tried to suggest in my Introduction and as I'll explain more fully in the next section of this chapter, absolute irony is meant to be understood as the most radical but also the most intrinsic or essential stage of modernist or disjunctive irony.

falling "Between the desire / And the spasm / Between the potency / And the existence" (p. 59), testifies to the frustration of the natural, intentional relation between self and world. Furthermore, what is true of this poem is even truer of *The Waste Land*, to which the metaphor of hollowness applies with still greater appropriateness and force. For from the conflict of disjunction and unity within the work—the opposed visions that absolute irony contains but does not resolve—there is generated a sense of acute negation: the estrangement, brought about by the inability to act (or, in a manner of speaking, by the enactment of a nonact), of consciousness from the world in which it is, to speak phenomenologically again, willy-nilly incarnated. Seen in this perspective, modernist depth —the primary target perhaps of the postmodern reaction—becomes a sign and, more, a space of absence, absence the figuration of desire, and desire the expressive form both of the poem and of the eternally arrested dialectic that, opening out onto the absence it creates, constitutes its shaping center.

At this point, it is hardly possible not to acknowledge what must in any case be clear, namely, that many of the terms I have been using were given special prominence and (some would say) notoriety by Cleanth Brooks in a series of essays during the thirties and forties.[10] Furthermore, however long and vexed the history of words like *irony* and *paradox*, it was, for most of us writing today, Brooks who made them current; and the debt needs to be acknowledged. My own aim, then, in stating my disagreements, is not to launch yet another full-scale attack on the New Criticism—the current hectic pursuit, as Oscar Wilde might just conceivably have said, of the unfashionable by the unreadable. It is, rather, to uncover the guiding principles of Brooks's critical enterprise, which, like all such principles, time invariably reduces to the status of unproved assumptions. Those assumptions I want to glance at now, taking them in what seems, from the perspective of the early eighties, to be an order of ascending vulnerability.[11]

To begin with: the notion of complexity. As I indicated in my discussion of *The Waste Land*, the poet must, according to Brooks, provide the *effect* at least of "chaotic experience." The better the poet, the greater his ability to recognize and articulate "conflicting elements" (*MPT*, p. 37), the "discordant" (*MPT*, p. 40), "the amorphous and heterogeneous and contradictory" (*MPT*, p. 43). In other words, the poem's method deserves praise in proportion to its ability to take into account, richly and fully, incongruities and tensions, qualification and conflict—so much so that Brooks is led to praise poetry "in which the opposition of the impulses which are united is *extreme*" (*MPT*, p. 42; my italics), and Murray Krieger is led to comment that, for Brooks, "the more complexity the better, so that this theory easily lends itself to the sanctioning of complexity for complexity's sake."[12] Nevertheless, I suspect that most modernists would, at this stage of his argument, agree with Brooks, given their sense of the world's disorder; and so too, allowing for a looser, untidier definition of complexity, would many postmodern artists. It is no accident, after all, that Robert Venturi's antimodernist manifesto, which quotes liberally from Brooks, is called *Complexity and Contradiction in Architecture*.

Complexity, however, is only the base of Brooks's aesthetic pyramid, and as soon as one begins to examine more closely the defining and controlling shape of complexity—to speak paradoxically of paradox—the lines begin to taper to their inevitable close. In the broadest sense, paradox is defined by Brooks as "a device for contrasting the conventional views of a situation, or the limited and special view of it such as those taken in practical and scientific discourse, with a more inclusive view" (*WWU*, p. 257). But that formulation only hints at a fact demonstrable everywhere in Brooks's essays and especially in *The Well Wrought Urn*: namely, that the contrasts and contradictions Brooks typically concerns himself with are only ostensible. Over and again, his metaphors of tension and conflict carry with them the same revealing qualification. We are directed not to the genuinely but to "the *apparently* contradictory and conflicting elements of experience" (*WWU*, p. 214; my italics). So it is, after all, seeming paradox that interests Brooks; not the irrefrangibly self-contradictory oppositions of the perfected dilemma but the provisional, melting balance of parts in search of a combinative whole. Paradox is, finally, "the assertion of the union of opposites" (*WWU*, p. 213).

And, in fact, it is the search for union that unifies Brooks's own essays, that furnishes them with their *telos* and their motive force. One has only to note in passing the words that repeatedly thread themselves through his discourse—*oneness, fusion, resolution, synthesis, harmony,* and so on—to recognize that complexity and paradox subserve the ultimate goal of unity, that their intensity guarantees the richness of "an achieved harmony" (*WWU*, p. 195). More is at stake, however. The writer who manages "to fuse the conflicting elements [of experience] in a harmonious whole" (*MPT*, p. 37) enables the critic, the contextual critic, "to find a criterion in the organization of the poem itself by assessing the relative complexity of the unifying attitude—the power of the tensions involved in it, the scope of the reconciliation which it is able to make, etc." (*WWU*, p. 256). But Brooks's criterion is not, in fact, an inherent property of the poem; rather, the poem provides an occasion for the critical detection of a hypothetical order, a "truth" he locates in the very nature of things. "The characteristic unity of a poem," Brooks writes, anticipating McGrath, ". . . lies in the *unification* of attitudes into a *hierarchy subordinated* to a total and *governing* attitude" (*WWU*, pp. 206-7; my italics). The key words of the quotation tell their own story clearly enough. What is implied is, not simply a notion of harmony and coherence, but a carefully graded, ranged and arranged relationship of part to part and parts to whole. Brooks's model of organic form, in its omnivorous, imperious resolutions, closes the door not only against time, as Spanos alleges, and against more casual conceptions of order and form (a story by, say, Barthelme or Coover), but also against the intransigence of unreconciled consciousness, the image of that genuine paradox Brooks persistently dissolves in the acid bath of aesthetically mastered experience.

I shall return to paradox later on, but for the moment it will be more useful to follow Brooks to the end of his argument, or rather, since we have arrived at the apex of unity that crowns the whole, to attend to the luminous glow of approbation that surrounds the resolved, perfected poem. No one, I think, will want to quarrel with Brooksian words like *sensitivity* and *richness*. *Sincerity* is perhaps a bit out of fashion, as is *depth*. *Coherence* and *integrity*, if too narrowly construed, may be expected to raise hackles. But the most problematic and troublesome of Brooks's terms of praise are surely the all too hearty and conclusive *tough-minded*, *healthy*, and, particularly, *mature*. This is no doubt unfair. The words I've cited are meant to stand in opposition to a sensibility that is "merely callow, glib, and sentimental" (*IPS*, p. 62), and since those unflattering adjectives are, in turn, directly contrasted with the principle of irony, it will be most appropriate to come at maturity by way of irony itself. Irony has, of course, several related meanings in Brooks's writings. Its function is "to make reservations, to notice by implication 'the other side' of the matter" (*MPT*, p. 30); it is "the most general term that we have for the kind of qualification which the various elements in a context receive from the context. . . . Moreover, irony is our most general term for indicating [the] recognition of incongruities" (*WWU*, p. 209). But the most comprehensive of Brooks's definitions claims for irony a good deal more. At issue is "a poetry which does not leave out what is apparently hostile to its dominant tone and which, because it is able to fuse the irrelevant and discordant, has come to terms with itself and is invulnerable to irony" (*IPS*, p. 62).

Now, Brooks's *apparent* paradox—the notion that only the fully ironic poem can withstand irony—is both ingenious and, at the most general level, persuasive, but the implications of various details of his definition are another matter. One can agree that *The Waste Land* or, to take another example, *A Passage to India* is a fully ironic work in that each "carries within its own structure the destructive elements," that is, takes account of "complementary impulses" and "correlative aspects of the experience" being explored, but it is something else again to assert that the writer "has reconciled [the structure] to [the destructive elements]" (*MPT*, p. 44). Certainly, both Eliot and Forster have managed brilliantly to *contain*, formally, aesthetically, the internal pressures of their works; but containment is not reconciliation, and still less is it a fusion of the discordant. Furthermore, it can be argued that Forster and Eliot "come to terms" with their paradoxes only in the sense that they, or their works, acknowledge them by expressing the dilemma into which experience shapes itself. And what results, as I suggested earlier, is a state not of mutual balance and support but of fierce, unreconciled opposition.

In effect, then, we are faced with two different models, superficially kin but, in the final analysis, subtly and determinedly at odds. In Brooks's, the writer, all passion spent, calmly stands above the experience he has wrought into unity, the master of all he surveys. In the other, the writer stands not only above but, as it were, against experience, his poem or novel indicating not a mastery of the world but a defensive maneuver prompted by it, a tacit admission of failure to come to terms with its complexity. The second model is, in other words, acephalous: the ultimate synthesis absents itself; like Forster's teasing Krishna, it "neglects to come."[13]

But what is it exactly that accounts for these differences and makes Brooks's criticism a not altogether reliable guide to much of modernist literature? It is tempting to answer summarily that there is a touch of complacency in his views—about art and about life as well. Certainly, he exhibits a somewhat naive delight in complexity, which is the very antithesis of most modern writers' gloomy perceptions of disorder: "these chasms," as Virgina Woolf puts it, "in the continuity of our ways."[14] Krieger comments aptly on Brooks's "unchecked multiplication of complexities, hell-bent for chaos" (*NAP*, p. 135). The last phrase is especially to the point. For writers like the Forster of *A Passage to India*, exclusion and inclusion are twin dangers, and the false order of the first is matched by the potential formlessness of the second. Brooks's disdain for imposed form, on the other hand, calls forth no answering suspicion of complexity—and for an obvious reason: complications and contradictions unnumbered are, for him, always susceptible of resolution—certain, if hard-won—in the ample embrace of organic form.

Organic form is a tricky concept, however. To begin with, one might argue that the most inclusive works of modernism—*Ulysses, To the Lighthouse, The Waves*, even *The Waste Land*—come closest to violating Brooks's inviolable union of form and content; that precisely those novels and poems whose internal complexities are most extreme exhibit the kind of structure Brooks most scorns ("'form' conceived as a kind of container, a sort of beautified envelope" [*WWU*, p. 226]), thereby ratifying Forster's insight that all-inclusiveness, or chaos, invites the

imposition of order fully as much as order imposed from without falsi-
fies the fullness of experience. But there is another and more important
distinction to be drawn, which requires further definition. If organic
form implies no more than that "each part modifies and is modified by
the whole" (*IPS*, p. 66); that the genuinely (as opposed to the *apparently*)
irrelevant has no place in art; that, finally, structure evolves (or is
discovered) in relation to the exigencies of the individual work and not
in accordance with some external set of rules (the three unities, say),
then most modernists would readily agree. Forster, for example, opposing rhythm to pattern, asserting that order is "something evolved
from within, not something imposed from without . . . an internal stability, a vital harmony" and that "a work of art—whatever else it may
be—is a self-contained entity," Forster in this sense is an organicist.
But—and it is a crucial but—for Forster, as for other members of
Bloomsbury, the order of art stands in contrast to the disorder of life
—"It is the one orderly product which our muddling race has produced"[15]—whereas for Brooks, the poet's task is not only "finally to
unify experience. He must return to us the unity of experience itself *as
man knows it in his own experience*" (*WWU*, pp. 212-13; my italics).[16]

   With this contrast, we come to what is crucial in the metaphor of
organicism. In Brooks's case, the theory of the organic work of art rests
securely on a Coleridgean belief in nature itself as organic. But is it
possible to share Brooks's view of art while simultaneously asserting the
disappearance (or death) of God and the disorderliness of life? Well,
yes, as Forster's case proves: the structures based on belief may long, if
not indefinitely, outlast the belief that once informed them; but poised
as they are over a void, they inevitably become both precarious and
rigid. The New Critical demand "that poetry be 'mature,' that it see all
around any experience and not cheat our life of its complexity, our
world of its body" (*NAP*, p. 132) evokes in Forster, by the time of *A
Passage to India*, not a euphoric response to complexity but a feeling of
metaphysical disgust. The detachment and objectivity that are two more
of Brooks's hallmarks of the truly ironic work (*IPS*, p. 62) are for
Forster—and for Eliot and Joyce, Woolf and Huxley, Auden and Isherwood—signs rather of a failure to engage the world: a standing apart
from experience, which inevitably reflects back from the characters
who dramatize this failure to their authors, who repeatedly and unmistakably betray in their narrative and poetic strategies their resemblances
to their fictional creations.

   Shall we, then, indeed can we, apply the criterion of maturity to
works that, far from expressing the harmonious unity of the assured
and settled mind, reveal instead, as a response to complexity and irresolution in the face of paradox, an overwhelming sense of nausea;

which view art as, at best, an ambiguous breakwater against the turbid flow of life? "Through control," Krieger writes, "[the poem] disdains the messiness of experience" (*NAP*, p. 26). But disdain is the prerogative of confidence and certainty. Calling unity itself into doubt, modernism—or at least those modernist works structured on the principle of absolute irony—expresses a sort of brave helplessness; and perhaps if one wants an honorific to apply to these writers, the appropriate term is not *mature* but *heroic*. What we confront finally is a different kind of complexity: the heroism of consciousness making art of its own uncertainty and expressing in its very form, in the express rejection of an easy resolution, the difficult aesthetics of crisis.

· · ·

Setting himself in opposition to Mies van der Rohe's orthodox modernism, Robert Venturi, by no means the most radical of postmodern theorists, writes as follows: "Mies refers to a need to 'create order out of the desperate confusion of our times.' But [Louis] Kahn has said 'by order I do not mean orderliness.' Should we not resist bemoaning confusion? Should we not look for meaning in the complexities and contradictions of our times and acknowledge the limitations of systems? . . . When circumstances defy order, order should bend or break: anomalies and uncertainties give validity to architecture."[17] Venturi's credo is useful in two ways. First of all, despite the diversity of beliefs I've already acknowledged as a feature of postmodernism, his words seem to me to articulate cogently the ethos of the movement: the perception, to start with, of experience as random and contingent ("confusion," "uncertainties") rather than—the modernist view—simply fragmented; further, an accompanying impulse not only to recognize but to *accept* variety and confusion; and, finally, the elaboration of an ethic of participation: the desire for experience unmediated by the moral and aesthetic imperatives of modernism. In the second place and as a corollary: if, as I believe, the nature of crisis becomes fully apparent only in its aftermath, only, that is to say, when a new path, among many possible and possibly unforeseen, has been chosen, then Venturi's statements, in their reactive force, help to establish more clearly the configuration of the modernist crisis. Unwilling or unable to accept, even as their sense of disbelief in all objective forms of order (exclusive *and* inclusive) grows, the consequences of their disbelief, the modernists refuse to admit the "limitation of all orders composed by man" (p. 47). Resisting Venturi's—and Kahn's—looser, more modest expectations, they cannot imagine the breaking or bending or, better still, the transfiguration of the order for which they continue to rage. And so they remain, as we now see, captives of an ideal less of order than of orderliness, asserting, in the teeth of a world gone inorganic and dead, those stubborn paradoxes that elevate visions of disorder to the unsteady heights of formal symmetry.

Not, of course, as I've already stipulated, all modernists and not even, to come closer to my subject, all ironists of this century. A more genetic approach to the problem makes immediately apparent the fact that irony, though it pervades the century, is far from monolithic. Satiric or mediate irony, for example, persists, however attenuated by the long decline of reason as man's master faculty and, more importantly (since twentieth-century satire tends in any case—with a few notable exceptions like Wyndham Lewis—to substitute primitivist for rational norms), by the evaporation of a "common sense" of things. But satire is, relatively speaking, a minor form in modern times, its notion of correctable error or folly superseded by what D. C. Muecke describes as "an awareness of life as being fundamentally and inescapably at odds with itself or with the world at large."[18] Muecke's "general irony," which, as he acknowledges, is by no means a twentieth-century discovery, seems to me a reasonable and suggestive account of the basic form of disjunctive irony in the modernist period; and in what follows I want to adopt his term, making some changes in its focus and taking it to contrast not only (as he means it to) with the specific ironies of satire but also with the more extreme and critical stage of absolute irony that develops from it.[19]

Muecke speaks of "one great incongruity," which is the basis for general irony: "the appearance of self-valued and subjectively free but temporally finite egos in a universe that seems to be utterly alien, utterly purposeless, completely deterministic, and incomprehensibly vast" (I, p. 68). The formulation makes an important point, but it may take for granted too great a consciousness of what it describes. The fact is that for most people Muecke's incongruity—or the awareness of it—is a more instinctive matter. By which I mean that theoretical ironic disparities are, again for most people, generally hypostatized as intrinsic features of the world or of the psyche. Thus Woolf's "chasms," and thus the gaps and discontinuities that modernist writers habitually explore and express, thematically and through their various techniques. It is not, then, so much a matter of "two systems which simply do not gear together" (I, p. 68) as of a world, inner or outer, perceived as inherently disjunctive.

Muecke would say, I suspect, that I am one of those robbing irony of "the 'central' feature of a contrasting appearance and reality" (I, p. 32); and in some respects at least, he would be right. My point is this: that as irony ceases to be merely the instrument of satire and becomes instead something more autonomous, it projects the doubleness that characterizes it as a trope into a lateral form, a disjunctive form, which creates in turn those attitudes and perspectives—distance and detachment, for example

—that we associate with irony as a strategy of noninvolvement or disillusion or defense. These various ways of reacting (or not reacting) are, however, secondary effects of something more basic: a way of "seeing" the world. Postsatiric irony seems to me, then, as it develops in the twentieth century from its roots in German Romantic theory, first and foremost a *vision* of existence. But where shall we situate it? Muecke's contrast of reality and appearance suggests that we place it precisely in the difference between man's perceiving consciousness and the world that is external to him. But if, as Merleau-Ponty holds, there exists "a natal pact between our body and the world, between ourselves [that is, consciousness] and our body," then these traditionally opposed elements are in fact inextricably entwined.[20] Or, to put it another way, the world both determines and is determined by consciousness, and whether we speak of a perception of disjunction or of a disjunct world, we are saying, effectively, the same thing. In short, Muecke's contrast is voided in a "world [that] is," to quote Merleau-Ponty again, "not what I think, but what I live through."[21] Furthermore, if what we are discussing is perception, an immediate response to the world that precedes conceptualization, then the fact of intention (as opposed to the phenomenological notion of intentionality), which Wayne Booth makes central to his rhetorical investigation of irony, becomes theoretically, if not necessarily, irrelevant.[22] Which is to say that the ironist is not, in the first instance, the manipulator (though he may be that ultimately) but the perceiver of disparities, inscribing his precritical vision in the form of his work.

We must look then, finally, to structure, as Brooks maintains, or, more appropriately, to acts of language to locate irony, for if irony is preeminently a responsive vision, still the vision must speak—be disclosed (or, as Mark Schorer maintains, be discovered)—in order to be recognized. Does this mean that, having set aside Brooks's ideal of achieved unity, one must adopt his principle of complexity? To do so, Muecke maintains—in speaking of the contextual model, which, for Brooks, underlies the valorization of complexity—is to give in to "a tendency to stretch the concept of irony to the point of making it the essential or distinguishing quality of imaginative literature" (*I*, p. 10). But in fact, modern art (modernist and postmodernist) *is* overwhelmingly ironic, however one chooses to define the word—and it is hardly surprising that it is so, given twentieth-century life for its context. The problem may lie, rather, in the definition of complexity, for what we require, in attempting to recognize and identify modernist irony, is not a criticism that attends simply or primarily to however many mutually modifying and qualifying elements, which can and, for Brooks, have to be made to coexist organically—the poem which "must perforce dramatize the oneness of the experience, even though *paying tribute to* its diversity" (*WWU*, p. 213; my italics).

We need instead to recognize specifically those techniques that translate the gaps and discontinuities in experience, that stress its broken edges and sharp corners, the scars of division and the palpable traces of absence —such stylistic and narrative devices as, for example, parataxis, montage, multiple point of view, the stress on discrete moments, or, in the case of absolute irony, genuine paradox. Which is to say that it is in the *formal* revelation of the *failure* to come to terms with experience that modernist irony makes manifest its bleak intuitions. So then, neither Muecke's contrast of reality and appearance nor Booth's stress on intention (rich and complex though their arguments are), and still less Brooks's mandatory reduction of disorder to unity, seems to me to make sufficiently visible the contours of irony in this century. If I am right about the way perception is encoded in modernist works of art, then the clue to the ironic vision lies, available to the reader, in forms that render not merely the fact of disparity but its informing principles, not only the unconnected elements of life but, more tellingly, the disconnection itself: those unbridgeable spaces that define as they disfigure the map of modern life.

In locating modernist irony in a vision of things side by side and not (as Muecke does) one behind the other and in finding its essence in the articulation of disconnection, I don't mean to rob human beings altogether of their sense of doubleness, which may be, after all, the chief token of living in a fallen world. In fact, I want to argue that *all* irony, regarded as a perceptual encounter with the world, generates in response to its vision of disparity (or in some cases is generated by) a complementary, more conceptual vision of wholeness or singleness, which I want to refer to as the *anironic.** Thus, if in mediate irony the world is perceived as deviating or lapsed from some preexistent norm, the anironic offers a contrasting societal or at least earthly vision of integration and connection, harmony and coherence: paradise regained and made reasonably or imaginatively terrestrial—where, to use Pope's words: "Earth smiles around, with boundless bounty blest, / And Heaven beholds its image in his breast."[23] By contrast, the modernist perception of fragmentation is balanced by an anironic vision of oneness or fusion: the jagged earth transcended, as in Yeats's Byzantium or, as in Mrs. Ramsay's "wedge-shaped core of darkness," interiorized and seemingly stilled.

---

*It's perhaps worth stressing that in coining the word *anironic*, I mean to suggest not a vision that stands in opposition to irony (not "anti-ironic") but one that complements it. There is, I recognize, a good deal to be said against the creation of new words, but no other term seems to me free both from extraneous overtones and from overspecificity. I have in the past used the word *sentimentality*—see my book *Christopher Isherwood* (New York: Twayne Publishers, 1971), chapter 1—but it now appears to me impossible to rid the word of its pejorative associations. See chapter 2, below, for a fuller discussion of this term and its meaning.

Does this formulation sneak an irony based on reality and appearance in by the back door after expelling it through the front? I think not. What it does, in denying fixed, essential realities and thus, too, illusory appearances, is to allow the coexistence of two mental structures or levels (which in mediate irony are perhaps one): an intuitive grasp of disparity (the ironic) and a secondary, frequently more self-conscious way of coping with disparity by creating alternatives (the anironic) to it. I'll return, less theoretically, to the anironic in a moment. The distinction between satiric and modernist, or disjunctive, irony can be left now. But the further division of the latter into general and absolute requires more detailed comment. To begin with, which works shall we agree on as representing general irony or, better still, what characters inhabit its unsettled regions? Prufrock, of course, and, to take less familiar examples, the heroines of Jean Rhys's novels, but the most striking may be Ford Madox Ford's John Dowell. Ejected from the world he has always known, a world, to use his words, of permanence and stability, he exposes himself as a man whose sensitivity has been unequal to his experience, who, faced with the sudden discovery that there are no certainties, can only repeat over and over throughout his long monologue: "I don't know. I know nothing. I am very tired."[24] Unprepared for what the twentieth century reveals to him, that the world lacks order and coherence and meaning, he is yet, in his dim, Laodicean way, the unwitting embodiment as well as the victim of his times. Perhaps his most revealing remark comes when, after his description of one of the novel's crucial incidents, he writes: "I was aware of something treacherous, something frightful, something evil in the day. I can't define it and can't find a simile for it" (p. 44). At which point he proceeds, as he constantly does, to look for one. The simile, that curious figure of speech which acknowledges, more, insists on, difference even while asserting likeness, which stresses the gap—the "like" or "as" or, Dowell's favorite, the still further estranging "as if"—between the things compared, the simile is in many ways the most tangible representation of Dowell's search for meaning in a world whose parts, mirroring his own flat, discrete, and fragmentary perceptions, stubbornly refuse to cohere. That his metaphors are, by contrast, totally conventional only underlines the point. Residual images of a lost order—paradise is his favorite—they function as anironic contrasts to his habitual sense of disconnection, his increasingly gloomy vision of "broken, tumultuous, agonized, and unromantic lives" (pp. 237-38).

Broken lives is in fact what Dowell's story is about, and his chief effort in tortuously reconstructing them is to find some meaning among the facts he recounts, to uncover or recover the continuity he once knew. He fails of course and remains to the end trapped in his shattered world, kept from total collapse only by a vestigial sense of duty and by his ludicrous identification with Edward Ashburnham. At one point, however, Dowell's irony threatens to evolve into a more complex form of response. Near the beginning of the novel, reflecting on the "little four-square coterie" (p. 5) of himself, his wife, and the Ashburnhams, he says, "Our intimacy was like a minuet" (p. 6) and then, shortly, goes on to contradict himself: "No, by God, it is false! It wasn't a minuet that we stepped; it was a prison—a prison full of screaming hysterics. . . . And yet I swear by the sacred name of my creator that it was true. It was true sunshine; the true music" (p. 7). For a moment Dowell holds in balance, as equally valid possibilities, the visions of hell and heaven, to use his metaphors, which elsewhere he opposes as reality (the ironic) and dream (the anironic). Here both together comprise his primary perception of the world, and we thus come to an adumbration of absolute irony. Dowell resumes his refrain, however—"I know nothing—nothing in the world—of the hearts of men" (p. 7)—and we may leave him now to concentrate on the concept he briefly suggests.

To put the matter schematically, what I am suggesting is this: if general irony is based on a perception of disjunction and implies a countervision of fusion, absolute irony joins these elements in a more comprehensively ironic view. In their interactivity, the world presents itself as more tensive and paradoxical, consciousness as more sophisticated and, in some cases, more self-aware. Dowell's hopeless confusion gives way to the self-consciousness of Cortázar's Horacio Oliveira, "weighing and accepting too readily the yes and no of everything, becoming a sort of inspector of scales."[25] But more is at stake. As the ironic and anironic of the earlier stage knit together in a new configuration, they assume, each of them, a more radical shape. Absolute irony, as I hinted earlier, embraces simultaneously the extreme of, on the one side, a world in which, as Forster's Mrs. Moore learns, "everything exists, nothing has value" (*PI*, p. 140)—a world, that is, in a state of total chaos—and, on the other, of a unity so inclusive as to be, for its part too, hardly distinguishable from chaos.

But what then of the anironic vision that complements absolute irony, if absolute irony has absorbed into itself the dream of oneness, the desire man feels, Dowell says, "to lose his identity, to be enveloped, to be supported" (p. 115)? The answer is tricky. In fact, at the level of absolute irony, that desire remains, but it is more narrowly and perhaps desperately channeled into an exclusive identification with art: "music heard so deeply," as Eliot writes in "The Dry Salvages," "That it is not heard at all, but *you are the music* / While the music lasts" (p. 136; my italics). Of course, art serves not infrequently as an ideal complementary to the vision of general irony as well, but not—and this is my point—in the same way. As the anironic of absolute irony, the modernist goal of fusion not only becomes specifically aesthetic; it is, as it were, transformed from the theoretical image of desire to its explicit form. Yeats's two Byzantium poems will help to demonstrate the difference. In "Sailing to Byzantium," the "artifice of eternity" is the ideal consciousness generates to express its dissatisfaction with the world it remains part of, an ideal correlative to the others Yeats expresses in the twenties: innocence, tradition, custom, and so on. But in the later poem, Byzantium is the shape of consciousness itself. From within the city, functioning here not as one of the poem's symbols but as its symbolic form, the speaker observes both the furies of complexity and the flood-breaking smithies of the Emperor; and, unable to choose between the extremes the poem projects or to resolve their antinomy, he materializes and stabilizes the dilemma through art. But it is the poet's art, not the Emperor's, that achieves this stability. The Emperor, violent and dynamic, is part of the paradox; the poet's art, the poem itself, is its transcendence. Is it any wonder that modernism speaks so insistently of anonymity and impersonality, and modernist critics of the intentional fallacy and the loss of the self? Art is, finally, the exiled artist's home, in which, remaining true to his perceptions, he is yet able—or so it seems—to bring consciousness to rest, its desire fulfilled in the attainment of order: "a *world*, or *mode of existence*," Valéry says in describing poetry's effect, "of complete harmony."[26]

But this transcendence, the pouring of paralyzed consciousness into the shape of the artwork it merges with, is at a cost. The situation that seems to Dowell true music is, viewed differently, a prison; and likewise, the absolute ironist's victory is, effectively, his defeat. For in seeking its loss, the self in reality finds itself implacably mirrored back by the form of the artwork, which, though sought as a liberation from consciousness, instead confirms consciousness and constrains it to see itself as precisely what it desired not to be in the first place: "estranged from the whole world to which [it] belongs." The words are Kierkegaard's and it is worth quoting a good part of the passage in which they appear. He is speaking of Socrates as ironist: "Thus he elevates himself higher and higher, becoming ever lighter as he rises, seeing all things disappear beneath him from his ironical bird's eye perspective, while he himself hovers above them in ironic satisfaction borne by the absolute self-consistency of the infinite negativity within him. Thus he becomes estranged from the whole world to which he belongs (however much he may still belong to it in another sense), the contemporary consciousness affords him no predicates, ineffable and indeterminate he belongs to a different formation."[27] It isn't necessary to pursue Kierkegaard's argument here. I simply want to pause for a moment over what his words might suggest in the context of this chapter. The "different formation" he attributes to the ironist and views in terms of an "infinite negativity within him" I would update and transform into that crisis of consciousness in a state of radical indecision to which I've already referred. Unable to make sense of the world but unwilling to forgo the ideal model of orderliness, the absolute ironist folds back on himself in the sanctuary of his art. Finally, the ironic and the anironic converge, and he finds in his supposed release only the inexorable reflection of his own equivocation.

Kierkegaard's metaphors of position are particularly suggestive as a description of the ironist's perspective. If general irony is distant and detached, absolute irony is more distant still, "hovering" in fact. The last image brings directly to mind one of Virginia Woolf's stories, which, because it exemplifies almost diagrammatically what I have been trying to expound here as theory, I want to look at now in some detail. The story, or sketch, or fiction—it is difficult to decide how exactly to name a piece of slightly over three hundred words that is virtually without characters or incidents—"Monday or Tuesday" has received little attention and less praise from critics, though Woolf apparently thought highly enough of it to use its title for the 1921 volume in which it first appeared. Perhaps it is best to regard the work as a parable: an exploration of various ways of perceiving and responding to the world and, as such, an invaluable guide to Woolf's preoccupations at least through the early thirties. Brief though it is, "Monday or Tuesday" is anything but simple in structure. Four short paragraphs, which enact a typically modernist dilemma, are framed by two others, in which both the narrator's perspective and the objects that solicit her attention shift so violently as to suggest that the central problem of the middle section has been, as is in fact the case, somehow bypassed or transcended.

I'll return to the frame in a while: it is between the narrative extremes that the initial perplexity defines itself. The first three of these paragraphs describe the desire (the narrator's, presumably, but perhaps that of human beings in general) for truth: "Desiring truth, awaiting it, laboriously distilling a few words, for ever desiring. . . ."[28] The phrase "laboriously distilling" suggests the attempted approach: a conscious and painstaking, active and repeated effort to extract, drop by drop, the essence of phenomena, the reality underlying appearance. The subject of the distillation is a series of impressionistically rendered cityscapes and desultory conversations, which reveals everywhere discord and conflict, triviality and bustle. But from time to time beauty too emerges, for this is, on the whole, as compared with the "Time Passes" section of *To the Lighthouse*, say, one of Woolf's more benign visions of disconnection and confusion. Still, even the moments of beauty constitute only so many more distractions in what Woolf was to describe a few years later as "an age of fragments."[29] More and more, as "wheels strike divergently" and "omnibuses conglomerate in conflict" and nameless Londoners exchange vaporous remarks, not only the quest for truth but even the ability to sustain the quest is called into doubt until, in the last paragraph of the three, truth appears one final time as an interrogative afterthought: "Flaunted, leaf-light, drifting at corners, blown across the wheels, silver-splashed, home or not home, gathered, scattered, squandered in separate scales, swept up, down, torn, sunk, assembled—and truth?" The passage is remarkable for the way in which it suggests the defeat of the narrator's project and her consequent disappearance, at least as a conscious seeker after truth. Lacking any finite verbs, almost devoid of nouns (all, except *truth*, appear in prepositional phrases), the sentence, or rather the fragment of a sentence, describes a world of pure appearance, in which truth, substantial and final, has no place or part.

But the sentence is not only an ending. Standing between the two preceding paragraphs—in which words seek to name and thus stabilize objects and actions, holding them in place so the narrator can penetrate from shifting surface to stable depth—standing between these and the passage that follows, in which words become transparent and suggestive, it also provides a transition to another mode of response. "Now to recollect by the fireside," the section begins, and the verb intimates not only, as compared with the activity of "laboriously distilling," a more meditative, intuitive process but, in addition, a summoning together of the self, an attempt, literally to *re*-collect what has been dispersed in the phenomenal world as a result of the search for truth. But in fact, though the narrator, first reading and then, book fallen, voyaging freely like Mrs. Ramsay through inner space, traverses vast, exotic oceans and continents, she attains only what William Troy, in speaking of Mrs. Ramsay, called "the range of *implicit* experience."[30] The passive surrender of consciousness to less logical and analytical forms of mental activity —the narrator's word is "closeness"—achieves, to be sure, a oneness or fusion of sorts (the intimacy of consciousness with its own imaginings or, in the final analysis, with itself), but it comes no nearer to capturing reality, as the final words of the story (the story within the story)—"truth? or now, content with closeness?"—make clear. For we are left at the end with a question and with a disjunction: that equal poise of opposites once more. There are, of course, various ways of translating or rephrasing the disjunction—objectivity and subjectivity, say, or, to be more Woolfian about it, night and day, or even Mr. and Mrs. Ramsay—but what matters is that the terms are perfectly balanced. Opposed and yet, subtly, effectively, the same—truth is engulfed by, while closeness evades, facticity—the two approaches describe twin failures to deal successfully with the phenomenal world to which the title, itself disjunctive, refers.

The story does not, however, acknowledge failure. What it does instead is present simultaneously valid possibilities, transforming disjunction into paradox and thereby creating the conditions for absolute irony. Unable to choose between truth and closeness, the narrator arrests choice and greets the alternatives with an equal eye, as the first and last paragraphs of "Monday or Tuesday" make evident. For if the sections I have so far described articulate the impasse, it is the frame that defines the narrator's final response, although obliquely. Removed as far as possible from the mundane activities of the rest of the story, the frame devotes itself to a description of the sky, "white and distant, absorbed in itself, [which] endlessly . . . covers and uncovers, moves and remains" and of a "lazy and indifferent [heron], shaking space easily from his wings, knowing his way." Whether the clouded sky, in its magisterial impartiality, is meant to suggest a constant reality hidden by the changing configurations of appearance; whether, to push conjecture further still, it is intended, in its self-delighting play of light and shadow, its mapping in gold and darkness of the landscape beneath it, to represent the self-sufficient, variegated world of art, I am not completely sure. But it seems to me beyond doubt that, however intended, the heron bodies forth the artist and, more, the ironic artist of Woolf's story. Lazy? Indifferent? Do the words apply? Yes, as contrasted with the descriptions of the narrator first laboriously distilling words in the search for truth and later, though more subdued, still seeking, this time for closeness. For the heron there is no search, no seeking; only casual attention to what is: the existent of which it is both part and not part. What exactly are we dealing with here? Surely, Kierkegaard's ironist, who "elevates himself higher and higher, becoming ever lighter and lighter as he rises, seeing all things disappear beneath him from his ironical bird's eye perspective." And surely too with what I have been calling the absolute ironist, "estranged from the whole world to which he belongs." Incapable of selecting either of her opposed perceptions of the world and incapable of fusing them into a Brooksian unity, the artist retreats from her paradox and from the world it figures, a remote, hovering observer now, saved from the impossible choice but condemned to its inevitable repetition. "Monday or Tuesday" is, then, a portrait of the modernist artist as absolute ironist, and in that sense it is as well a parable of the aesthetics of crisis: it presents an order, no doubt, and, in its own way, a solution, but the vision of paradox remains, unresolved and, lacking a new way of apprehending reality, unresolvable.

· · ·

One other major problem remains, which leads, appropriately enough, to a critical paradox, though only, as I hope to show in examining it, an apparent one. Let me get at this by a question. If I have been arguing primarily, in my attempt to establish a category of absolute irony, against New Critical assertions of resolution as the mark of the successfully ironic work, am I then committed by my opposition to defining the structure of absolute irony as not only nonresolved but open? Many critics have argued that modernist literature is, in fact, characteristically open or open-ended, and, among them, none more persuasively than Alan Friedman in his exemplary study, *The Turn of the Novel*, which concerns itself with the form of "an ethical vision of continual expansion and virtually unrelieved openness in the experience of life." "In this discussion of structure in the novel," he writes, "a form conceived as in motion and as a process, I am going to use 'closed' or 'open' to refer to the full and final shaping of the flux of experience. . . . By a closed novel, then, I mean a novel in which that underlying ethical form, the stream of conscience, is finally contained [or, as he says on the following page, "checked and brought to rest"]. By an open novel I mean a novel in which the stream of conscience is finally not contained."[31] Now, if one regards the description as a comment on the twentieth century as a whole, including, as Friedman does not, postmodern fiction, it is hard to resist its general validity. But I have to add that, in those works whose structure is defined by absolute irony, we have, for reasons I shall try to specify, the exceptions that prove the rule. In such poems and novels, though resolution does not take place, expansion, as in Friedman's *closed* novel, is nevertheless checked—if hardly brought to rest. Still dynamic, experience is arrested in flight, made negative in a sense, by the equivocal balance of consciousness; the movement to expansion is turned back on itself, linearity made endlessly circular, the energy of the movement imploding inward and held, if not stilled, only by the exigency of form.

In speaking of absolute irony, then, I mean to assert, in response to those who see the shape of modernist literature as organic, its failure to fuse its contradictory elements, and in response to those who view it as expanding, I mean equally to assert its abrupt arrest of outward or onward movement. I have admitted, however, that such works are *formally* closed, and I would add now that they are open as well, if openness is seen to locate itself as an irresolution *within* the confines of the novel or poem. For Friedman, "the expanding flux of conscience in modern fiction is left finally open . . . in one of three senses: finally uncontained, finally unreduced, or finally still expanding" (p. 30). In the works I am describing, it is both contained and, to that degree, reduced and, if still expanding, then in a troublingly reflexive way: desire straining against the constraining form it has itself devised as the only possible response to its impossible hope for fulfillment. So, in "Monday or Tuesday," the unanswerable question—"truth? or now, content with closeness?"—continues to echo and reecho, as the narrator transcends the open, phenomenal world and ascends to the framing order of art. Of course, Woolf is, in may ways, a special case. The endings of the middle novels—from "For there she was" to "I have had my vision" to "*The waves broke on the shore*"—increasingly and with increasing emphasis bolt shut the door on their questioning, meditative visions until, in *The Waves*, absolute irony triumphs and we are left not with "the world seen without a self" but with the self absorbed into its own world of art, the paradox of life both affirmed and denied, left behind, frozen.

Friedman himself, in his remarks on *To the Lighthouse*, shows, I think, some discomfort with his formula: "the need to *suggest* a nonexistent containment," he writes, ". . . persists" (p. 33). But is it only a suggestion, and is the containment nonexistent? And might not one do better to rephrase his earlier comment—"The final attainment of the lighthouse, there in the book's world, is no containment but actually an unstopped movement of still disturbed conscience" (p. 31)—by saying that the unstopped movement of still disturbed conscience is, in fact, contained, so much so that the novel's fluid, interrogative texture is almost fatally rent? In any case, most modernist poems and novels are less obviously final in their endings, and it will be fairer to Friedman's hypothesis to test it against some other works. What of expanding experience in Yeats's "Blood and the Moon," for example? After three sections in praise of tradition and beauty and purity, Yeats reverses himself in the fourth:

> No matter what I said,
> For wisdom is the property of the dead,
> A something incompatible with life; and power,
> Like everything that has the stain of blood,
> A property of the living. . . .

Opting for the crude energy of life, he moves toward "virtually unrelieved openness" in every sense. But the poem does not end here. The concluding lines—"But no stain / Can come upon the visage of the moon / When it has looked in glory from a cloud"[32]—represent not another volte-face, still less a casual afterthought, but the acknowledgment of a paradox that turns the imagination of the poem back to the contemplation of its own unresolved but contained elements.

A Passage to India illustrates the same point in a different way. Friedman's comment on the novel's ending—"This is not still another reversal of the book's direction. But it *is* an expansion of conscience blocked, a direction left uncertain, a new and final opening outward left incomplete" (p. 128)—is incisive and suggestive and, read purely as thematic criticism (which is not what Friedman intends), it is, I think, indisputable. The notion of expansion blocked is exactly right, but the suggestion of an opening outward, even if left incomplete (Friedman quotes Forster's dictum: "Expansion. . . . Not completion"), seems to me to misconstrue the novel's final effect. I shall try to demonstrate more fully in the next chapter that, from the very first sentence of the book, Forster begins to establish the focus of absolute irony.[33] Here, I want simply to glance at the last paragraph: "But the horses didn't want it—they swerved apart; the earth didn't want it, sending up rocks through which riders must pass single file; the temples, the tank, the jail, the palace, the birds, the carrion, the Guest House, that came into view as they issued from the gap and saw Mau beneath: they didn't want it, they said in their hundred voices, 'No, not yet,' and the sky said, 'No, not there'" (*PI*, p. 312). Certainly, the passage directs us, thematically again, toward a distant, unresolved future. The implication of another time and another place does assert itself against the cacophony of dissenting voices. But surely the passage, regarded in a more formal way, tells another story. Almost all of the effects that for Barbara Herrnstein Smith contribute to a sense of closure are present here: verbal repetitions, monosyllabic diction (there are almost four times as many monosyllables as there are polysyllabic words, and of the latter, all but one is disyllabic), formal parallelism, balance, alliteration, metrical (or in this case rhythmical) regularity, unqualified absolutes, and closural allusions.[34] In this sense, there is no question of a direction left uncertain. Once again, the movement is reflexive. Friedman's comparison of the endings of *A Passage to India* and *Women in Love* serves, as I see it, only to emphasize the difference. Next to Lawrence's genuinely open-ended novel, Forster's suggests a backing away from what I agree is its *potential* for openness, its dimension of desire. What we have, in place of the untamed energies of Lawrence's characters, is the withdrawal of the artist from chaotic experience and, less explicitly but no less certainly than in *The Waves*, into the containment of his art.

This image of aesthetic fusion naturally associates itself with the aesthetic theories of Stephen Dedalus. "The personality of the artist," he announces in the passage on the progression of artistic forms, ". . . finally refines itself out of existence, impersonalises itself, so to speak."[35] But there is, as criticism abundantly shows, no easy way to establish how we are to react to Stephen or, indeed, to the *Portrait* as a whole. Whether Joyce's protagonist is, as the book ends, creator or forger, artist or aesthete, is only the final question about a novel that commentators have worried with as much imagination as persistence. "Well," Wayne Booth asks, "which *Portrait* do we choose, that of the artistic soul battling through successfully to his necessary freedom, or that of the child of God, choosing, like Lucifer, his own damnation?" and he ends by asserting that "we cannot believe that it is *both* a portrait of the prisoner freed *and* a portrait of the soul placing itself in chains."[36] Friedman, quoting this passage, sees in it the rhetoric of a criticism that demands clarity, the evidence of the author's intention, at all costs; and, as we would expect, the novel is for him one more example of literary openness. But Booth has a point, though his penchant for "stable ironies" leads him to miss its implications. "The truth seems to be," he says, "that Joyce was always a bit uncertain about his attitude toward Stephen" (p. 330), and he goes on, discussing now the earlier version of the book, to say this: "A supreme egoist struggling to deal artistically with his own ego . . . [Joyce] faced, in the completed *Stephen Hero*, what he had to recognize as a hodge-podge of irreconcilables." His solution, in moving to *A Portrait* was, according to Booth, "a retreat": "simply present the 'reality' and let the reader judge" (p. 332). But can't we, less hot for univocal meaning, read Joyce's uncertainty differently and see the *Portrait* as yet one more thematically open but formally contained work of absolute irony? Isn't the locus of the irony precisely the aesthetic and aestheticizing consciousness unable to solve or resolve the dilemma it posits, except by hovering over it in the sublimity of form? Like *The Waste Land*, "Monday or Tuesday," *A Passage to India*, and "Blood and the Moon," *A Portrait of the Artist* arrests its complexities and contradictions in one of modernism's variations on the basic, artistically perfected shape of paradox, inviting not the puzzle solver's ingenuity but the willingness to recognize, as at least a possible mode of response, the intractability of genuine crisis.

I don't want to prolong indefinitely my catalogue of absolute ironists, though one could add such names as Gide, Kafka, and Faulkner, taking in along the way (minus its final chapter) that sacred cow of modernism, *Ulysses*, and ending with Molloy's "mania for symmetry" and Moran's final words: "Then I went back into the house and wrote, It is midnight. The rain is beating on the windows. It was not midnight. It was not raining."[37] What matters, in any case, is surely not the number of works that conform to the specifications of absolute irony but their individual and, still more, their representative importance, since, as I've been attempting to indicate throughout this chapter, absolute irony defines the crucial point, the furthest perceptual thrust of the modernist movement. Heirs to a tradition they revolted against—the whole tradition, some would maintain, of Western, Aristotelian logic—the modernists proved incapable either of accepting chaos or of denying it, and equally incapable of reformulating what seemed to them the inherent, inescapable shape of order—harmony, in a word, or organicism, or "significant form." So, first reducing confusion to superficially more manageable antinomies and dilemmas, they then framed their visions of disjunctiveness in the more than usually patterned order of art. Thus fixed and steadied, the paradox, the aesthetic embodiment of absolute irony, constitutes the emblem both of the ironist's intuition of disorder and of his compelling desire for at least the *appearance* of form: Moran's desperate confusion contained in Molloy's empty, isomorphic gestures.

In short, a world threatening incoherence is first stabilized and then distanced. But instability attends. Closed in a sense (not Brooks's sense), works of absolute irony are in a way open too, but it is not Friedman's way. Is it any wonder that works like those I have been describing seem so often on the point of exploding from within? One can speak, of course, of the marvelously controlled tension of modernist works, but at times the control is too obvious and the tension too great. Woolf's delicate web of questions in *To the Lighthouse* will not be encompassed by the great symbolic resolution—or only forcibly so; Stephen and Bloom, at least from the seventh chapter of *Ulysses* onward, are coerced by the novel's self-conscious proliferation of techniques. The openness of absolute irony is a space within the work of art, the gap between desire and its realization; for crisis, if it is genuine, must lead either to breakdown or to the reformulation of the problem (as Forster reformulated his in *The Life to Come* or Woolf hers in *The Years* and *Between the Acts*), and thus to a new form of desire. Institutions, it has been said, rigidify just before their collapse (or reformation), and so too movements. The dissatisfaction and frustration that are everywhere apparent in modernism progressively channel themselves into more and more rigid structures, which simultaneously externalize and turn inward the pressures that threaten to shatter them. For a moment—it is the definition of crisis—the flow of an unresolved energy is dammed up, arrested, before it breaks forth and floods the postmodern world, leaving in its wake a series of remarkable testimonies to the struggles of an age's consciousness, which, despite themselves no doubt, predict a new, more haphazard conception of order and an end to the aesthetics of crisis.

· · ·

I want to close by dipping gingerly into that flood, thereby reestablishing the postmodern perspective I alluded to earlier. But first it will be useful to take a brief look at the downward slope that leads to it. No movement terminates abruptly, least of all modernism, and crisis, in any case, is not termination, in literary periods any more than in drama. So it is hardly surprising that modernism continues on—not only in isolated pockets, as it does today—but, at least until the Second World War, as a definable (if increasingly unstable) movement with its own special characteristics, most notably in England in the nineteen thirties among the members of the so-called Auden Group. The fact is that the major preoccupations of the earlier decade are still visible in the late modernism of its successor, and the writers of the thirties reveal themselves to be, if anything, still more self-conscious, yet more aware of the rift between self and world than their elders. But differences there are, and for my purposes it will be most illuminating to focus on one in particular.

The thirties, a decade on an altogether smaller scale than its predecessor—though a noisier one perhaps—is, fully as much as the twenties, a time of paradoxes. Indeed, external events forced on the thirties writers a series of troubling contradictions, centering in particular on the rival claims of artistic vocation and political commitment, which they then proceeded to debate publicly in the endless manifestos and declarations of those years. But whether arguing art and politics, exploring the contrary tugs of past and future (C. Day Lewis's "In Me Two Worlds"), investigating the mysterious inconsistencies of personality (Isherwood's Truly Weak Man), or tracking down the sources of perverse and destructive evasions (Auden's negative inversion of the will), in all these cases the writers disclose their faith that contradictions are susceptible of resolution. The genuine paradox of the twenties gives way to apparent paradox, metaphysics to social science. Consciousness, no less initially confused and divided against itself, marches behind the banners of Marx or Freud (or both), trampling down in the process all of the mythical monsters of the decade: the old gang and the wicked mothers, the politicians and the clergy, and not least the craven doubts and hesitations of the self. So Auden, in a poem called "Crisis" (in the *Collected Poetry* of 1945), answers his opening question—"Where do They come from? Those whom we so much dread"[38]—by demonstrating not only that we are ourselves responsible for the horrible anxieties, fears, and neuroses that afflict us, but, in addition, that we have "failed as their pupils," that in continuing, however obliquely and ruinously, to resist the "Terrible Presences" we create, we open ourselves to a better future. So, first awareness, and then action and choice: the proper exercise of the will. It is the age's formula and its promise of relief. The aesthetics of crisis yields, in the decade's most characteristic metaphor, to the image of travel and to the resolving vision of a "New Country."

But this is to make things too simple. From the start, the decade's enthusiasm for change rings a bit hollow. Auden's *Paid on Both Sides* counsels love and migration: the difficult journey to a new life (New Country again) undertaken in a spirit of active but not histrionic commitment. But from time to time, the Chorus belies the social hope, shifting its attention from the local feud that is the major subject of the charade to the unchangeable human condition: the sense of "Man divided always and restless always,"[39] to quote from *The Dog Beneath the Skin*, in which the same call to choose another life is undermined by the same covert intuition of the hopelessness and uselessness of choice. In *Paid on Both Sides*, Anne Shaw expresses, while rejecting, the thought of "divided days / When we shall choose from ways, / All of them evil, one" (*EA*, p. 14). And throughout Auden's (and Isherwood's) work in the thirties —from "1929," where "a sudden shower / Fell willing into grass," symbolizing the unthinking natural world and "making choice seem a necessary error" (*EA*, p. 37), to *The Ascent of F 6*, where the Abbot recommends, mysteriously, given the general direction of the play, "the complete abnegation of the will" (*TGP*, p. 154)—there runs the belief that any choice, because conscious, implies division and is therefore evil. I'm suggesting, in other words, that, in addition to the apparent paradoxes the decade traffics in, there are genuine paradoxes as well, but that these, half buried and contravened by the bugle calls to action, work not to define a present crisis, as among the earlier modernists, but to intimate the inevitability of one in the future.

Of course, the decade was in any case moving, thanks to the economic and political events of the time, to its own more public crisis, but I doubt that the Auden Generation would, in the long run, have made substantively different decisions or expressed substantively different attitudes had events been otherwise. In retrospect at least, modernism appears to have been sliding toward a state of exhaustion and impasse. Jogged from the heights their elders held, defensively and with a kind of aesthetic bravado, the writers of the thirties, and particularly the decade's ironists, found themselves more bewildered than heartened by their frequently superficial involvements: troubled by the detachment that, as they recognized, still afflicted them but uneasy in their demand for participation in a world whispering, beneath the shrill slogans and hopeful therapies, of disaster beyond the reach of politics and psychology and of disorder not to be stabilized by the symmetries of art. The chief paradox of the decade—the inevitable but unintended subversion of depth through a relentless attention to surface, undertaken in an attempt to change both self and world by rendering language transparent—this paradox marks the effective end of modernism and of the attitudes that made absolute irony possible.[40] Symptomatically, perhaps, Auden and Isherwood turned to religion in the forties, seeking a final resolution of modernist paradox, intractable now to art as well as to politics. In the philosophic city of Auden's "Spring 1940" man's doubleness is recognized and, sub specie aeternitatis, accepted. New Country has been transvalued and left behind.

Younger writers have turned elsewhere, in so many directions, in fact, that it sometimes seems impossible to identify the goal because of the superabundance of movement. What can be said with some assurance is that postmodernism tries in any number of ways to refute—or simply rejects—the very bases of modernist beliefs. Distance, detachment, depth, essentialism, anthropomorphism, humanism, analogies, and the privileging of sight have all been anathematized, most famously perhaps by Robbe-Grillet in *Pour un nouveau roman* (though I don't mean to attribute all of these rejections to him) and more recently by writers like Raymond Federman, Ronald Sukenick, and other participators in the "literary disruptions" described in Jerome Klinkowitz's book of that title.

Most important may be what Erich Kahler views, with considerable asperity, as "the disintegration of form in the arts."[41] Given Kahler's examples, there is much to be said for his diatribe, but it is possible too to speak, with Venturi, of an expanding, more comprehensive form, aiming, as he says, to fulfill through contradiction and complexity "the obligation toward the difficult whole" (pp. 89-103). Symmetry, shapeliness, and binary oppositions (*pace* Lévi-Strauss and the structuralists) are clearly at a discount; and if Derrida is right in asserting that, since all oppositions are implicitly hierarchical, one of the two terms is always more valued, then still more so is the notion of genuine paradox.[42]

We begin, then, with an antipathy to at least certain kinds of order. But that is only the beginning—or only the manifestation—of the change. Modernism reaches through order toward stability, and in Derrida's antimetaphysics the very idea of presence undergoes increasing deconstruction, revealing only and always an elusive absence. The high modernists, it should be said, had themselves begun to dismantle the infrastructures of their universe, making visible everywhere the shadow of the abyss, but what is at issue here is as much an attitude as a vision. In the movement from depth to surface, from an orderliness defined in terms of harmony or stasis to a more kinetic sense of order, from the high seriousness of the modernists (even at their most whimsical or witty) to contemprary ideals of play, there is a further and more basic shift. To speak metaphorically first, paradise, once lost, is now abandoned: Dowell's desperate desire not to concede the passing of the "true sunshine; the true music" is transformed, more or less cheerfully, into an antiessentialist *je m'en foutisme*. The modernist nostalgia over origins is replaced by a dismissal of them; the frustration of being unable to resolve a dilemma gives way to an acceptance of the impossibility of making any sense whatever of the world as a whole. Acceptance is the key word here. Modernist irony, absolute and equivocal, expresses a resolute consciousness of different and equal possibilities so ranged as to defy solution. Postmodern irony, by contrast, is suspensive: an indecision about the meanings or relations of things is matched by a willingness to live with uncertainty, to tolerate and, in some cases, to welcome a world seen as random and multiple, even, at times, absurd. Forster's vision of simple contiguity has been naturalized, so to speak, transformed from a bleak intimation of unbearable meaninglessness into an acceptance of life as sometimes messy and vital, sometimes more prosaically quotidian, and, at worst, as manageably chaotic. The last phrase is possibly too self-contradictory to pass without comment. I mean simply that, at the least, postmodernism has managed to establish enclaves of occasionally odd and curious pleasures, "the smaller pleasures," Forster calls them in *The Life to Come*, while continuing (in some cases) to acknowledge, if only covertly, the confusion that attends and surrounds them.

All of this is to say that the conditions that made possible the modernist imagination of crisis have now gone by the board. Yeats was righter than he knew. The center has indeed not held—and for a good reason: to all intents and purposes, it has disappeared, taking with it the fulcrum on which the modernist dilemma turned or, rather, supported itself. Paradox has become quandary, the scales have been unbalanced, and we have come, depending upon how one chooses to read the present, either to what Spanos calls "this silent realm of dreadful uncertainty," where and only where we are "likely to discover the ontological and aesthetic possibilities of generosity" (pp. 167-68) or, according to Kahler, to "the triumph of incoherence" (pp. 73-109). Neither alternative is all that joyful, though Spanos at any rate sees hope in the break from the modernist tradition. I don't think it would be inaccurate to assert that, as the large, imposing structures that embody the modernist crisis become, from the thirties onward, increasingly modest and various, crisis itself, redefined as an almost continuous response to a decentered or uncentered world turns, quite simply, into anxiety, that uneasy burden of contingent existence. And for Spanos, anxiety is exactly what the postmodern artist ought to be aiming at, as a way "of undermining the detective-like expectations of the positivistic mind, of unhoming Western man" (p. 167). Barthelme's Thomas puts the case more lightly but with similar intent in *The Dead Father:* "Things are not simple. . . . Things are not done right. Right things are not done. There are cases which are not clear. You must be able to tolerate the anxiety. To do otherwise is to jump ship, ethicswise" (*TDF*, p. 93).

Tolerating the anxiety. It is a reasonable, if not complete, definition of the postmodern sensibility, in any case of its ironic wing. And there, for the moment, I want to leave that sensibility, at least as something to be contemplated for its own sake. It is time to focus backward again, using the present as a vantage point from which to survey the past more accurately. The question that remains (it is the one I posed at the outset and left hanging) is this: how are we to evaluate and respond to the practitioners of absolute irony, the modernist masters whose reputations are in many cases currently under siege? For the response, Barthelme's portrait of the Dead Father once more comes neatly to hand. As I suggested earlier, that colossal relic of the past is Barthelme's myth of modernism: imperious (his murderous temper); commanding (his "Authority. Fragile, yet present" [*TDF*, p. 67] and his fondness for issuing ukases); aesthetic (he is an art connoisseur manqué and the novel's most spacious and rhetorical speaker); a devotee of organization and order ("What purpose? What entelechy?" [p. 168] is his question to two of his children); and, finally, someone who, as he admits, enjoys "having it both ways" (p. 15). Certainly, it is a comprehensive, if parodic, account of the modernist myth, critical but not without humorous sympathy; and it is wholly appropriate that Barthelme's postmodern version of *The Waste Land* discovers the possibility of redemption in the death of its Fisher King. But though Thomas oversees the burial with which the book closes, as the Dead Father descends still unwillingly into his grave, he disclaims responsibility: "Processes are killing you," he says, "not we. Inexorable processes" (p. 158). The remark echoes what may be the novel's central comment, which appears at the end of the interpolated book within the book, "A Manual for Sons." "Patricide," the anonymous author of the "Manual" writes, "is a bad idea. . . . It is not necessary to slay your father, time will slay him, that is a virtual certainty. Your true task lies elsewhere. Your true task, as a son, is to reproduce every one of the enormities touched upon in this manual, but in attenuated form. You must become your father, but a paler, weaker version of him. . . . Your contribution will not be a small one, but 'small' is one of the concepts you should shoot for. . . . *Fatherhood can be, if not conquered, at least 'turned down' in this generation*—by the combined efforts of all of us together" (p. 145).

The strategy is typically Barthelmean: the small-scale effort to disenchant or demystify inherited beliefs and imperatives informs all of his work.[43] And typical too is the novel's climactic revelation. In its final chapter, where, unequivocally now, the rains do fall, the Dead Father learns that the Golden Fleece he has all along been seeking (for him the journey is a quest to recover his youth) does not exist—or not in the shape or place he had imagined:

No Fleece? asked the Dead Father.
Thomas looked at Julie.
She has it?
Julie lifted her skirt.
Quite golden, said the Dead Father. Quite ample. That's it?
All there is, Julie said. Unfortunately. But this much. This where life lives. (*TDF*, pp. 174-75)

Together with the antipatricidal message of the "Manual for Sons," this interchange makes Barthelme's related points: the value of a not too vigorous stand against the largeness of absolute values; the effort to participate in an admittedly confused world; and the acceptance of life, however drab, as the only source of the smaller pleasures. So then, the largely ritual nature of the journey that loosely structures the book suggests a debunking of the insistent modernist quest, in *The Waste Land* and elsewhere. What you find, the novel implies, is what you already have under your nose—or, in this case, under Julie's skirt. As a low-keyed restatement of the anxiety of influence, *The Dead Father* contrasts a modest present with a too solid past, all moral bluster and aesthetic retreat, and proceeds, in a final parody of Eliot, to its own "burial of the dead." Allowing for rather too much and too derivative artfulness of its own, a sometimes numbing indulgence in nonreferential play, the novel succeeds wonderfully well in dramatizing its refusal of the sustained, the coherent, and the organic and, equally, its affirmation of the provisional and suspensive—in asserting, in short, the validity of local, uncoordinated pleasures against the claims of entelechy. But does the portrait of the Dead Father stand up to the facts of modernism? If I'm right in what I've been saying all along, then the answer is no, although Barthelme's summons to smallness provides a helpful clue to the truth. What is required, I think, is less a "turning down" in the present of modernism's overwhelming fatherhood, as the novel conceives it, than a recognition that the modernists were themselves somewhat less monumental than they are now taken to be.

Earlier, rejecting Brooks's criterion of maturity, I described the modernists as heroic, but that word may be as inadequate as the other for the scale and condition I'm trying to suggest. Isherwood's phrase "the antiheroic hero"[44] (used to describe Forster) comes closer to the mark perhaps, but even qualified, the idea of heroism is not likely to sit well with an age like the present, so resolutely seeking, exceptions like Pynchon notwithstanding, to miniaturize both its aspirations and its forms. No, not even the antiheroic hero: it is too easy to conjure up an endlessly receding line of statues, their heads drooping disconsolately but each upper lip still defiantly stiff. What word will do then? To find it we need to recognize in the unresolved quality of modernist irony (to return to the essential mode of its art) a refusal of easy answers and, at the same time, to acknowledge in its absolute poise not confidence and rest but crisis and arrest—to concede, that is, the *humanity* of the modernist enterprise. At the heart of that enterprise one discerns the intense need to shape a disordered world —not, in the first instance, either to reform or escape it but, instead, to establish, if only negatively, a relationship with it. The search for relationship is what links the modernist attempt with the postmodern effort now in process; and if the latter has, by reformulating the problem, brought the specifically modernist crisis to an end and opened the door to new solutions, it has sometimes succeeded only too well in packaging them in severely attenuated containers. I'm not sure that anyone can declare today what the mainstream of postmodernism is, but it is at least possible to discern, here and there within the movement, the danger on the one hand of a too flaccid acceptance of disorder and, on the other, of a too easy retreat into a reductive, minimalist aestheticism that makes Clive Bell's pronouncements seem hardy by comparison. For what characterizes the modernist consciousness above all is the energy of its desire. And where postmodernism succeeds, it does so by embodying that energy, though, to be sure, on a less heroic scale. In these cases, the sons have become the fathers, as Barthelme says, their achievement, as he also implies, not only a weakening of the originals but a redirection of their energy, so that the sons manage, in the unobtrusively symbolic phrase of *Between the Acts*, to "touch earth,"[45] as the modernist ironists, for all their perfervid primitivism, ultimately failed to do.

Between the Acts, odd though it may sound to say so, seems to me still the most impressive of *postmodern* novels, and all the more interesting for representing an awareness of and a response to the crisis I've described, not by a later generation but by one of the major modernists reacting to the dead end her own earlier work reveals. For the awareness and the response seem to me unquestionably deliberate. Far more fluid and open in its form than novels like *To the Lighthouse* and *The Waves*, Woolf's final work contrives nonetheless to allude to the paradoxes of absolute irony. Throughout the book, we are presented with an insistent structure of opposites, which culminates in the contrasting *"Unity—Dispersity"* (p. 235) the pageant ends with. (The reference at one point to "the donkey who couldn't choose between hay and turnips and so starved" [p. 74] neatly summarizes the inevitable consequences of absolute irony's arrested poise.) But the oppositions, the novel makes clear, are *thematic*—merely conceptualizations of life's ineradicable ambiguities; and to that degree, equally true or equally false or—and this is the most accurate way of viewing them—equally irrelevant: "'Yes,' Isa answered, 'No,' she added. It was Yes, No. Yes, yes, yes, the tide rushed out embracing. No, no, no, it contracted" (p. 251). What we have here is not modernism's balanced "either-or" but, as contemporary critics are fond of saying, postmodernism's more comprehensive "both-and."

In any case, it is not on the level of theme but of texture that the novel's final vision asserts itself: in its enormous density, its heterogeneous materials, its constant reference to the absolute dailiness—the "Monday or Tuesday"—of the life it presents. Within the context of its omnipresent noise—and its silences ("We are always in a plenum, in being," Merleau-Ponty writes, ". . . just as silence is still a modality of the world of sound" [*PhP*, p. 352])—things seem to exist, as they do not in the earlier novels, in their own right; not simply as avenues to transcendent vision but, like the animals passing in and out of the barn or the fish swimming "in their self-centered world" (p. 55), as themselves. For *Between the Acts* maintains and expresses a contact with things as they are: the world as perceived. The reference to touching earth derives from an allusion to Antaeus, and Antaeus is precisely the right emblem for Woolf's novel and for the postmodern imagination as well. Thus, later in the book, starlings attack the tree behind which Miss La Trobe, the exhausted author of the pageant, has been concealed, and she witnesses "a quivering cacophony . . . birds syllabling discordantly life, life, life, without measure" (p. 245). There is nothing placid about the scene, as the world (the starlings) imposes itself on Miss La Trobe's being (her consciousness incarnated in the tree), but that is the point. The unsought activation of perception begins again the process of vision, and "from the *earth* green waters seemed to rise over her"; "words of one syllable sank down into the *mud*. She drowsed; she nodded. The *mud* became fertile" (pp. 246, 247-48; my italics). What *we* witness is the affirmation of the *Lebenswelt*, or, rather, we are given an image of vision arising out of and rooted in it: an acceptance of the gaps and discontinuities that were once, for Woolf and other modernists, the source of horror and now, between the acts, become the basis of life and creation.

If Woolf's affirmation defines the nature of postmodern irony, it also releases the energy of desire contained in the earlier novels and in "Monday or Tuesday." And so too, it seems to me, postmodernism in general—or at its best—fulfills the blocked energies inscribed in the modernist crisis. Thus Ferguson, the narrator of Max Apple's "Vegetable Love," failing in his modernist attempt to discover depth (his center) and his late modernist effort to become transparent (the name he assumes is Glass), realizes that "starting from himself and stretching right to the farthest astronaut hitting a golf ball on the moon, there was a line of chaos as direct as the plumb line that went through Ferguson." "Who had absolutes?" he asks himself, and answers, simply, as he prepares for a new life, "I have tried."[46] The tone resembles nothing we associate with modernism, and no more do Ferguson's final attitudes: the rejection of certainty and the acceptance of chaos—the attainment, in other words, of suspensiveness. But the roots of his quest point backward as surely as his solution points ahead. The breaking up of paradox, then, can be interpreted not as the discrediting of modernism but as the release of its humanity; and, retrospectively, we can now see, in distance and detachment, in the search for order and its creation through absolute irony, not moral smugness and aesthetic complacency but, to say it one last time, the dynamics of consciousness in crisis. By humanity I intend, I should say, not whatever may result from the personal revelations about Woolf and Strachey, Forster and Eliot, and the rest, which, in exposing clay feet that leave prints no different from our own, threaten, in some instances at least, to simplify the problematics of their work. The evidence I'm referring to, the case against the dehumanizing and dismissal of modernism, exists in the texts themselves. Biography will shed its light no doubt, but all the rest—and it is what counts, after all: the still vital legacy of modernism to its rebellious sons and daughters, inevitably attempting once again to make it new—all the rest is literature.

TWO

Injunctions and Disjunctions

"I used to admire Forster's work much more than I do now," Angus Wilson announced recently in an interview, adding: "Forster has receded from me as a figure."[1] The comments apparently address different aspects of the Forsterian heritage, although, because of the particularly strong inherence of Forster's characteristic tone not only in the essays but in the fiction, it would be too simple to designate these as the writings and the man. Nevertheless, some such distinction is implied, and, accepting it for the moment, one recognizes that the second remark, conjuring up by way of contrast memories of Isherwood's "antiheroic hero," is in many ways the more devastating of the two. No doubt it is a fortuitous circumstance that Wilson's key word is one employed by Lionel Trilling over a quarter of a century ago: "He [Forster] is not merely a writer, he is a figure";[2] but the echo, like one from the Marabar Caves, is no less unsettling for being coincidental, and no less telling. For Trilling, Forster represented a particular kind of figure: one who "acts out in public the role of the private man"; and the description, which is in some ways as penetrating as it is representative of its times, suggests Forster's status, so congenial to Trilling and other earlier critics (I include myself), as—along with the not altogether different D. H. Lawrence—the principal moralist of his age. "As for his other traits," writes P. N. Furbank, Forster's biographer, "I think the most characteristic was his passion for moralising. He was moralising busily when he was twenty; and he continued, without intermission, for the next seventy years. He plainly regarded it as the business of life; one was on earth to improve oneself and to improve others, and the path to this was moral generalisations."[3] In the light of these observations, Wilson's reaction takes on more than individual significance, becomes, in fact, symptomatic of a larger change of attitude, which has its roots in a revaluation not only of Forster but of modernism as well.

To speak of a revaluation and, by implication, of a devaluation of Forster is, I recognize, to invite a good many objections and a good deal of contrary evidence; and I'm more than willing to admit that there has been no perceptible slackening of academic interest in him or in his works. Indeed, given the critical activity surrounding both in recent years—the eleven volumes that have so far appeared of the late Oliver Stallybrass's Abinger Edition, Furbank's illuminating biography, and Frederick P. W. McDowell's compendious and intelligent bibliography of secondary writings, not to mention the steady outpouring of books, essays, and conference papers—given all this, it might plausibly be argued that we are in the midst of a Forster boom. But whether, to return to Wilson's remark one last time, Forster and the values associated with him retain outside the academy the vitality and influence they once possessed is another and more complex matter; and it's perhaps more to the point I'm making to note that Forster is not for contemporary *writers* the presence he so obviously was for the young men of the thirties and even for novelists and poets of later decades. The voice that appeared at one time, and not so long ago, to speak with such quiet authority, the more persuasive for its hesitant and tentative discriminations, seems to have grown fainter or (to call upon Renata Adler's narrator again: "There they all are, however, the great dead men with their injunctions. Make it new. Only connect") to have hardened into a tone designed for fussy, hectoring, and objectionable pronouncements.

Adler's reference to *Howards End* makes clear what I've already intimated, that Forster's "injunctions" are as much a property of the fiction as they were, according to Furbank, a feature of the man. In other words, the "figure" and the novels are after all—or seem to be—inextricable, and it is reasonable to assume that disenchantment with the one will, as in Wilson's case, entail a rejection of the other. But to accept this formulation is very likely to simplify both terms of the equation and, with it, the nature of modernism. That Forster *is* a modernist, as Adler's placing of him among "the great dead men" implies, needs perhaps to be stressed. The moralizing strain of the work notwithstanding and notwithstanding various of his critical positions—the deprecation of too great a concern with point of view; the preference for the looser structural device of rhythm over the tighter organizational principle of pattern; and the talk of writers who bounce their readers and of novels that open out—Forster is fundamentally at one with his contemporaries in his formal concerns, in his allegiance to an aesthetic of art for art's sake, and in his sometimes unwitting pursuit of resolution and closure. Furthermore, and to turn the matter around, we are surely in a position now to recognize just how pervasive—if less overtly so than in Forster's writing—the moral impulse of modernism was, even in writers like Joyce and Woolf: to what a large degree form enacts in these works, even as it disguises, moral statement. It may well be, then, that what appears old-fashioned about Forster's fiction today derives not from the ubiquitous "moral generalisations" and their vehicle, his intrusive narrators, but from the too exacting translation of the need for order into inadequately realized or overly insistent redemptive characters and symbols (Stephen Wonham, Mr. Emerson, Mrs. Wilcox, Pan, the egregious hay of *Howards End*) and into shapes that belie and at times coerce the tensions of the works they enclose.

To recognize these tensions is, I'm suggesting, to learn to read Forster differently—can one do otherwise after the publication of the posthumous fiction, particularly the homosexual stories of *The Life to Come*? And it is just possible that in forgoing some of our assumptions about the novels' and stories' aesthetic coherence we will discover heretofore unrecognized levels of complexity, which make of the books, if less perfect and autonomous creations, at any rate a more authentic record of Forster's (and modernism's) struggles. No doubt there is an apparent danger in this enterprise of sacrificing literature on the altar of psychology; and I may be accused of making a silk purse *into* a sow's ear—worse, of proclaiming the sow's superiority. My concern, however, is not with the origins of Forster's contradictory impulses as they are to be discovered in the events of his life but with their manifestation, their inscription, in the very fabric and texture of his fiction: a concern, in short, not with the man behind but with the figure *in* the works, who, more and more with the passage of time, appears to act out, in defiance of those works' implied claim to finality (and of Trilling's neat summary) a variety of different and incompatible roles.

None of the fictions is free of these contradictions, not even the minor and major triumphs, *Where Angels Fear to Tread* and *A Passage to India*, that frame Forster's career as a novelist; and the rest, I'm tempted to assert, retain their interest in direct proportion to the irresolutions they manage (barely) to contain, the tensions they (inadvertently) define. *A Room with a View* remains a charming and genial fairytale, provided one is willing to ignore the problems raised by the presence of George Emerson, just as *Howards End*, so long as one chooses to focus on Margaret Schlegel, represents a memorable attempt to register the difficulties inherent in the effort to achieve satisfactory personal relations. But the resonance, the fascination of these books has its source elsewhere: precisely in those characters—George with his everlasting Why, Helen Schlegel with her never fully explored intimations of the abyss—who threaten to negate the ostensible tendencies and destinations the novels too facilely proclaim. As for *The Longest Journey* and *Maurice*, the books that meant most to Forster himself, they are, or so it seems to me, almost unreadable today—unless, that is, one opts to view them, even more than the other fiction, as battlegrounds of contending values and aspirations. The metaphor is commonplace but accurate: from first to last, the fiction reveals an internecine warfare, in which Forster's moral stance is increasingly undermined and finally subverted (if never, in either case, completely), first by an awareness and then, in part, by an acceptance of life's and the self's profound disunities.

Seen in other and, for my purposes, more relevant terms, Forster's career portrays the progression and interrelations of the century's different ironic modes, as mediate gives way to disjunctive and disjunctive to suspensive irony. This is again to make things too neat, of course, and in several ways. To the degree that Forster's irony is satiric, irony and morality coalesce, but, except in some of the earlier stories, the moral imperatives never issue forth unshadowed by forces that threaten to disrupt the hegemony of a corrective and stabilizing consciousness. It follows that in most of Forster's fiction Adler's "injunctions" are less the expression of a serenity so assured as to impose itself on others in the form of a minatory *sagesse* than they are the reflexive response to an intuition of disjunctions only partly and unwillingly acknowledged by Forster as determining factors of his more urgent vision. Furthermore, as we become familiar with that urgency, we come to recognize as well that Forster's irony generates the compensations not only of an integrating morality but of a more anarchic, freewheeling desire; and if the former contribute to the novels' visible structure and immediately audible voice, the latter, hidden or at least disguised, constitute the subtexts of the fiction: the dimension of what cannot, even in the posthumous *Maurice*, be said directly—at least not until, in some of the final stories, desire is liberated at last, revealing itself not as anything so simple as the homosexuality that covertly informs a number of the earlier novels but as the release from a whole range of constraints that consciousness, usually with marginal success, dictates throughout the fiction.

The amorality or, more properly, the new morality of these stories (oddly, in this last phase of his career, morality and irony, both reconstituted, more or less come together again for Forster) is not, however, a feature of all the work in *The Life to Come*; and one ought not to be surprised, in the light of what has been said, to discover even at the end a vacillation between different forms or dreams of self-realization. In fact, the vacillations, the tensions, the contradictions are, as I read it, the very meaning of Forster's life's work, which lies not in its unstable resolutions but in the intensity of its desperate search; and, in turning now to a more specific examination of some of the novels and stories, I want—not as a fashionable exercise in deconstruction but by way of recovering, salvaging, what seems to me the essential Forsterian spirit—to focus on this inconstant constant that manifests itself, variously, in the contention of consciousness and desire, in the shifting moral impulses the works reveal, and, above all, to come to the controlling perspective of the sections that follow, in the persistent intensities of Forsterian irony (even when most seemingly comic and assured) and of the anironic countervisions it calls into existence.

COSMOS, CHAOS, AND CONTINGENCY

The moral Forster is nowhere more in evidence than in *Where Angels Fear to Tread*, which, in its mediate irony, is among the most coherently satirical of his works. Written with an exuberance that even the most sanguine of the later novels lack (perhaps one ought to make an exception of the still earlier conceived *A Room with a View*), *Where Angels Fear to Tread* testifies to Forster's faith, as he later recalled it, that a "new age had begun"[4] and to Leonard Woolf's that society "should [and would in the future] be free, rational, civilized, pursuing truth and beauty."[5] Clearly, there existed in the early years of the century a group, whatever its size, sharing common standards and aspirations and furnishing that community of belief upon which satire depends. Whether Forster's first novel conforms completely to Woolf's revolutionary fervor or indeed to his own optimism is another matter; and it may be best at this point to state again that, however congenial to him throughout his career, satire proved a confining and often inadequate vehicle for his fundamental sense of life's complexity. Nevertheless, although it ultimately exposes the limits of what he was able to do with the form, *Where Angels Fear to Tread* obviously intends to be, and in some respects at least approximates the condition of, a satiric novel—holding up to ridicule as it does, through its controlled and witty verbal strategies, the triviality, complacency, and dishonesty of the lives exposed in its pages and, more importantly, presenting as the basis for its attacks a comprehensible and coherent world, embodied in the symbolically central figure of Gino Carella.

Gino and his city give a definite shape to the universe of *Where Angels Fear to Tread*, encompassing, as Philip sees it, everything between heaven and hell (p. 90) or between "the sun or the clouds above him, and the tides below" (p. 113). The novel's world may be mysterious and terrible, but it is ultimately limited and contained: an extrapolation (in Pierre Francastel's terms) from a "cube scénographique au centre duquel se déplace l'homme-acteur," "l'image d'une Nature distincte de l'homme, mais à la mesure de l'homme et de ses réactions."[6] Though he is seen by Caroline at one point as "greater than right or wrong" (p. 109), almost a transcendent force, Gino is very much of *this* world, conceived "à la mesure de l'homme," extending but also defining its boundaries.

In other words, Gino is the image of nature in the novel, and despite his occasional brutality (or because of it) a symbol of cosmos, of order. But his order is not Sawston's, and his function is not only to articulate the human limits of *Where Angels Fear to Tread* but to give its world a sense of dimension, to ratify its concern with views, which are as central to this as to Forster's other Italian novel. "Astride the parapet, with one foot in the loggia and the other dangling into the view" (p. 104), Gino exists, without being aware of it, in spatial and moral depth. He is part of the view, at one with, perhaps identical with, the phenomenal world and the world of value into which he merges. As contrasted with the superficial, morally conventional life of Sawston, Monteriano embraces, stretches, unifies (most notably at the opera), absorbing and accepting the melodramatic moments that are part of the texture of its life.

I've suggested already that in *Where Angels Fear to Tread* irony functions largely as a rhetorical weapon in the armory of satire. But the novel reveals as well another kind of irony: the perception of disparities or incongruities inherent in the very nature of existence and consequently resistent to the corrective thrust of satire. Furthermore, this other, disjunctive irony can be seen as the response to as well as the perception of a discontinuous and fragmented world, a world lacking order and coherence and, finally, meaning, as meaning is increasingly located not objectively in the cosmos but subjectively in the eye of the beholder. Longing to cross the gulfs and abysses that scar the landscape of modernist literature, the ironist (Francastel's "l'homme-acteur") is trapped in the dubious safety of distance and uninvolvement.

Gino stands outside this kind of irony. As the vehicle of Forster's satiric vision, he makes clear that the aim of the satire in the novel is to break down barriers, to achieve through a sort of transparency or harmonizing unity a coherence that will make more radical ironies impossible. But Gino is less a solution than an ideal. Like his opposite number, Harriet Herriton, who has no view, no ability to see in depth, Gino is, for very different reasons, irrelevant to the whole problem of disjunctive irony. Absorbed in depth, as she is excluded from it, he has only a limited bearing on the problems raised by Philip, Caroline, and the narrator. Thus, though he continues to mediate Forster's satiric vision to the end of the novel, he comes to seem increasingly less effective as he is juxtaposed with these figures, who, standing on the periphery of the view, can recognize but cannot come to terms with the depth it is Gino's function to express.

Possibly unintended, these more recalcitrant ironies become apparent as soon as one moves to the more general level of moral inquiry on which much of the novel is conducted. So, in the principal normative statement of *Where Angels Fear to Tread*, the narrator contrasts "a sense of beauty and a sense of humour" with "human love and love of truth" (pp. 54-55), a suspiciously resounding collocation of what C. S. Lewis once called "the great abstract nouns of the classical English moralists."[7] Indeed, these abstractions, called upon to carry more conceptual freight than they can easily bear, produce in the reader a sense of slightly blurred vision, and one is hard put to specify the values they are meant to designate. Granted that Philip does in fact transcend the unpleasantness of his early laughter and the crudity of his youthful art-worship, still, more fundamentally, the trajectory of his short career reveals some puzzling insights into Forster's hypothetical ideal. That Philip's instruments in attaining truth are in fact an ingrained irony and what I've elsewhere called "the aesthetic view of life"[8] (that is, variants of what he presumably leaves behind), may be put down to Forster's own deliberate irony at the expense of the limited growth of his ironic protagonist. But it is more difficult to rationalize one's perception that love and truth are not, as Forster's formulation of the ideal suggests, coordinate but disjunctive.

Truth may be granted to Philip, if the word is meant to suggest his increase in self-knowledge and his ability, as the book ends, to "see round" the whole situation "standing at an immense distance" (p. 147). But the abortiveness of his love for Caroline seems, in the final analysis, less the result of circumstance or even of character than of Forster's failure to realize the implications of that love—or, indeed, of Caroline's for Gino. It is difficult to overlook a sense of distaste for sexuality, evident in Philip's thoughts and in Caroline's hysteria, more difficult still to avoid the conclusion that Forster has constructed a fable of impossibility: the offer of love or truth—but not both. What is at issue then is not simply the awareness of "the complexity of life" (p. 89), which Philip and Caroline share, but, more ambiguously, Forster's own notion of human relationships.

Early in the novel, the narrator describes, as a central feature of Italian life, "that true Socialism which is based not on equality of income or character, but on the equality of manners" (pp. 35-36). The passage goes on to envisage the possibility of a relationship as close as David's and Jonathan's, because free from "feminine criticism and feminine insight and feminine prejudice." My point is not, to return to Caroline for a moment, simply that her love is frustrated by her exclusion from this world of masculine camaraderie (as Lilia's to a large degree is), any more than it seems to me adequate to explain away her retreat in terms of the mores of 1905. The problem hinges, surely, on the word "manners," which suggests first and inevitably the drawing-rooms of Sawston. The manners of Italy are very different of course: in the open-air world of the piazza, "in the democracy of the *caffè*," rooms and walls are dissolved, the domesticities of Sawston overturned, transparency and union achieved in "the brotherhood of man." But is the ideal proposed here any less artificial than the decorums of Sawston? "He will spit and swear, and you will drop your h's," the narrator comments, presenting, it would seem, a rather paltry end-product of socialism, democracy, and the brotherhood of man. It appears that we have been offered not a transcendence of but merely an opposition to Sawston, an inversion of its values; and, as a corollary, too feeble a structure to support the weight of the novel's satire.

In fact, it makes a good deal more sense to read the passage as a comment not on brotherhood but on sexuality, specifically homosexuality, and more concretely still, on a particular kind of homosexual relation. "He achieved physical sex very late," Furbank writes of Forster, "and found it easier with people outside his own social class" (*TPF*, p. 62). Seen in these terms, everything in the passage falls into place: David and Jonathan, the destructive "feminine insight," and not least the (Italian) spitting and swearing and the more verbal, passive *h*-dropping of that "you" (Philip, Forster, or the English reader?) who deliberately, artificially remakes his manners to achieve (I am quoting Furbank again) "a kind of private magic . . . an almost unattainable blessing, for which another person was merely a pretext." What hope for Caroline, then, in a book where the unacknowledged truth is sex and in which sex is finally seen as antithetical to love?

I want to make clear my major point here, which is *not* that Caroline as a woman can find no fulfillment in the homosexual world of the piazza. Indeed this observation seems to me trivial as compared with what is implied by the opposition of character and manners. "Equality of manners" is the end-product of a reductive process, a stripping away of all that individualizes two sexual partners, a minimal, anonymous unity achieved by the suppression of complexity. But Caroline cannot forgo her complexity to join with Gino any more than she can retain it and love the disconsolate Philip; for if "equality of character" implies the possibility (and no more) of love, it also entails self-consciousness, division, and an irony more subversive than any implied by Forster's intended satire. If it is too simple to substitute sex for truth in Forster's formula, then truth needs perhaps to be seen as the incompatibility between love and sex: an ironic intuition of disconnection that shadows almost all of Forster's fiction.

There is, I'm aware, a danger of making too much of the passage I've been commenting on. And yet it seems to me that the total effect of the novel, as articulated in its various techniques, substantiates my reading of it. The predominance of air, light, and view notwithstanding, *Where Angels Fear to Tread* is a sad and chilly book, a novel whose tensions are held in check but not resolved. The sadness, no doubt, is intentional: a conscious and normative irony directed at the protagonists of the story, who have learned much but accomplished little. The lack of warmth and the sense of irresolution are another matter. Forster's signature is partly stylistic, partly narrative, and each of his techniques is in effect double. So the essentially paratactic style is at odds with the predilection for rhetorical figures and occasional high-sounding words and, too, with the addiction to inverted sentence order. The effect of this overlay of slightly old-fashioned elements on a predominantly simple syntax is to create a sense of a voice both fastidious and mannered, a combination which, for all the apparent intimacy of that voice, helps to keep the reader and the characters as well at a distance. Philip, we are told, "always adopted a dry satirical manner when he was puzzled" (p. 59), and the description suits Forster's tone too, if one allows for occasional modulations into enthusiasm and sentimentality.

As for Forster's notorious melodrama, the appearance of violent moments in the context of the book as a whole suggests, paradoxically, a quality of containment. The incidents themselves threaten to explode Forster's world, but the violence of imagination is constantly checked by the coolness of the treatment, by the disconcerting flatness with which even the most emotional incidents are described. This distance from the events (like that from the characters) makes for an understated power in the novel, but it also confirms, through its tonal and stylistic checks, Forster's resemblance to Philip. Viewing his fictional world aesthetically and (to use the word with all of its modernist resonance) ironically, Forster creates more light than warmth; and there is some question as to whether the novel itself manages to express the "human love" its author apparently desires.

The problem of "love of truth" is more complex still. The sexual question apart, it is clear from the start that the very search for truth is compromised by the blurred perspective Forster adopts in his pursuit of it. The stable foundations of satire contrast with the subjective, shifting ground on which disjunctive irony rests. And to acknowledge the transformation of the one into the other (or the uneasy balance between them) is to recognize that an apparently ordered world is about to give way: the objective standard of a solid, essentially unchanging world is threatened by the ambiguous, personal vision of a world in flux. In short, irony, unmoored from satire, becomes autonomous—a vision of the universe held together only in the troubled consciousness of the individual observer. Nevertheless, what is finally important about *Where Angels Fear to Tread* in Forster's career is that, at this stage, these two perspectives are able, however tenuously, however fragilely, to coexist, providing at least an aesthetic coherence Forster was not always able to achieve in his succeeding novels. My aim here, however, is not to pursue all of the byways in the development of Forster's irony. The high road leads to *A Passage to India*, where both the nature of the observation and the sense of control undergo a definitive change. In the metaphysical universe of Forster's final novel, modernist irony, absolute at last, is the dominant vision.

In *A Passage to India*, the humanized conception of a three-dimensional, orderly universe gives way to something vastly larger and less comprehensible. Space and time as well are defined no longer "à la mesure de l'homme" but in terms of infinity and eternity. And if the narrator comments at one point that "vastness [is] the only quality that accommodates them to mankind" (p. 141), it is because man has tried to make over even these ultimate abstractions into analogues of "Heaven, Hell, Annihilation—one or other of those large things, that huge scenic background of stars, fires, blue or black air" (pp. 197-98). But for Forster and for Mrs. Moore, who "in the twilight of the double vision" after the caves, "can neither ignore nor respect Infinity" (p. 198), there is behind the blue or black air only emptiness, silence, and indifference. Distances in Forster's final novel are incomparably greater than in *Where Angels Fear to Tread*; depth has become a bottomless abyss. Beyond the arches and vaults of the book, there is "that further distance . . . last freed itself from blue" (p. 3). Over and over, among the negatives that thread the novel together, the eye seeks rest in a perspective that offers no point of convergence but only "an impartiality exceeding all" (p. 34). With the dissolution of Forster's earlier cosmos, nothing any longer contains—except "the echoing walls" (p. 37), which drive the characters back into the uneasy worlds of their own consciousnesses.

Fielding's momentary belief "that we exist not in ourselves, but in terms of each other's minds" (*PI*, p. 237) may stand as a symbol for how the self responds to the de-anthropomorphizing of the universe. From the first chapter, where the views of Chandrapore form and reform with changes of perspective, the relativism of human perception asserts itself. In the land of the hundred Indias, truth is splintered; the pretension to it, the subject of the narrator's bitterest scorn. And the conception of love as rape and (in Mrs. Moore's disillusioned thoughts) as "centuries of carnal embracement" (p. 127) completes, notwithstanding the more hopeful relations of the novel, the reduction of "human love and love of truth" almost to the point of travesty. Forster's outlook has become, in short, ironic in a way that *Where Angels Fear to Tread* only begins to suggest. Which is to say that *A Passage to India* articulates a vision of life in which everything disappoints or deceives; in which appearances are equivocal and the possibility of a reality behind them at best a question;

in which all things are subject to interpretation, depending upon how, where, and in what mood they are perceived; in which, at the extreme, meaning, no longer supported by value, is dissolved "into a single mess" (p. 220) and even the extraordinary is reduced to nothing.

The word "nothing" echoes through the novel, undermining, like the winds and airs in the middle section of *To the Lighthouse*, all pretension to human structure. But (to recall the argument of the last chapter) I've called irony absolute in *A Passage to India* not primarily because of its despairing vision, which is common to all disjunctive irony, but because of its form. Central to Forster's novel is the unresolvable dilemma—not the disparity between right and wrong or real and pretended on which satire thrives, but the discordant and equal poise of opposites. So in Forster's meditation on unity, carried on through the description of the two well-meaning missionaries, the irony is only superficially at the expense of Mr. Sorley, who "admitted that the mercy of God, being infinite, may well embrace all mammals" (*PI*, p. 32). More fundamental and more unsettling is the awareness that inclusion and exclusion are alike impossible. It is, as I have suggested in my book on Forster, between these poles that the drama of *A Passage to India* takes place: the factitiousness of any attempt to impose order on the one hand and, on the other, the recognition of the unbounded as the chaotic. "In our Father's house are many mansions," but "We must exclude someone from our gathering, or we shall be left with nothing" (p. 32).

Nothing again; and inevitably one comes to the caves: "Nothing, nothing attaches to them"; "Nothing is inside them . . . if mankind grew curious and excavated, nothing, nothing would be added to the sum of good or evil" (*PI*, pp. 117-18). The use of the caves to symbolize the infinite and eternal is in itself ironic. The small, discrete, claustrophobic enclosures are made to represent their apparent opposite, the limitless, formless, agoraphobic universe both because men "desire that . . . infinity have a form" (p. 201) and because, as in the Kawa Dol, which is at the same time something and nothing, the extremity of opposition is identity. In the caves, immeasurable space and immeasurable time are flattened out in Mrs. Moore's horrified awareness that "everything exists, nothing has value" (p. 140).

With this sentence, we come to the heart of Forster's irony, as it manifests itself in his final novel. In the disconnection between existence and value; in the failure of simultaneity to entail relation; in the disappearance of the dimension that value and relation imply, there is a collapse of the book's various metaphorical "bridges" and a confirmation of its pervasive "gulfs." And there is a collapse too of that depth and of those views that shape the cosmos of *Where Angels Fear to Tread*. "Visions are supposed to entail profundity, but—," the narrator adds,

"The abyss also may be petty" (*PI*, p. 198). The repeated emphasis on smallness, when what is at issue are the inconceivable reaches of the universe, has to do with the final reduction of meaning to a neutral co-existence in chaos. The amorphous and the illimitable come together when "the horror of the universe and its smallness are both visible at the same time" (p. 197). We are, in short, in a world of surfaces, where appearances, unresonant and reflexive, signify no meanings beyond themselves and where life, nonprogressive in its linear disconnection, "went on as usual but had no consequences" (p. 132).

The reduction of the metaphysical to the temporal and spatial dimensions of the caves parallels the transposition, accomplished through the mediation of consciousness, of the metaphysical into the psychological. Like the Anglo-Indians retreating from the implacable sun, the self, confronted with the silence of Forster's infinite spaces, folds in on itself. Viewed subjectively—and how else to view it when everything is "infected with illusion" (*PI*, p. 132)?—the universe dwindles into Mrs. Moore's cynicism and Fielding's solipsism.[9] If microcosm and macrocosm retain, conceptually and aesthetically, a metaphorical correspondence, effectively, self and world are disjoined. As J. Hillis Miller puts it: "When God and the creation become objects of consciousness, man becomes a nihilist. Nihilism is the nothingness of consciousness when consciousness becomes the foundation of everything."[10] In the shadow of the caves, the lesson of the Marabar is internalized, and causality gives way, with signification, to the terrified vision of simple contiguity: "Pathos, piety, courage—they exist, but are identical, and so is filth" (p. 140).

The perception of life as mere surface is a prefiguration of *The Life to Come* in the same way that the personal relationships of Forster's first novel look forward to those of his last. I'll return more fully to the question of depth and surface later on; but to a degree it bears on the human level of *A Passage to India* as well. The two paradigms of relating, mooted in *Where Angels Fear to Tread*, are here both clarified (to a degree) and polarized. Fielding and Adela, we are told, "spoke the same language, and held the same opinions, and the variety of age and sex did not divide them" (*PI*, p. 252); and of Ronny and Adela, the narrator similarly comments: "Experiences, not character, divided them" (p. 77). As defined by Adela's relations with the two men, "equality of character" comes to suggest an essentially static conception of character: predicated on the acceptance of the self; grounded on the belief in the possibility of rational understanding; and threatened both by the eruption of unacknowledged emotions and, more simply, by the conjunction of love and sex. Forster's strategy is to show that those who assume the stability of the ego are precisely those threatened by the depths of their own personalities. The intention, however, is not simply to expose the incompleteness of reason (Adela's imperious need to *know*) but, more profoundly, to test conventional notions of psychological depth (as he tests those of metaphysical depth in the caves) in order to reject them.

The point needs further explanation, involving as it does still another paradox. The relationships that dramatize "equality of manners" (Aziz's with Mrs. Moore, with Ralph, and with Fielding) are precisely those that seem, in their acceptance of mystery, instinct, and intuition, to arise from and to thrive on depth. But Aziz's friendships are not an answer to Adela's inability to touch bottom; they suggest, rather, a revolt against psychology, character, and the ego. Based not on being and knowing but on acting and doing, they are a pushing away from conventional psychological depth toward a new kind of human surface, as yet only partly realized in *A Passage to India*. In any case, one begins to see that Forster repeatedly constructs his ideal fictional relationships (the earlier stories and novels, particularly, as we shall see, *Maurice*, provide examples too) in terms of some initial abrasiveness—race, religion, class, age, nationality —which, overcome, yields what is, in essence, not the acceptance of the self but a creation of a new and desired self.

To a degree at least, the characters themselves consciously share Forster's belief. Aziz thinks of Fielding and Mrs. Moore: "He loved them even better than the Hamidullahs because he had surmounted obstacles to meet them" (*PI*, p. 134). And in his last ride with Fielding, he turns aside his friend's attempt at personal conversation and begins deliberately, almost artificially, the political argument that leads to the assertion of friendship with which they part. The novel's ending is a reminder, however, that the achievement of "equality of manners" depends not only on the transcendence of old patterns of relationship and the transformation of the self but still more on a conception of the universe in which the self can find its fulfillment. Where there is existence but no value and where, as Lawrence implied of Forster,[11] there remains the desire to act on a belief no longer believed in, love, friendship, and sex alike are futile.

It will be objected at this point, rightly, that I have arrived at the end of the novel without more than a glance at its third, Hindu section. So much has been written on the issue of "whether *A Passage to India* reveals a pessimistic or optimistic view of the universe,"[12] that I am reluctant to stir the pot once again. Something, however, needs to be said about the relation of "Temple" to the question of irony. Frederick McDowell has written that the Indian essays in *Albergo Empedocle and Other Writings* "weight the balance . . . in favor of anti-rationalist, pantheistic, mystical, religious, and quasi-Hinduistic interpretations of the novel."[13] And he notes, correctly I think, that the essays counteract Forster's remarks in *The Hill of Devi*. I am more willing than I once was to admit that the *desire* for what Hinduism represents throbs through the novel as the most perfect consummation of that transformation of the self I've already referred to. And no doubt my concentration on the caves has obscured the change in mood (signaled by the reappearance of views) that part 3 represents.

Still and all, even before we arrive at "Temple," we are back on the horns of a dilemma no less potent than, indeed related to, the inclusion-exclusion paradox of part 1. If Mrs. Moore's perceptions as she travels back across India and Fielding's as he returns to Venice represent a re-assertion of phenomenal reality independent of the transfiguring self, a return to depth; then Godbole and his Hinduism, already anticipated in Fielding's conversation with Aziz (*PI*, p. 265), are a denial of it. Forster's assertion that the Hindu festival represents the same thing as the scene in the cave "turned inside out"[14] seems to me to suggest not a disavowal but an alternate view of the meaning of the Marabar: a shift of perspective, which equivocally suspends questions of true and false. Throughout the novel, possibilities are mooted, but desire is not realization; and it is no easier for the reader to fix Forster's meaning than it is for Godbole to prolong his vision.

If I seem by now, in my attempt to question the legitimacy of reading "Temple" as a plunge into oneness, to be questioning as well my reading of "Caves," it is what I intend. The lesson of the criticism of the last fifteen years or so seems to me to be that, thematically considered, *A Passage to India* can be made to yield totally opposed and equally valid interpretations and that on this level no argument is ever likely to be accepted as final. I wrote some years ago, in a mildly existentialist reading of the novel, that, at its close, *A Passage to India* directs the reader back to life. It appears to me now that, more powerful than any suggestion of thematic open-endedness is the effect, described in the last chapter, of formal closure. In short, it is neither in the explication of its discursive content nor in the exegesis of isolated symbols that the key to the novel is to be found but in an examination of its pervasive and controlling technique.

Beginning with the opening sentence of the novel, in which, subtly but firmly, syntax establishes a dizzyingly ironic focus for the reader, Forster's strategy emerges. If Forster's cosmology undergoes a radical change between his first and last novel, the comparison of technique suggests an intensification rather than an alteration of basic approach. To put this another way, the collapse of Forster's earlier world seems to have called forth not a corresponding transformation in aesthetic form but, by way of compensation it would seem, a firmer sense of control. The result, predictably, is an enormous tension in the novel, manifest first of all in the style, whose still essentially paratactic structure supports and holds in check a texture that, in the density of its images and symbols, of its diction generally, is so much richer and fuller than that of the first novel and, too, so much more restrained. With the first view of Chandrapore, the urbane and cultivated voice of the narrator establishes his distance from the scene, the reductive tone expressing, along with the distance, a certain distaste. Matching the abundant stylistic qualifications —the careful *excepts*, *rathers*, and *thoughs*—the tone, for all its apparent casualness, is ultimately self-conscious, academic, fussy, almost precious in its attempt to produce "the coin that buys the exact truth [which] has not yet been minted" (*PI*, p. 12).

And so it is throughout the book. His tone verging at times on cynicism, the narrator continues to play down what is positive, to question what is taken for granted, to qualify what is whole. Laying out his narrative as a series of tableaux, discrete and contained despite the violence of the action they describe, he is the embodiment of artistic control surveying an incomprehensible world. Nothing within *A Passage to India* but *A Passage to India* itself is Forster's "self-contained harmony," which gives "us the illusion of perspicacity and of power" (*TC*, p. 57; *AN*, p. 44). Thus it is that, as one comes to "Temple," the ubiquitous irony of the novel plays over Hinduism, as over everything else, enforcing and at the same time questioning its own paradoxes. Forster's description, very near the end of the novel (and anticipating its "No, not yet," "No, not there"), of the "emblems of passage" expresses perfectly the attitude of aesthetic poise: "a passage not easy, not now, not here, not to be apprehended except when it is unattainable" (*PI*, p. 304). Like this fragment, the book as a whole achieves a stasis of equivocation: the accumulated negatives playing off against the imagination of desire. Suspended between the equally valid polarities of "nothing" and "extraordinary," *A Passage to India* is not so much open-ended as forever ironic in its simultaneous and equal assent to the contradictory possibilities man can entertain. If the fictional world of *Where Angels Fear to Tread* is chilly, *A Passage to India* is (like Virginia Woolf's *The Waves*) frozen, its "wintry surface" (p. 8) directing us, finally, back to itself through the extraordinary perfection of its art.

When Sir Richard Conway, surveying the remainder of his dull, country weekend, thinks to himself: "The visit, like the view, threatened monotony" (p. 97), he gives perfect expression to Forster's sense of ordinary existence in *The Life to Come*. Not the metaphysical terror of the caves but the monotony of "normal" life serves as the background of these stories, and their heroes, unlike Mrs. Moore or Fielding, who react by a movement inward, accept that monotony as an inevitable part of life's texture, while actively accommodating themselves to what are now seen (in a dramatic reversal of Forster's attitude in his last novel) as the intermittent pleasures of life's surface. At least, most of them do. Of the stories I am concerned with (those which, according to the dates offered in Oliver Stallybrass's admirable edition, were composed at about the same time as or later than *A Passage to India*),* three deal with love. Significantly, "The Life to Come," "Dr. Woolacott," and "The Other Boat," which I'll examine in greater detail later on, are closer in feeling and strategy to Forster's earlier work. More ambitious and morally more ambiguous than the other five stories, they are also more obviously sentimental, sometimes, as in the opening of "The Life to Come," embarrassingly so. And in the first two at least, the attempt to render love leads to a style that is poetic by intention, yet curiously flat, thin, and conventional.

More striking is that fact that each of these stories ends with death. And although it is possible, given their orthodox psychology, to regard the endings as inevitable effects of causes specified in the stories, it is difficult to avoid the sense that what is being revealed more clearly still is a psychological pattern in Forster. If *Maurice* is predicated on a happy ending,[15] these stories express the more typical lure of failure in matters of homosexual love. Or, rather, not homosexuality as such but, as I've suggested, the conflation of love and sex. To combine the two is, in Forster's imaginative world, to invite, indeed to ensure disaster. To the last, as "The Other Boat" makes clear, Forster was unable to envisage the stability of complete human relationships in a universe of temporal and psychological change. What his imagination sought and intermittently found was a nondynamic world, freed from the impersonal determinations of causality as from the more subtle connections of love. It is, in part, the world to which the endings of many of the earlier fantasies (and of "Dr. Woolacott") unsatisfactorily point; it is also the world of the remaining five stories: "other kingdom" brought down to earth.

The deliberate avoidance of love in this second group has as its corollary the acceptance of sex as sex and for the moment. What Forster is after is described perfectly in "Arthur Snatchfold" as "the smaller pleasures of life," a one-time affair conducted "with a precision impossible for lovers" (p. 103). "Equality of character" gives way totally in *The Life to Come* to a series of unequal confrontations; and now that physical contact is out in the open, the abrasiveness I spoke of earlier is still more apparent. Indeed, the looser, freer structures of most of the sexual stories create, for the first time, a fictional world congruent with the asymmetric relationships they celebrate—one in which the new allegiance to surface

*See Stallybrass's introduction and the dates on p. xii, which indicate that these stories run from 1922 to 1958. For convenience, I shall use the title of the whole volume to refer to the eight homosexual stories that run from p. 65 to p. 197. The other five stories, written between 1903 and 1906, are not relevant to this discussion. The eight I do plan to examine can most conveniently be subdivided into "sexual stories" and "love stories."

is revealingly defined by means of the curious psychological discontinuity that marks their heroes. Even in "The Other Boat," Lionel, in the midst of his affair, forgets "any depths through which he might have passed" (p. 178). In the sexual stories this habit of mind is endemic: characters forget the men to whom they have been attracted, with whom they have had an affair, indeed by whom they have been raped—thereby ignoring or refusing the depth implied by memory and created by continuity of feeling. In all these stories, depth—spatial, temporal, and psychological—is inessential, inimical, or impossible: a force operating against the disequality of character that is now more than ever a positive good, a barrier not to be minimized or ignored but to be pleasurably overcome.

But the relationships achieved make for an "equality of manners" that needs to be further defined with reference to Forster himself. Furbank's comment: "He valued sex for its power to release his own capacities for tenderness and devotion, but he never expected an *equal* sexual relationship" (*TPF*, p. 62) indicates that equality is, in fact and paradoxically, inequality: a peculiarly limited, discrete moment, in which connecting becomes coupling and love, of course, sex. It is in the contact alone that the participants are leveled—equal in their enjoyment of their unequal pleasures. And so it is in the stories. Freed from sentiment, if not from sentimentality, they represent a movement from Forster's familiar "as if" to a very different "as it is": self joining with world in an unresonant acceptance of amoral pleasure.

It is part of the donnée of *The Life to Come* that pleasure remains the object of general disapproval, and so Forster continues to attack his old enemy Mrs. Grundy and her relations, who, in the chronological progression of the stories, go down to increasingly violent defeat. Each of the stories has its villain; all are the object of Forster's sometimes unpleasant satire, the corollary to the single-minded assertion of his ideal relationship. Where sex is refused or scorned or rejected, there is, in all eight of the stories, an eruption of violence and vengeance, darkened at times, as in the curious nastiness of "The Classical Annex," by the shadow of sado-masochistic impulses. But Forster's antipathies are more wide-ranging still. The cruelty directed at Hilda in "The Obelisk" derives presumably from Forster's rejection of her rhetoric of salvation, which, whether or not it was so intended, comes across as an inversion and parody of almost identical language in *Where Angels Fear to Tread*. Philip's attitude is clearly no more acceptable by now than his sister's. The search for romance and the mating of character, like the transformation of sex into idealized love, define the attitudes of those who cannot accept the smaller pleasures of life.

The passage of time obviously made imaginative assent to his sexual ideal more of a possibility for Forster. In "Arthur Snatchfold," the first of the group, Forster seems unable as yet to conceive of pleasure triumphant and unpunished, and the story in fact registers a defeat for the smaller pleasures. In the second story, the obelisk that symbolizes them may, in its fallen state, undermine the sense of phallic potency—though one would hardly judge so from the activities of its two sailors. But there is, in any case, no question about the other three stories, which are in every sense tumescent. Forster's rising joy is, however, no guarantee of the reader's sympathy. Unless one accepts the criteria that determine Forster's approval (and which so markedly exclude large areas of human needs and desires), it is hard to accept the repulsive Ernest of "The Obelisk" or the sadistic gladiator of "The Classical Annex" or even Mirko, Forster's generally attractive *porte-parole* in "What Does It Matter?" who includes among the things that do matter "baiting the Jews" (p. 141). All three are presumably meant to be "natural," but from Gino and Stephen Wonham onward, naturalness is more than a little suspect in Forster's writings: a Nietzschean temptation unrelieved, as it is in Gide, by a consistent moral alertness. And it is at the least curious that Forster can accept, if not approve, Mirko's statement.

Still, it is easy enough to see what Forster is after. "What Does It Matter?" is subtitled "A Morality," and, along with Sir Richard and the Roman Marcian, Mirko is the most genial expression of Forster's ethic: the need for diversity and tolerance, especially in sexual matters. The Pottibakians, "do[ing] as they like" (p. 144) inhabit Forster's utopia of activity and participation and acceptance. And so too does Marcian, after the destruction of the basilica and its *virgo victrix* in "The Torque." The movement of the story's final pages is, by way of the animals, who "clucked and copulated as usual," away from Christianity and ascetic morality toward a "natural," sexual life, in which where he is is enough for Marcian. "There was nothing to exorcize," the Bishop unhappily discovers, "and Marcian became gay and happy as well as energetic, and no longer yearned nostalgically for the hills." Despite its misplaced touch of fantasy at the end, "The Torque" attains to Forster's final vision of the here and now. Marcian, with his take-it-as-it-comes philosophy, is, along with Mirko, a natural inhabitant of a world "equally dispossessed of good and evil" (p. 165) and thus immune to conventional ethical categories.

Taken together, the sexual stories in *The Life to Come* define the final stage of irony in Forster's work: an acceptance of contingency that is perhaps best illustrated, by its absence, in the figure of Count Waghaghren, the villain of "What Does It Matter?" and a man "unaccustomed to incidents without consequence" (p. 132). Obliquely, the description hints at the suspensiveness of Forster's irony and at the priapic ethos of the sexual tales. For Forster's late figures are, to repeat, men unconcerned with consequences; and the stories explore and celebrate, precisely, a world without causality, sequence, or depth. The results of this change of attitude, apparently so striking, need to be recognized and understood. In the movement from cosmos to chaos and, further, from the melancholy awarness to the feverish acceptance of surface; from redemptive moments to desperate snatches of pleasure; from "the power to love and the desire for truth" (p. 19) of "Albergo Empedocle" (and *Where Angels Fear to Tread*) to the truth of that discordant sexuality heretofore at least partly concealed in Forster's fiction, what has most strikingly disappeared is the all-embracing ideal of connection set forth in *Howards End*. Along with the asymmetry of relationships comes, or seems to come, the acceptance of randomness and multiplicity as the very definition and condition of life and its satisfactions; and, in the light of Forster's earlier work, the acceptance is as radical as it is surprising. In *The Life to Come*, Forster goes beyond not only *A Passage to India* but the prewar fiction of his chief disciple, Christopher Isherwood. *The Berlin Stories* take place, as it were, "in the cave": cosmos is gone, chaos is unthinkable; one tries (uncomfortably) to live in time and space. But the overriding concern of Isherwood's novels with disconnection and discontinuity[16] implies the ability still to imagine the theoretical possibility of wholeness and unity as an ideal.

Forster's is a further step: not merely from logical sequence to simple succession but from surface conceived of as the limited and limiting prison of the self to the perception of it as the open ground of the self's sporadic but total fulfillment—an area something like what Wylie Sypher describes as "a visual field, which is quite unlike the visual world we 'know' . . . [and which] cannot be perceived all at once."[17] In other words, we have moved into a world where, although everything continues to exist by contiguity alone, that state of affairs is now for the first time accepted and indeed welcomed. Looking back at the prewar years, W. H. Auden described the need for the writers of his generation to adopt irony as a style of writing and, it is implied, of living:

> And where should we find shelter
> For joy or mere content
> When little was left standing
> But the suburb of dissent?[18]

The Life to Come positions itself quite differently: situated neither between heaven and hell, nor in the shadow of infinity, nor yet "in the cave," it exists, by intention at least, firmly in the midst of the suburb of *assent*.

To invoke the notion of assent at this point is to trespass on the problem of the anironic, a subject I want to explore in connection with Forster further along in this chapter; but there is no easy way of separating into discrete bundles the complementary visions of acceptance and assent: the ironic and anironic impulses that together define Forster's ultimate response (or, since my concern for the moment is still with the sexual stories, one aspect of it) to his world. The fact is that just as Forster's acceptance of contingency leaves behind, or seems to leave behind, mediate and disjunctive irony altogether, so it provides the basis for the anironic counterpart of suspensive irony, namely, the desire for unmediated experience, for direct participation in the world. And indeed, despite the continuation of satiric impulses, Forster is essentially the celebrator, not the critic, of the world he fictionalizes in his final stories. Furthermore, the total collapse of Forster's characteristic distance from his subject matter is, far more than in the love stories (though without their rhetorical infelicities) an assent to a unity achieved through "equality of manners" and "the smaller pleasures of life."

But as one begins to examine more closely the nature of these pleasures, something odd and unsettling emerges, which calls into doubt, as it does in the case of those later and lesser writers Forster adumbrates in *The Life to Come*, both the thoroughgoingness of his acceptance and the vitality of his assent. To begin with the latter: as one surveys the opposite ends of Forster's career, taking as terminal points the stories in *The Celestial Omnibus* and those in *The Life to Come* that I've been discussing, it becomes clear that if the early ones express the need for love (compare again too the "human love" of *Where Angels Fear to Tread*) and the later ones for sex, still what is central to both is the idea: the *idea* of love, the *idea* of sexuality—"Maîtresses de l'âme, Idées."[19] And as the early stories subdue Pan, their tutelary and informing presence, into an urgency made conformable to the demands of consciousness, so the later, priapic tales, for all their often attractive exuberance, remain equally and curiously theoretical: blueprints of desire, amusing schemata of passion, which, because of their abstractness, qualify, in their comparatively decorous way, as at least quasi-pornographic.[20]

Forster's assent is, then, something less than it seems at first glance: not genuine participation but, again, the *idea* of participation. But that is not all. Like the early stories, the later ones achieve their ends through a process of exclusion or substitution. Which is to say that Forster's suspensiveness is less genuine, less comprehensive than it appears; that a world of insupportable density and facticity has been replaced by a more manageable, because more abstract, version of it. Consequently, Forster's response to the dilemma of *A Passage to India* is less a transfiguration than an evasion of his earlier problem: the awareness that "everything exists, nothing has value" is not so much overcome and faced as it is neutralized by the foregrounding of occasional intensities at the expense of the random, incoherent world they imply. What purports to be a movement toward inclusion is in fact the extreme of exclusion: a spurious unity superimposed on a still fragmented world, whose fragmentation is only partly acknowledged. In short, the inadequacy of the sexual stories is twofold. On the one hand, Forster's earthly paradise speaks of assent, of passion, vigor, and sexuality, but the thinness of the dream belies its reality—if not the longing for it. On the other hand, and more importantly, the naturalization of Eden, which is what, in the context of Forster's career, the sexual tales represent, refuses at the last to recognize or to accept fully the background against which the new Eden is made to arise: the contingent world that is in fact its source and meaning. The resolute and deliberate affirmation of a small part of life's possibilities may be stoic or tragic—even and especially the origin of a limited joy. But to act, while celebrating local and discrete pleasures, as if the whole had been embraced and all its parts connected is a delusion and an illusion: the ground equally of pathos and, for the reader aware of the discrepancy between intention and result, of an irony of an altogether conventional kind.

The Life to Come bears most immediately on Forster's own earlier work, and it has already called forth reinterpretations and revaluations of it; but it has other implications as well, which become apparent when one views it in a larger context. The growing insistence in recent years that art is definitively rejecting depth[21] involves not only an animus against ultimate realities and Newtonianly-ordered world views but a reassertion of the relationship between the self and the phenomenal world. "Il est clair, dès à présent," Francastel writes, celebrating the end of Renaissance space, "que le nouvel espace sera un espace construit davantage en fonction de nos comportements que de notre réflexion" (p. 205).

But the movement from Sein to Dasein, "the return to the surface,"[22] has assumed at least two radically different alternative forms. On the one hand, there are those writers who, beginning with an awareness of modernist irony, move beyond or transform it. In the writing of Merleau-Ponty, for example, with its repeated invocations of "horizons" or its notion of co-presence, there is implied, as in Between the Acts, a dynamic interaction of consciousness and world leading to a new kind of creation. The world suggested may be predicated on surface, but it is neither fragmented nor static nor flat—as Forster's so conspicuously is.

The Life to Come, on the other hand, predicts not phenomenological art and thought but figures such as Warhol and Robbe-Grillet, certain of the photo-realists, and, in general, those contemporary writers, both French and American, given to the celebration of reflexivity. As in the works of these novelists and artists, Forster presents a surface that is opaque and unresonant; and like the painters in particular, he points to the problem involved in the discrepancy between intention and response.

Obviously less neutral than they, he resembles them, by way of his subject matter, in his manifest but not fully realized abandonment of the Arnoldian responsibility for seeing life steadily and whole. From "the smaller pleasures of life" to Campbell's soup cans the psychological and aesthetic leap is not that great; nor is it from Forster's ultimately drab assent to a comment made by one recent painter: "I'm not saying that what I picture is good or bad. It's up to the viewer to make his own response."[23] Whether deliberately or not, the burden of commitment and subjectivity has been shifted to the reader or viewer—along with the recognition that in these cases the artist's uncertain acceptance of his content *is* the irony.

A less ambiguous but finally more evasive approach to the question of intention is to be found in the critical writings of Robbe-Grillet. The business of the novelist, he writes, is to record distances "and to insist further on the fact that these are *only distances* (and not divisions)."[24] The implications of this statement are enormous. If there are no divisions, then all of the anguish of modernist literature is meaningless. Indeed, to see separation as disturbing is to assume that there is such a thing as depth or interiority or transcendence. But there is, in fact, only surface: "The world is neither significant nor absurd. It *is*, quite simply" (p. 19). The attitude is, again, one of acceptance, but the acceptance is achieved not, as in the case of Merleau-Ponty or the later Virginia Woolf, by a restructuring of the relations between self and world but by a semantic sleight-of-hand, whereby the ominous "division" becomes the neutral "distance."

Forster's strategy is the same: redefinition becomes the solution to the problem—in his case, the problem of connecting. The final irony of Forster's suspensive irony is, however, that in The Life to Come he does achieve a connection of sorts. But it is a connection by reduction: the joining of self and world at the expense of consciousness. Man is not incarnated in his body; he *is* body, his sexual self, finally an object, a thing. At the last, it is a sad, pinched, meager vision of life that The Life to Come expresses. "Give pain, give pleasure an outer body," a character thinks in The Years, "and by increasing the surface diminish them."[25] The words suggest the impulse behind Forster's final stories, written one feels, not simply, as he acknowledged, "to excite [him]self" (p. xii) but for personal salvation. They may well have served their purpose, but the diminishing of pain is, inevitably, the circumscribing of pleasure as well.

DESIRE AND CONSCIOUSNESS

From the start, Forster's familiar ideal of permanent connection—which provides the not altogether solid basis for his belief in "personal relations" —is more or less openly subverted by an attraction to the pleasures of passing contact. Generally, connection is made to triumph. Only in *The Longest Journey* among the early books is a protest lodged, not without ambiguity, against "the code of modern morals," with its slogans of "Eternal union, eternal ownership" (p. 292); and even in that novel "Romantic love" is acknowledged to be greater than Stephen Wonham's more prosaically independent notions about marriage. Still, Forster's occasional tributes to the discrete and discontinuous relationship, however much qualified, act (or should act) as potential threats to the reader's perception of his moral design, which, in the novels from *Where Angels Fear to Tread* to *Maurice* (1914), depends upon the possibility of integration. Divided against themselves, Forster's characters are invited to overcome *through* consciousness their consciousness of isolation in a disordered and incoherent world. Encouraged to "live in fragments no longer" (*HE*, p. 184), they are asked to undergo a process of transformation by adding to or absorbing into themselves the primitivist values of the novels' symbolic figures and landscapes. Becoming is the goal of these characters; choice the instrument Forster offers them; and their ambience, "the sense of space, which is the basis of all earthly beauty" (*HE*, p. 202).

In a world so conceived, there is, so far as personal relations are concerned, room for failure certainly but not for successes that abort the psychological depths and temporal continuities implied by the attainment of "connecting." And yet both Forster and his characters entertain the notion of just such final and depersonalized encounters. So Philip Herriton, in a manuscript passage excised from *Where Angels Fear to Tread*, addresses (with no irony intended either by him or by Forster) the "dear friends of mine whom I have made in Italy! cabmen, waiters, sacristans, shop assistants, soldiers . . ." and ends, after his perfervid praise of these chance, passing acquaintances: "oh thank goodness, I shall never see one of you again!"[26] What is at issue (and there are connections to be made between this passage and Philip's subsexual relationship with Gino) is an immediacy of gratification to which the discriminations of consciousness are antithetical and for which the fact of essential personal disequality is prerequisite. Margaret Wilcox's praise of "eternal differences" (p. 336) is a civilized response to the difficulties of human interaction, the tolerance of a consciousness secure in its own individuality; Philip's unequal friendships are, rather, a welcoming of anonymity, an escape from the disintegrated self in the interplay of frictional surfaces.

More revealing still are the remarks Forster makes in his own voice (or in his narrator's)[27] in *The Longest Journey*: "Love, say orderly people, can be fallen into by two methods: (1) through the desires, (2) through the imagination. And if the orderly people are English, they add that (1) is the inferior method, and characteristic of the South. It is inferior.

Yet those who pursue it at all events know what they want; they are not puzzling to themselves or ludicrous to others; they do not take the wings of the morning and fly into the uttermost parts of the sea before walking to the registry office" (p. 66). Two rather large assumptions enclose Forster's analysis, namely, that both of the "methods" he describes are properly called love and that both will inevitably eventuate in marriage. The second may be merely a concession to Edwardian proprieties; the first appears, in a fundamental way, to place Forster himself among the orderly people he mildly ironizes. The fact is that Forster's early novels display both a devotion to discriminations and a certain reluctance or inability to pursue the implications of the abstractions that make the discriminations possible. It is easy enough to understand in the context of the novel what is meant by the contrast of the desires and the imagination; it is less easy to see why, since Rickie's method of falling in love inevitably invites disaster, the other is acknowledged as inferior.

The answer lies in a redefinition of Forster's terms. Forster's love is in fact desire; desire, sexuality; and imagination, love—or at least a form of it. Further, if imagination suggests the distortion of consciousness, desire implies its absence; and Forster at this point is no more able to accept unmediated desire (that is, sexuality) than he is able to imagine the successful combination of sex and love. Or at any rate to present it convincingly. Presumably Mrs. Elliot and her lover Robert are meant to suggest the ideal, but Forster's treatment of their relationship—a sketchy, discursive interpolation into the main body of the narrative—demonstrates how theoretical the ideal in fact is. Forster's early novels are filled with "moments" that resonate with sexual feeling or that displace sexuality with violence and death, but the major relationships of these books belie the idea of passion, subordinating it (where it is not rendered impossible) to "the comradeship, not passionate, that is our highest gift as a nation" (HE, p. 265).

Paradoxes begin to emerge. Love is integrative for Forster, sex partial and temporary. Yet sexuality achieves for its brief moment a unity of desire for which connecting strives in vain. The assertion of consciousness, exigent in its demands for the total and enduring, produces the meager Lucy and George of A Room with a View, the devitalized Margaret and Henry Wilcox of Howards End, but nowhere the intensity of feeling of Helen Schlegel, for example, who is "led to that abandonment of personality that is a possible prelude to love" (HE, p. 21). It is worth quoting at length the passage in which Forster comments on the incident of Helen's kiss, since nowhere else in his work is there so great a tension between the Edwardian moralist and the "amoralist" who emerges in The Life to Come:

But the poetry of that kiss, the wonder of it, the magic that there was in life for hours after it—who can describe that? It is so easy for an Englishman to sneer at these chance collisions of human beings. . . . It is so easy to talk of "passing emotion," and to forget how vivid the emotion was ere it passed. Our impulse to sneer, to forget, is at root a good one. We recognize that emotion is not enough, and that men and women are personalities capable of sustained relations, not mere opportunities for an electrical discharge. Yet we rate the impulse too highly. We do not admit that by collisions of this trivial sort the doors of heaven may be shaken open. (*HE*, p. 22)

Imagination or desire, to revert to Forster's terms for a moment? Both, obviously. The Paul who kisses Helen is no more "real" than the Agnes with whom Rickie falls in love. The object of the emotion has once again been misapprehended. But the emotion itself, the passage insists, is authentic. Desire and imagination coalesce; and that is precisely the point, or the beginning of it. Not only Forster's vocabulary but his problem needs to be reshaped. In the final analysis, what is central is neither the method of falling in love nor the reality of the object; it is instead the radical subjectivity of desire, revealed in the conflicting attempts of consciousness either to fulfill itself in "sustained relations" or to obliterate itself in the apocalyptic moment of "passing emotion."

But that is to simplify the problem. Forster's comment, in its carefully balanced, modulated progression, means to do full justice to "chance collisions" like Helen's, but only up to a point. As moral statement, its intention is not to ratify an equality of opposites but to assert the ultimate superiority of Margaret's efforts to connect. Rhetorically, however, the passage (which I have quoted only in part) tells another story. Its brief, normative defense dissolves into the two longer, fuller, and more lyrical tributes to poetry and magic by which it is surrounded and engulfed. And so with the novel as a whole: the manifest ideal of integration, buttressed by all of Forster's symbols and "harvest predictions,"[28] convinces less than the sisterly affection of Margaret and Helen on the one hand and Helen's sexual collisions on the other. In short, if, as I have suggested, the early novels in general demonstrate—though they are far from acknowledging—the incompatibility of love and sex, the series starting with *A Room with a View* and ending with *Maurice* are something more: a determined, conscious effort to strike a balance (the "proportion" of *Howards End*) between irreconcilables, thereby generating from the discordant vocabulary of prose and passion (to use Margaret's words) a logical syntax of desire.

There is, of course, some imbalance between the contrasted elements that subtend Forster's arc of desire. Margaret's "very good kind of prose" (*HE*, p. 171), as she describes her feeling for Henry, is less vivid than Helen's electrical discharges, but it is more congruent with the novel's thrust toward an all-embracing harmony. As in *A Room with a View*, where Lucy seeks "equality beside the man she loved" (p. 110), so in *Howards End*, love and comradeship effectively take precedence over the sexuality that is theoretically part of the final amalgam.* But in *Arctic Summer* (1911-12), as far as one can judge from the fragmentary nature of the book,[29] and certainly in *Maurice*, the balance shifts toward the activation and realization of passion. Integration remains the objective, but the priority of the physical threatens to skew the ideal, to dissolve the complexity of becoming in the indivisible finality of passing emotion. *Maurice* does not quite do that, but its allegiance to connecting is precariously maintained. It, and not *Howards End*, as we can now see, is the last stage of Forster's early work: the final defense and also the implicit defeat of consciousness as the redeemer of a fragmented world.

The presumptive flight of Maurice Hall and Alec Scudder to the greenwood defines both the goal and the limits of Forster's novel. In Alec, or rather in the relationship with him, Maurice's "part brutal, part ideal" (p. 23) boyhood dreams resolve the familiar divisions of the earlier books. Initially the realization of Maurice's first dream of "a nondescript whose existence he resented," Alec is eventually meant to suggest the "friend" (p. 22) of the second dream as well. Yet for the reader he remains more persuasively the vital antagonist: if the comrade, then the *sexual* comrade of the greenwood. That is so because the greenwood itself remains so oddly vague. There is little in *Maurice*, not much more in the appended terminal note, to suggest its contours, although it is, as the note makes clear, the symbolic space toward which the whole of the novel moves. Inevitably one is reminded again of the early tales, in which characters repeatedly manage to leave their drab, confining situations for one or the other of Forster's "other kingdoms": those ecstatic and static enclaves beyond change and beyond choice, which are so congenial to his imagination.[30] In them, one finds the clue to *Maurice*, for like "other kingdom," the greenwood is, even more than concept masquerading as symbol, a space of fictional absence; and it is the irony of Forster's most overtly sexual novel that it fails at the last quite literally to embody its abstract ideal.

But that is to get ahead of Forster's story. As Maurice's dark, confused "secret life" (p. 23) externalizes itself first in love for Clive Durham and then in sexuality, the novel recapitulates the shifting configurations of desire throughout Forster's prewar fiction. Clive, theoretical, platonic, is

---

*Compare with Helen's responses those attributed to Margaret: "And she had often 'loved,' too, but only so far as the facts of sex demanded: mere yearnings for the masculine, to be dismissed for what they were worth, with a smile" (*HE*, p. 162). We are also told, apropos of Howards End, that "house and tree transcended any simile of sex" (*HE*, p. 203).

the aestheticizing heir of Forster's earliest protagonists, and the love he imposes on Maurice expresses perfectly both a recurrent Forsterian ideal and the limitations that preclude or diminish a variety of relationships elsewhere in the novels. It would no doubt be foolish to overlook the fact that Maurice and Clive are homosexual, but it would be a more egregious error still not to recognize that the problems inherent in Forster's treatment of homosexuality are only a specific instance of how his imagination responds to the conception of personal relations throughout his career.[31] The value of *Maurice* lies in the opportunity it provided Forster to deal directly and openly with his own desire; but there is no reason to believe that he regarded the psychological dynamics of homosexual and hetero-sexual love as different in kind—or indeed to assume that they are. The analogues to Maurice and Clive are to be found not in the quasi-sexual feelings of Philip for Gino or Rickie for Stephen or in Mr. Beebe's watery release,[32] but in that quite different and more sober group of relations —Caroline and Philip, Rickie and Agnes, Martin and Venetia, Ronnie and Adela—which assume, in Clive's words, that "it's character, not passion, that is the real bond" (p. 128).

Clive's formula may be regarded as a rationalization after the fact of his discovery that he is no longer homosexual (earlier his ideal had been "love passionate but temperate" [p. 98]); but the contrast, as we have seen, is one Forster himself—his personal sense of division possibly re-inforced by Cambridge mentors and Bloomsbury friends—makes in effect from the time of his first novel onward. Although the later, private stories move increasingly toward the celebration of passion for its own sake, Forster's public declarations carry on even more deliberately the defense of character, which is to say, the stable self. So, in "What I Believe" he writes: "Psychology has split and shattered the idea of a 'Person,' and has shown that there is something incalculable in each of us, which may at any moment rise to the surface and destroy our normal balance. . . . [but] For the purpose of living one has to assume that the personality is solid, and the 'self' is an entity, and to ignore all contrary evidence" (*TC*, pp. 65-66).

The solidity of character, the congruence of depth and surface, is in turn the basis for Forster's defense of personal relationships, most notably in *Howards End* and in the essay I've just quoted from. Of course, the Philips and Carolines and the others whose relationships founder or fade do little to sustain Forster's belief. And yet the love of Clive and Maurice, the paradigm of all the relations based on character, is such as to have led Noel Annan to argue that "Forster does not deprecate or diminish this platonic affair. For him it is as valid and as real as consummated love."[33] In the context of the novel as a whole, this is surely a misreading, but it is also testimony to Forster's empathetic imagination. By now biographical reasons have become available to explain Forster's attitude (Annan speculates that he "had never had a sexual affair until he was in his forties," that is, 1919 at the earliest),[34] but the published works offer sufficient evidence. The fictional delineation of "personalities capable of sustained relations"—the stable self defining itself through continuity in time—is meant as concrete proof that connecting is possible: the sign of that ordered, coherent world Forster longed for, even in the face of contrary evidence, throughout his life.

The words used to describe the love Maurice and Clive achieve—"consistent," "permanent," "affectionate," "sensible," "calm" (p. 98)—suggest the moderating deliberateness of consciousness. But they imply something more. "They themselves became equal" (p. 99), Forster writes of the two men; and it is, precisely, "equality of character" that defines the shape of their relationship. Not that they are in any obvious sense alike. The point is rather that their assumptions (more accurately, Clive's, which are accepted by the "humble and inexperienced and adoring" [p. 251] Maurice) are the same. Together they inhabit Margaret Wilcox's tolerant, rational, complex world of "eternal differences," in which Maurice, acknowledging his homosexuality, discarding his superficial religion, is able to grow without abandoning his outwardly "normal" life or the class structure he and Clive share. In short, Clive invites Maurice into a world without change, which, ironically, his own change destroys.

Clive's defection, however, important though it may be to Forster's plot, is not the central issue. His sympathy with the relationship notwithstanding, the price it exacts is one Forster is no longer able or willing to pay. It may be that for Maurice "the idealism and the brutality that ran through boyhood had joined at last, and twined into love" (p. 63); but it is idealism that is in fact the keynote of their love, and idealism, as Forster now partly recognizes, is the disease of consciousness. Looking back from Clive to his many predecessors, one can see that character in Forster is not fate but a guard against it: an index to that inexorable demand for order and stability (Forster's as well as Clive's), which tempers passion with comradeship and transforms the integrating consciousness into self-conscious distance and restraint.

"Passion and the instincts," Lawrence's Birkin tells Hermione Roddice, "—you want them hard enough, but through your head, in your consciousness";[35] and the analysis of modernism's characteristic debility suits still better the fundamentally ascetic Clive. It is against the imperialism of the head that Forster launches his counterideal of total sexual union, and, as he does so, equability gives way significantly to violence. Though there are precedents in his earlier work, Forster nowhere else (until the stories of The Life to Come) delineates so strikingly as in Maurice's growing feeling for Alec Scudder the contours of a relationship generated out of antagonism. Maurice's feeling of cruelty as he first sees Alec; the altercation with him over the tip; the two suggestive scenes of his inadvertently "colliding" (p. 190) with the gamekeeper; and finally the blackmail episode, with its anger and threats—all make for an intensity of opposition that disrupts the continuities of consciousness and disintegrates the stable self.

To what end becomes apparent in the aftermath of the hostile encounter in the British Museum when the two men spend the night together. "Only a struggle twists sentimentality and lust together into love" (p. 218), Forster writes, and the redefinition of love, heretofore a twining of idealism and brutality, provides the necessary clue. The reductive weakening of the first term and the specific intensification of the second indicate that love is now sexuality and sexuality something altogether different, and in every way, from the earlier platonic love. For the stress throughout the second relationship on physical and mental struggle leads not only to the body's fulfillment but to a new psychic equilibrium. So, in the midst of the surface hostility of their encounter in the Museum, Maurice announces: "my name's Scudder" (p. 223); and as Alec leaves him, presumably for the last time, he thinks: "In a way they were one person" (p. 233).

Oneness (or fusion) is for Forster a far more radical state than integration, comparable in its movement toward unity of some sort but otherwise virtually opposed: the substitution, one might say, of an irreducible finality for the hovering tentativeness of complexity. More fully articulated in *Maurice* than in the earlier novels, it reveals itself in retrospect as a potentiality of Forster's thought from the beginning. Like Philip Herriton, Maurice and Alec find in the anonymity of surface the body's answer to the too exigent mind. Oneness, then, is the reward of activity: the violence, lust, antagonism, and "reaction" (p. 226) that contrast with Clive's Olympian theorizing. Its foundation, not surprisingly, lies in a total dissimilarity of character: the antithetical materials from which struggle fashions an indivisible, if temporary, whole. Maurice's identification proceeds directly from his sense of "some infuriating inequality" (p. 225) that is generated between them, and it symbolizes both his and Forster's rejection of equality of character as the basis for relationships—and indeed the rejection of character itself.

For the passage from disequality to oneness assumes the possibility that "personality [can] melt and be subtly reformed" (p. 209). That Maurice's conscious wish at this point is to become heterosexual is irrelevant or ironic. What matters is that the concept of re-forming is central to *Maurice* and that it implies not simply amendment or growth but the making over of character into something altogether different and new. The change Maurice undergoes is both personal and social—involving on the one hand the full acceptance of his homosexuality and of himself as a physical being: "flesh educating the spirit . . . and developing the sluggish heart and the slack mind against their will" (pp. 151-52); and on the other, his growing challenge to the idea of class. The appropriation to himself of Alec's name takes place, fittingly, in the presence of Mr. Ducie, the first of the novel's representatives of society and authority and marks the climax of both his social and his personal transformation.

But in some ways the reorientation of Maurice's ideas about class is the more difficult and more basic step, so largely is his sense of himself defined in terms of his social identity. His progress from priggishness to guilt brings him at last to the recognition that "if the will can overleap class, civilization as we have made it will go to pieces" (p. 207). And when he is willing to accept that possibility, he is able to admit that Alec "too was embedded in class" (p. 227) and to reject the entire system. As he now sees, coming to terms with his homosexuality parallels, indeed depends upon, a willingness to move beyond notions of class altogether. The "crack in the floor" (p. 197) that is Forster's recurrent symbol for society's artificial and destructive divisions (and for the homosexual "fault" it sees in his hero's psychic landscape) is Maurice's final barrier; and as he overleaps it, he discards the factitious order of civilization for the more kinetic, abrasive world of sexuality, dissolving Clive's self-conscious *idea* of love in the darker intensity of "primitive abandonment" (p. 226).

But Forster wants something more from his hero (after Alec's apparent departure for the Argentine) than the chastened recognition that "love was an emotion through which you occasionally enjoyed yourself" (p. 233). Though most reviewers have agreed with Lytton Strachey (as quoted by Forster in his terminal note) "that the relationship of the two rested upon curiosity and lust and would only last six weeks" (p. 252),*[36] Forster is not yet ready to accept consciously and fully (as he will later in his career) the disjunction between sex and love. Connection still remains the ideal, the need for integration returns, and Forster chooses at the last to have things both ways. The final chapters of the novel are a deliberate and determined effort to surround the intermittencies of sexual satisfaction with the continuity of comradely affection. "A happy ending was imperative," Forster wrote in 1960, ". . . I was determined that in fiction anyway two men should fall in love and remain in it for the ever and ever that fiction allows" (p. 250). By comparison, the final scenes of *A Room with a View* and, still more, of *Howards End* are, despite the inclusive symbols of water and hay, equivocal in their effect. *Maurice* ends "without

---

*Actually, Strachey used the words "lust and sentiment" and predicted "a rupture after 6 months."

twilight or compromise" (p. 246)—that is, with the promise of absolute salvation in the unrealized and unresonant spaces of the greenwood.

Beneath the mild belligerence of Forster's defense of his ending there can be heard a more plaintive note: a tacit admission of the gap between the disorders and disappointments of life and the order of which art is capable. But Forster's art is at odds with itself. The exiguous symbol of the greenwood affirms his desire but in its aesthetic emptiness belies the object of that desire. Which is to say that connection is theoretically attained but in fact betrayed. The vacillation between the ideals of integration and oneness—variously, and at times confusingly, conceived as "the actual and the ideal"[37] or comradeship and sexuality or love and truth—occurs everywhere in the prewar fiction; and though in *Maurice* Forster gestures again toward integration, he does so ambiguously—or in a way different from what he intends. Unable to forgo the possibility of reconciliation and equally unable to actualize it in the world Maurice and Alec inhabit, he circumvents it finally by opting (in Yeats's words) for "That quarter where all thought is done."[38] In short, the attempt to restore consciousness by joining the values of Maurice's first relationship with those of his second reveals instead the need to transcend it—to achieve in oneness an absolute freedom from contingency. "Love and Truth—" Forster writes in *Howards End*, "their warfare seems eternal. Perhaps the whole visible world rests on it, and if they were one, life itself, like the spirits when Prospero was reconciled to his brother, might vanish into air, into thin air" (p. 227). The comment is striking in its relevance to *Maurice*. The novel's dilemma is overcome only through the illusive linking of contrary ideals in a hypostatic kingdom of imagination, where, to quote Yeats again, "intellect no longer knows / *Is* from the *Ought*, or *Knower* from the *Known*— / That is to say, ascends to Heaven." For Helen Schlegel, a chance collision shakes open the doors of heaven; the attempt to provide Maurice and Alec with a sustained relation bolts the doors firmly behind them. In the sanctuary of depth offered by the greenwood, the more human vision of equality and integration gives way not to an equally human sexuality but to an eternal moment of fusion, as consciousness melts into fantasy; and Forster's heroes flee, improbably joined, into thin air.

Throughout his career, Forster's various formulations of the ideal relate directly to the changing nature of his irony, in fact depend upon it. So the notion of connecting, for example, correlates, reactively, with the mediate, satiric irony of his earliest writing; or to put it another way, the prewar novels define worlds whose deviations from a presupposed norm are apparently remediable. Theoretically at least, it is possible for Philip to learn the lessons of Gino and Italy, for Rickie to acknowledge the reality that is Stephen; and Lucy does in fact accept the Emersonian gospel and passes from darkness into light. By the same token, the drift from the normative certainties of satire toward a more radical vision of the inherent and unresolvable complexities of life—the disjunctive irony of Forster's second phase—entails the compensating desire for an escape into oneness: the need to transcend rather than to encompass and integrate the discontinuities of life. In brief, and as I've already intimated, the ironic determines the aironic in all of Forster's fiction. It seems to me worth repeating that if irony is best viewed as a mode of perceiving the world and if that perception involves in one way or another a fundamental sense of disunity, then it is hardly surprising that ironists generally, if not inevitably, react to the lapses, discontinuities, or randomness that confronts them by positing, in the face of an unsatisfactory world, redemptive or at least consoling visions of unity. In this respect, the aironic is distinct from but also dependent upon and, finally, in the broadest sense, part of the response initiated by the ironic imagination. As noted, the aironic, inevitably and necessarily, undergoes transformation as irony itself is transformed, and nowhere more clearly than in the fiction that spans Forster's long life. Set beside the ideals of other modernist writers —Yeats's "unity of being," Eliot's "still point," Lawrence's "star-balance," Woolf's ecstatic moments, or Auden's "affirming flame"—Forster's are in some ways more extreme but, closer to the point, they are more various, since Forster, moving as he does through different forms of irony, facing always new and unstable horizons, enacts more spaciously than most of his contemporaries (in this respect at least) the characteristic dialectic of recovery and fall that the aironic and ironic impel.

More raggedly, however, than the preceding paragraph indicates. Disjunctive irony, we've seen, is adumbrated even in the earliest of the novels (though it is only in *A Passage to India* that it becomes, in assuming its most extreme shape, absolute); and, as I have tried to show, there are uneasily contained contradictions between the first two of Forster's aironic ideals in all of the fiction through *Maurice*. What is clear is that the disintegrative vision of the caves in *A Passage to India*, asserting what is only implicit in the prewar work, establishes unmistakably and unconditionally the second stage of Forster's irony and leads to the equally extreme and apparently unqualified vision of oneness in the novel's third section. I don't intend here to argue again Forster's final position in *A Passage to India*.* For present purposes, the final adjustment of meaning between caves and temple is less to the point than what is implied by Forster's opposition of the two. Consciousness is, if

---

*Briefly, as I suggested in the last section, Forster's irony seems to me to rise above both of his symbolic extremes and above the paradoxes they constitute in an affirmation of the *formal* unity of the novel: the oneness of the artist with his art.

not annihilated in the cave, then effectively reduced to the status of witness—witness to the chaos of disconnection it can no longer hope to
control. And in the novel's next and final section even Godbole fails
when he is "seduced" by "logic and conscious effort." His success, on the
other hand, derives from his ability to impel Mrs. Moore "by his spiritual
force to that place where completeness can be found" (p. 277). Thus the
anironic counterideal of part 3 can only be formulated as the subduing of
ordinary consciousness to that completeness Godbole temporarily and
with difficulty achieves—a state in which, while it lasts, both the nothingness of the caves and the ineffectual human awareness of it give way to "a
spiritual unity in which all races and species and sex shall one day be
merged."[39]

An extreme position, certainly, particularly congenial to those critics
who read the novel as Forster's endorsement of Eastern religion. But in
the light of his later (and hardly mystical) fiction, it is important to judge
just how extreme. In fact, the "loss of the self" (as the once popular
phrase had it) toward which Hinduism looks is only superficially a loss
and more fundamentally the discovery or recovery of another, more
authentic self. In this sense, the attitude dramatized in *A Passage to India*
is by no means as radical in its implications for the idea of consciousness
and the concept of the self as that which underlies the homosexual stories
of *The Life to Come*,* where, in Forster's third and final period, there is a
cutting loose from all essentialist beliefs in an ultimate, absolute reality—even the negative reality symbolized in the caves.

The existential bias of *The Life to Come* is, as one would expect, most
apparent in the five "sexual stories" which, putting aside the earlier ideals
of connection and permanence or of transcendent unity, attempt to
reclaim the phenomenal world for and through unmediated desire. With
randomness ostensibly accepted, even welcomed, as the condition of
immediate gratification, irony is transformed again; and in taking as their
desiderata " the smaller pleasures of life," the stories place at their center
a self—if one can still use that word for what has been reduced to a sort
of behavioral tropism—that is the vehicle solely for sexual satisfaction.
In one sense, these exclusively sexual stories mark too the culmination of
the anironic impulse in Forster: the celebration of Maurice without the
greenwood, and even without Alec; the apotheosis of Helen's chance
collisions, unencumbered by the demand for either integration or completeness. There is more to it than that, however, as becomes apparent
when one turns to the remaining homosexual stories of *The Life to Come*,
in which, probably because, as in the novels, sexuality is once again

*As in the previous section of this chapter, I am concerned only with the last eight stories of
the volume, though my focus here is on the three remaining "love stories," which I have so
far only briefly glanced at.

associated with love, the interplay of ironic and anironic is more complex. Of the three, "The Life to Come" (1922) and "Dr. Woolacott" (1927) precede the "sexual stories" and suggest that Forster had not yet completely abandoned his primitivism or, in the second, his need for total union. By contrast, "The Other Boat" (1957-58), the last and finest story in the volume, unambiguously confirms the values implied in the sexual stories. In a sense, then, the "love stories" retrace the three stages of the anironic in Forster. But at the same time, in what they reveal, if not in what they intend, the stories are sufficiently alike to constitute an identifiable, if evolving, group, in which sexual repression plays havoc with all three protagonists and provides the key to what Forster is about. Obviously, repression is meant to indicate the reasons for the sudden and overwhelming attractions in the stories and to mitigate their improbabilities: Lionel March, for one, finds that "sex had entirely receded—only to come charging back like a bull" (p. 193). But more importantly and paradoxically, the rejection of sexuality *creates* consciousness and forms those hidden depths, which in turn give rise to introspection and guilt and constitute the traditionally divided self. Inevitably, the men so affected return to the conformities of society, yielding to the pressures they have internalized, or, following the true direction of these stories, die.

It becomes apparent that the "stable" self of *Howards End* and the books that precede it is, as compared with the empty, static self of the sexual stories, at best a complex equilibrium of contending forces. The love stories, with their uneasily shifting perspectives, stand somewhere between the two, and the earlier of them are still equivocally poised between the attractions of depth and surface. So "The Life to Come" begins, as it were, in the greenwood and manages to reverse the progression of *Maurice* quite literally with a vengeance. Ostensibly concerned with Paul Pinmay, the story chronicles the missionary's fall from sexual grace with a crudely satirical irony reminiscent of Forster's Egyptian books. But the details of his decline are less important than its initial cause, the guilt that overcomes him as he realizes: "Sooner or later, God calls every deed to the light" (p. 68).

Conscience and consciousness, God and light, are then the repressive enemies of Paul's unexpected and ecstatic encounter with the native chief Vithobai in "the depths of the woods" (p. 68). But Forster's imagination, as well as God, militates against depth—or, rather, betrays through stylistic incompetence and an excess of violence its disbelief in what it means to affirm. In the most fundamental sense, it is not the thwarting of love by Paul and the Christianity he embodies but Forster's own covert assumptions that make the conjunction of love and sex more than ever impossible and lead to Vithobai's unforeseen triumph. For it is Vithobai who is the more authentic ideational center of "The Life to Come"; and his belief that "it is deeds, deeds that count" (p. 80) is ultimately Forster's too, in this and in all of the other homosexual stories. Not yet fully acknowledged here, it is nonetheless dramatized at the story's climax. Attracted for an instant by Paul's promise of "Real and true love!"—that is, a prolongation of their initial union (as he understands it) into eternity —the dying man suddenly rejects the offer and, stabbing the missionary, experiences "the most exquisite [moment] he had ever known. For love was conquered at last" (p. 81).

What is at stake in Vithobai's conquest is as much the manner as the fact of it; and the additional chapter Forster projected, in which Paul becomes Vithobai's sexual slave in the afterlife, reveals even more clearly the inner logic of the story's movement from sentimentality toward disequality, revenge, and sadistic cruelty. "If the reverse side of accidie is violence," John Fraser has recently written, "this is partly because violence is felt to promise not merely a titillating but a radical relief from accidie."[40] In other words, what determines the action of "The Life to Come" is a reaction not to the failure of Forster's unlikely dream of union but to a growing disbelief in the value of existence itself. Ahead lie the caves of *A Passage to India*, with their destructive negations; and, anticipating Mrs. Moore, Vithobai comes before his death to a querulous perception of the chaos of values. The irony at this point, so much more corrosive than that directed at the perversion of Christian *caritas*, suggests that "The Life to Come" is Forster's attempt to stave off the vision of the caves in a frenzy of violence. But if the story looks toward the caves, it looks beyond them as well. Directed against the notion of an afterlife, "The Life to Come" nonetheless projects one, as if to compensate for the impossibility of love. And in its static eternity, a distorted image of the original greenwood, it adumbrates the world that, after *A Passage to India*, Forster reconstitutes in his sexual stories—the surface world of unrepentant pleasure.

But not without a final and revealing attempt to salvage the more comprehensive values of his earlier work. "Dr. Woolacott," a slight story whose confusions may be mistaken for complexity, resembles "The Life to Come" in its conflation of love and sex but presumably moves in the opposite direction: roughly, from Clesant's initial repression to his fulfillment in both sex and love. Like "The Life to Come" again, "Dr. Woolacott" is both sentimental and violent, though the violence is now largely psychological and, like the sentimentality, partly, if not successfully, masked by fantasy. Dramatizing Clesant's internal struggle by externalizing the more vital half of it in his handsome farmhand lover works reasonably well, though the young interloper is somewhat overburdened by symbolic meanings. The real problem, both ethical and semantic, begins with the story's all too obtrusive message: "What's life after twenty-five? Impotent, blind, paralytic. What's life before it unless you're fit?" (p. 90). The opposition implied by these questions—prolonged, tepid, self-conscious existence versus a short, intense burst of passionate living —is sufficiently familiar to any reader of Forster; but in the special context of "Dr. Woolacott" the shrill insistence on those things, and those things alone, that make sexuality possible provides a facile and disturbing estimate of life as a whole. Furthermore, the culmination of Clesant's desire, as he accepts the nameless farmhand's invitation to accompany him to the grave, where "we shall be together for ever and ever" (p. 96), defies satisfactory translation. Forster's fantasy implies not simply that death is preferable to invalidism or to a socially acceptable but sexually barren life but that death *is* life: the achievement hereafter of that fullness of union Dr. Woolacott and society deny.

This is to be literalist about fantasy, no doubt, but since the afterlife has no substantive meaning for Forster, there is no other way to read his metaphor for dynamic living than as an emblem of stasis, no other way to view the unity of desire than as the total blankness of death. And yet the story is, whatever its contradictions, in its own way instructive. The finality of death that "Dr. Woolacott" exposes is the inevitable complement of the presuppositions that underlie the stories written after it; which is to say that the stress on a particular kind of fulfillment here and now creates, in the absence of that fulfillment, no possible alternative but death. Oliver Stallybrass reports that "The Life to Come" "embodied what Forster described as 'a great deal of sorrow and passion that I have myself experienced' and came, with 'Dr Woolacott,' 'more from my heart than anything else I have been able to turn [out].'"[41] One can see why. The two stories are a turning point for Forster; after them, the recognition that love leads inevitably to death is finally accepted. The hero of Forster's first sexual story, "Arthur Snatchfold," recognizes "that little things can turn into great ones, and he did not want greatness" (p. 112). And no more does Forster. Henceforth, however reductively he celebrates it, the phenomenal world is the locus of his concern.

For this reason, "The Other Boat," though tragic in tone, is akin in spirit to the sexual stories that precede it. What these, in their allegiance to surface assume, "The Other Boat" makes explicit: not, as in "Dr. Woolacott" and "The Life to Come," the impossibility, but instead the *destructiveness* of love and of the psychological depths it entails. Given this intention, Forster's choice of Lionel March as his hero is at first sight unlikely—or would be, were it not for the precedent of Maurice. But Lionel, though as average, dim, and conventional as the other, achieves almost in one step the goal toward which Maurice develops so painfully and slowly. Partly, no doubt, because Lionel's "prejudices were tribal rather than personal" (p. 174), but also because Forster supplies him, some four decades later, with different sorts of expectations and needs. Writing to T. E. Lawrence in 1929, Forster commented on "how over-rated and over-written [love] is, and how the relation one would like between people is a mixture of friendliness and lust."[42] The description accords admirably with the feelings Lionel instinctively brings to the relationship in which he finds himself involved.

In fact, though connected with society and automatically responsive to its codes, Lionel is, far more than Cocoa, his half-caste seducer and lover, capable of the smaller pleasures of life. "Nordic warrior" (p. 174), "half Ganymede, half Goth" (p. 178), "a Viking at a Byzantine court" (p. 180), he is cousin to the soldiers, sailors, gladiators, and barbarians of the sexual stories. It is Lionel, I've noted, who forgets "any depths through which he might have passed" (p. 178) and who tells himself: "Enjoy yourself while you can" (p. 180). So long as he gives himself to his rela-tionship, Lionel incarnates Forster's ideal form of desire, in which emotion adds a grace to the urgency of lust—or, as Lionel himself thinks of it: "luxury, gaiety, kindness, unusualness, and delicacy that did not exclude brutal pleasure" (p. 180).

Lionel's thoughts of his mother as "blind-eyed in the midst of the enormous web she had spun" (p. 193) identifies her with the sense of fate that overhangs the story. But fate is only the outward sign of an inner necessity, and Mrs. March is more importantly a potential within Lionel himself: consciousness waiting to reassert the social conformities and sexual antipathies of the tribe against his homosexual affair. Furthermore, the apparent polarization of Mrs. March and Cocoa into the story's principal antagonists simplifies, even distorts, the situation. Unlikely as the conjunction is, the two are, from the beginning of the story, sym-bolically identified, and so they are throughout, with good reason. Cocoa, however exotic and bizarre, is in fact closer to the Englishwoman than to her son in his ways of thinking. The web in which he and his lover are "caught" (p. 174)—to use the story's key word—by the fatality of Mrs. March, parallels directly the "net" (p. 183) in which Cocoa himself seeks to entrap Lionel. Anxious, planning, and plotting, Cocoa is "the deep one" (p. 178), unable in his self-conscious awareness to accept the moment without fear or anxiety or to make do with less than the "ever and ever" of "Dr. Woolacott." If, then, Mrs. March is the ultimate, Cocoa is the proximate cause of the disaster. And everything that happens in the final, melodramatic pages of the story, from Lionel's recovery by convention to the murder and suicide, is set in motion by the force of Cocoa's too exacting love. In this way, "The Other Boat" confirms a connection that is shirked in the earlier love stories. On the other side of the grave, there is perverse fulfillment in "The Life to Come," a unity of sorts in "Dr.

Woolacott"; but in "The Other Boat" there is only silence—the unequivo-cal finality of death, which follows implacably from the assertion of love.

That is not quite all, however. Early in "The Other Boat" Cocoa complains about his long wait for his lover, saying, "I thought I should die." And Lionel's answer, "So you will" (p. 173), if it looks forward prophetically to the ending, suggests more immediately the sexual act that follows at this point and also the traditional association of sex with death, which in some ways underlies the sexual stories from "Arthur Snatchfold" to "The Torque." For the love-death of "The Other Boat" is not the opposite but the analogue and mirror of that state of intense but intermittent response which, in the world of Forster's sexual stories, is the condition of the smaller pleasures. Or, to phrase more simply this seem-ingly bizarre conclusion, the anironic complement to *both* groups of tales is, effectively, the same. In *Howards End*, Helen Schlegel insists that "Death destroys a man; the idea of Death saves him" (p. 236). But Helen's conceptualization, her appeal to consciousness, is precisely what Forster rejects in *The Life to Come*. Not the idea of death but the death of the idea now saves; and Helen's statement of "the vague yet convincing plea that the Invisible lodges against the Visible" has no place in the surface world of Forster's final stories, where the anironic, whether conceived in terms of sex or love, points inexorably in the same direction: toward death or the death of consciousness, the physical or psychological ob-literation of the self.

The Life to Come is, then, taken as a whole, a set of variations on a theme. Although, as compared with much recent fiction, the book remains formally conventional (this is relatively true even of the more loosely organized sexual stories), its vision is not. The point has some general importance, since it runs counter to the notion of a sharp break between modernism and postmodernism. It bears repeating that Forster and a significant number of his contemporaries as well come increasingly in the course of their careers to recognize (or to sense) the impasse to which their assumptions have brought them and are led to search out alternate ways of responding. The crisis point, therefore, needs to be located not after, but, more properly, before the war—in Lawrence's rethinking of "the old, stable *ego* of the character," in *Finnegans Wake*, in *Between the Acts*, in the ambiguous allegiances of late modernism, and, however much smaller its literary merit, in *The Life to Come*. If modernism repre-sents, among other things, the imposition of the mind's structure on the external world, then Forster's stories are no longer modernist. Wylie Sypher's notion of "methexis" is relevant here. "The distance between life and art," he writes, "is no longer fixed or definable even as minimal. . . . There is participation as well as observation." And again: "The immediate occasion is sufficient unto itself. . . . If the significance is on the surface, then the need for depth explanation has gone, and the contingent, the everyday happening, is more authentic than the ultimate or absolute."[43] The self-confessed auto-eroticism of Forster's stories falls in its minor, narcissistic way precisely within this ethic of participation, although (and it should be said that Sypher is not discussing Forster) it hardly validates its interest or importance.

The excitement of Philip's anonymous contacts and of Helen's chance collisions translates, when these come to dominate Forster's fiction, into a way of life that is dispiritingly minimal and aleatory—like a good deal of the current art that goes by those names. Not that an allegiance to the phenomenal or to the suspensive necessarily implies a thinning out of either self or world. But in Forster's stories exactly that happens (explaining, perhaps, why Forster found himself unable any longer to deal with the more extended form of the novel). The dissolution of the self—not, as for the structuralists, in a web of language but in the peremptoriness of desire—leaves the self just as effectively a fiction. Hovering and havering in the world to which they have been abandoned, Forster's attenuated heroes are prescient of Beckett and the Surfictionists, and of the chaotic or baffling spaces of the *nouveau roman*. For all their violence, there is something exhausted about Forster's final stories. One has come a long way from the conceptual moments of the earlier fiction, which, however discrete in form, are intended to provide and enforce the opportunity for reflection and change. In the resolutely limited, sexual world of *The Life to Come*, moments exist for their own sake or for the sake of the minimal, limited activity generated by them. What Sypher, following Nietzsche, refers to as the "pathos of distance" (p. 128) gives way to a more pathetic capitulation to simple, disordered sensation.

Forster's stories, particularly after "The Life to Come" and "Dr. Woolacott," are a refusal of compromise in fantasy and a rejection of *Howards End*'s belief in the possible connection of life's antinomies. The injunctions of that novel give way at last, in the enervated suspensiveness of Forster's final work, not simply to the disjunctions that are in fact a feature of his work from the beginning but to something that is both more random and, oddly, more restricted as well. And if the stories become as a result more honest, at any rate less equivocal, still their values are sadly diminished, even reversed, in the process. No longer intent on the disappearance of the visible world, Forster abandons too the attempt to reconcile love and truth. Materializing the greenwood, so to speak, he creates a world in which the unexamined life is the only one worth living. Lionel March's murder of Cocoa in a final, sexual act is described as "part of a curve that had long been declining, and had nothing to do with death" (p. 196). Fate, then, presumably, or, more accurately, inner necessity; but tending no less surely toward the literal or psychological extremity of death. If so, the curve is, mutatis mutandis, Forster's too, fictionally elaborated throughout his career in a movement from Philip's ill-understood desires to their realization in the impoverished relationships of *The Life to Come*. Like Lionel's, a barren climax; but also Forster's dubious passage to the contemporary scene.

PART II

The Aesthetics of Surface

THREE

Language and Surface

Commenting on *The Berlin Stories* in a recent talk, Christopher Isherwood suggested: "If I had made the 'I' character homosexual, it would have made him too interesting. I wanted to treat the other characters and the situation."* What is important about the remark is not the allusion to homosexuality (most readers, I suspect, took for granted, even before the appearance of the latest, autobiographical works, the nature of Isherwood's and of his narrators' sexual preferences) but the suggestion of an intentional underplaying of the roles of William Bradshaw and "Christopher Isherwood" in *The Last of Mr. Norris* and *Goodbye to Berlin*. There is no reason to doubt Isherwood's explanation of his motives, but it is also not implausible to wonder whether the avoidance of depth in the presentation of his narrators' inner lives is simply a matter of narrative strategy or whether it is at least as much a question of prior and, in part, less conscious choices—specifically psychological and linguistic choices.

Isherwood's relation to his narrators, especially his first-person narrators, is nothing if not ambiguous. Claiming at times that these figures are simply a literary convenience, "nothing more,"[1] admitting at others that "It's always myself really that I'm talking about," he has managed successfully so far (and despite the "revelations" of *Christopher and His Kind*) to blur the degree and, more importantly, the intention and meaning of his autobiographical involvement. The problem seems unusually dramatic in Isherwood's case—thanks to his repeated use (and abuse) of his own name, which he so frequently and symptomatically twists, truncates, and dismembers—but it is not, in the largest sense, uniquely his among writers of the nineteen thirties. Others, especially those popularly associated with the Auden Group, similarly reveal an extraordinary

*Isherwood's talk was delivered at a meeting of the Modern Language Association, 27 December 1974. Any remarks attributed to him in the course of this chapter and not otherwise documented were made at that time.

absorption with themselves, along with a tendency to generalize or typify their autobiographical material. The result, a curious tension between situating and at the same time voiding the particular identity of the self, is nowhere more explicitly suggested than in Isherwood's description of the subject of *Lions and Shadows:* "A young man living at a certain period in a certain European country, is subjected to a certain kind of environment, certain stimuli, certain influences. That the young man happens to be myself is only of secondary importance: in making observations of this sort, everyone must be his own guinea-pig."[2]

It is easier to accept Virginia Woolf's contention that the writers of the thirties were "great egotists" than to agree that they "wrote about themselves honestly."[3] Which is not, however, to accuse them of dishonesty but of a peculiar kind of obtrusive reticence. What seems to be at issue is the belief that only the desire to move beyond the self validates the obsessive concern with it. Thus Michael Roberts writes in his preface to the anthology *New Country*—speaking presumably for his contributors as well as for himself—of the satire of "our own past interests. . . . which is intended to free us from our own preoccupations and indulgences so that we may stop the pitiful waste of thought and energy, which has made us as powerless and contemptible as we are."[4] But Roberts's explanation, while it locates in a general sense of guilt and social impotence the source of the decade's desire for a therapeutic self-abnegation, fails to recognize the compromise effected by most of his contemporaries whereby the self survives the call for total renunciation—a compromise that shows itself in the characteristic method and the oddly indeterminate irony of the thirties. For most of the "New Countrymen,"[5] certainly for Auden and Isherwood, the freedom to which Roberts alludes lies in indirection and retrenchment, in what may be seen as an allegiance to autobiographical *surface.* What their practice suggests is that the remedy for an uneasy self-consciousness—which cannot or will not refuse consciousness entirely—is to be found in the attempt simultaneously to exploit and to minimize the facts and also the subjective resonance of the author's private life.

The purely psychological roots of this striking aesthetic discipline push, one senses, into rather boggy, libidinal areas. They suggest, above all, a kind of defensive maneuver that turns testingly upon itself, asserting a brave, unsentimental austerity while fearfully undercutting what it cares most to assert. But this ought not to deflect attention from the literary superstructure these roots support. What is apparent is that the equivocal treatment of the self correlates closely with the decade's characteristic attitude toward language, which, perhaps originally determined by the refusal of depth, curtails in turn the possibilities of moving beyond the given or chosen limits of surface. Language, in other words (especially but not only in the thirties, of course) is both affected by and affects the nature of immediate perception and of conceptual choice. But it is, finally, the texts that offer themselves for direct scrutiny, and in them it is the determinative, transitive role of language that signifies, as it articulates and fixes the expressive range of consciousness.

Proceeding inductively is all the more necessary, since the writers of the thirties are (apart from some notable academic critics) almost totally unoriginal in their theories of language, though they are no less passionate and insistent on the subject for being commonplace. From right, left, and center, poets, novelists, and essayists pour out endless complaints, warnings, and recommendations—contemptuously refusing the rhetorical "tracery of pen-ornament," ironizing the uncritical ascendency of "the Roaring Boys," calling for "a tongue that naked goes, / Without more fuss than Dryden's or Defoe's."[6] Less aesthetically radical than earlier modernists, they adapt to their own pragmatic and utilitarian ends the ideals of simplicity, plainness, and directness already set forth by Pound, Hulme, Aldington, and other imagists and illustrated less programatically for the writers of the decade by Forster in particular among the preceding generation of novelists.

But what, more than anything else, unifies the writers I'm describing is the ethical stress they bring to their examination of language; and in this area at least theory does help to illuminate practice. Typically, in their slightly post-thirties handbook, *The Reader over Your Shoulder*, Robert Graves and Alan Hodge write: "Faults in English prose derive not so much from lack of knowledge, intelligence or art as from lack of thought, patience or goodwill. . . . The writing of good English is thus a moral matter."[7] Still more to the point because of its tacitly subjective emphasis and its larger sense of personal imperfection is the statement in Michael Roberts's *Critique of Poetry*: "If we can give precise verbal form to our thoughts and feelings, we can control them."[8] Morality and control are, in fact, the clue to the whole thirties venture: the presumably parallel intentions (roughly, the desire to know and transform the external world and the need to come to terms with the self), which prove, however, not always compatible in practice. And they are in particular the key to Isherwood's undertaking, both to what Auden described in mid-decade as his friend's "strict and adult pen"[9] and to what may, less charitably, be seen, in Isherwood's own words, as "a kind of void in the books" that make up *The Berlin Stories*.

To begin with the more obvious of these problems—that of overt moral concern: it is clear that the language of *Mr. Norris* and *Goodbye to Berlin* is meant to establish a norm against which the reader gradually comes to measure the linguistic (and, by extension, the social, political, and psychological) situation in prewar Berlin. At one point, William

Bradshaw addresses himself directly to the state of affairs around him, and it is worth quoting the passage at length:

The murder reporters and the jazz-writers had inflated the German language beyond recall. The vocabulary of newspaper invective (traitor, Versailles-lackey, murder-swine, Marx-crook, Hitler-swamp, Red-pest) had come to resemble, through excessive use, the formal phraseology of politeness employed by the Chinese. The word *Liebe*, soaring from the Goethe standard, was no longer worth a whore's kiss. *Spring, moonlight, youth, roses, girl, darling, heart, May:* such was the miserably devaluated currency dealt in by the authors of all those tangoes, waltzes and fox-trots which advocated the private escape. Find a dear little sweetheart, they advised, and forget the slump, ignore the unemployed. Fly, they urged us, to Hawaii, to Naples, to the Never-Never-Vienna.[10]

Bradshaw's remarks are sufficiently explicit to require no gloss, but it is revealing to examine the ways in which the narrator's choice and arrangement of his language themselves comment on the substance of his observations.[11] Although one misses some of the typical features of Isherwood's style—notably the general sense of anticlimax in the apparently offhand architecture of his paragraphs—still the overall effect is unmistakable. the informal and generally simple diction; the casual sentence structure; the occasional reductive or incongruous image; the unemphatic stress; the absence of connectives, with its consequent effect of syntactic discontinuity; the unobtrusive ironies—all imply the need for linguistic deflation and for a revaluation of the events betrayed by the empty vocabulary of politics, propaganda, and escape. Isherwood's aim is, generally, to produce in the reader the response of yet another of his first-person narrators when confronted by Lester, the World War I veteran of *Lions and Shadows*, whose "quietly told horribly matter-of-fact anecdotes . . . had the knack of making all those remote obscenities and horrors seem real" (p. 256).

Style, then, does its judgmental work throughout *The Berlin Stories*, but William's comment is uncharacteristically explicit, Isherwood's methods generally more subtle and oblique. Since the two novels of Berlin life are, above all, concerned with the public consequences of private acts, their attitude to the larger political and social scene is more typically revealed through the dramatization of personal communication—and nowhere more tellingly than when it involves the deceptively charming Arthur Norris and Sally Bowles. Norris's language is a model of evasion and equivocation: polite and formulaic, full of meaningless repetitions, *chevilles*, insipid jokes, semantically vacuous *really*s, *indeed*s, and *rather*s, nervously wooden *oh*s, *dear me*s, and *my dear boy*s. It would be a mistake, however, to attribute to Arthur, with his creaturely instinct for self-preservation, too much or too conscious an intention. His verbal habits are significant finally not because they facilitate his deceptions, still less because they point back to his much regretted nineties, but because they point to nothing at all—are, in fact, almost totally nonreferential. If a standard is to be found for the self-enclosed linguistic system by which Norris has been effectively absorbed, it can only be a somewhat meager notion of formal adequacy, that is, a purely and thinly aesthetic criterion.

So when William, after his abortive confrontation with Arthur, acquiesces in a return to their old relationship, he notes: "The moment of frankness, which might have redeemed so much, had been elegantly avoided. Arthur's orientally sensitive spirit shrank from the rough, healthy, modern, catch-as-catch-can of home-truths and confessions; he offered me a compliment instead" (N, p. 165). *Elegant, compliment:* the words go to the heart, or rather to the surface, of Arthur's being, which is continuous only in the way it adheres to verbal and visible proprieties, mysterious only in its possession of secrets, which William (hardly one for home-truths and confessions himself!) repeatedly mistakes for depths.

Sally's case is comparable and can be dealt with more summarily. Certainly she rivals, perhaps surpasses, Arthur in her lack of linguistic discrimination. Substituting emphasis for politeness, her conversationally vivid but imprecise language, a fluid succession of *terribly*s, *marvelous*es, and interminable, hollow superlatives, amounts to a kind of italic prose, directed, again in aesthetic terms, essentially at performance rather than meaning. In short, what Sally does in *Goodbye to Berlin* and what Arthur does throughout *Mr. Norris* is to frustrate the rules of social interchange by dislocating the relationship assumed to exist between word and thing in the essentially "realistic" thirties.

The Communists gathered to listen to speeches about the Chinese peasants are instinctively right in their "uneasiness" over Norris's "graceful *rentier* wit" (N, p. 50), in their sense of the disparity, which William also notices, between the stipulated matter and the more instinctive manner of his talk. And they are equally right in feeling that, attending to Bayer, who, if anyone, is the novel's hero, they are "listening to their own collective voice" (N, p. 48). For Bayer's speech is as transparent and self-effacing as Arthur's is deceptive and self-serving; and the implications of the audience's reactions to the two men make clear that what *Mr. Norris* is most centrally about is the nature and conditions of social compact. Richard Ohmann's notion, borrowed from J. L. Austin, of "'illocutionary acts': acts performed *in* speaking" is relevant here. "When a text violates syntactic or semantic rules," he writes, "cognitive or logical dissonance ensues. Violating the rules for illocutionary acts also produces a kind of chaos, but predictably a *social* one."[12] Speaking of the telegrams Norris receives from "Margot" (which in the course of the book involve manifold betrayals of "friends" and party), Fräulein Schroeder tells William: "I believe it's a kind of secret language. . . . Every word has a double mean-ing" (*N*, p. 96). Ludicrously wrong though she is in her interpretation of that meaning, she is altogether right in recognizing the intention to conceal. The opacity of the words in which Arthur and Sally traffic makes personal intercourse a sham and, more, inevitably threatens the linguistic and social breakdown of public and national life as well. Norris serves not only as symbol but as symptom of the Nazi domination soon to come.

Despite their superficial attractiveness, it is relatively easy to account for Sally and Arthur in the moral scheme of *The Berlin Stories* and, of course, to find them wanting. The difficulties that surround William and Christopher are more recalcitrant and also more central, since, as I've suggested, their own language determines the verbal norm upon which the ethical burden of the novels rests. How, in other words, are we to reconcile the moral function of Isherwood's two narrators with their obvious and severe limitations? The answer apparently lies in the fact that, as compared with Arthur and Sally, Christopher and William are at any rate aware: conscious of problems they cannot yet match with appropriate responses and behavior. (Christopher, less gullible than his predecessor, is perfectly able, at least when he is angry, to recognize that Sally has "the vocabulary and mentality of a twelve-year-old schoolgirl" [*G*, p. 65].) Consequently, if they are demonstrably deficient in any number of ways, they nonetheless resemble the hero of Edward Upward's story "Sunday," who thinks to and about himself, as he decides to overcome his neurotic fears and anxieties by joining the Communist Party: "It will take time. But it is the only hope. He will at least have made a start."[13]

Making a start: it is this kind of restricted and even hypothetical commitment that ratifies the language of *The Berlin Stories* and that offers, in this most self-conscious of decades, the promise, if not the achievement of the goal. But what goal exactly? The answer is complex, but some help can be found in Isherwood's collaborative effort with Auden, *The Dog Beneath the Skin*. Early in the play, the chorus outlines the nature of the journey Alan Norman is about to take through the false forms of love—predicting in particular his narcissistic relationship with a shopwindow dummy whose lines he speaks at the play's climax—and promises that, at the end, love (and Alan) will be "disenchanted."[14] Disenchantment, in fact, expresses exactly the character of the thirties enterprise: the attempt, on the one hand, to reestablish a unified, func-tional self by freeing it from its delusive, self-centering pain or desire and, on the other, to acknowledge, by the new clear-sightedness this disen-chantment entails, the objective autonomy of the world.

The two projects, the psychological and the epistemological, are, then, by intention at least, interrelated; and the connection is made again, more subtly, in *Goodbye to Berlin*. The famous camera image with which the novel begins ("I am a camera with its shutter open . . ." [*G*, p. 1])[15] is associated, when it returns at the end of the book, with the far more characteristic image of the mirror. And in fact, even in the first section of "A Berlin Diary (Autumn 1930)," the world outside Christopher's window is much less the object of his photographic scrutiny than a subjective and expressionistic reflection of his state of mind. Unlike Fräulein Schroeder, who instinctively accommodates herself to the changing conditions around her, "like an animal which changes its coat for the winter" (*G*, p. 207), Christopher typically annexes the world to his own imperial concerns. Isherwood leads us from the Gidean *fausse piste* of the camera eye to the rude awakening of the mirror, as if to bear witness to the failure of an intended objectivity, a failure that is, above all, moral. This in itself is remarkable. The thirties had not heard of Herbert Marcuse, nor yet of a "primary narcissism" that may force its way joyously into the outer world and rearrange the parts according to its own comprehensive "theory for government, education, or society."[16] Isherwood's sterner and guilt-ridden mirror signifies a refusal to see or to face necessarily unpleasant or unredeemable realities. Consequently, the need in him and in the thirties writers generally to prove their adequacy by interiorizing the prevailing, strenuous notions of a "reality principle" and to end, paradoxically, in the persistent self-concern and self-doubt that pervades their work. More to the point, however, Christopher's open shutter, for all its abortive passivity, expresses an intention at least that is as much linguistic and psychological as moral. The *reportage* to which he and other authors (or their personae) of the period are commonly thought to be addicted derives precisely from a new and, one might say, puritanical use of language—one they naively hoped would disenchant language into transparency or into a mediative purity. Unlike the shameless hedonism of Arthur's and Sally's speech, it would be, with a laconic vengeance, directly referential. "Good prose," as Orwell remarked, "is like a window pane."[17]

Isherwood and his fellow writers see language, then, not, in symbolist or postsymbolist fashion, as a means of discovering or evoking some final and ultimate "Truth," but as a way of releasing the self and of thereby making the phenomenal world once more the scene of purposeful action—the site, even, of the decade's much-fabled New Country, that socially, politically, and psychologically unified realm "Where," in Auden's words, "grace may grow outward and be given praise / Beauty and virtue be vivid there" (*Dog*, p. 112). But, as we have seen, the self is not easily released to "grow outward" like grace or to become the pellucid verbal medium through which objective realities shine like the sun. To acquire the body and texture of a pane of glass requires the special "control" of "thoughts and feelings" through verbal precision of which Michael Roberts speaks—a kind of personal ascesis that, in practice, in their chosen literary exercises, has implications and results these writers could hardly have contemplated, results that complicate and delimit their positive achievement. When so much effort is expended on becoming so linguistically thin, we wonder about the motive and method of the regimen and about the final resultant configuration, much as we have every right to puzzle retrospectively over the last canvas in one of Matisse's reductive series. Evidently, behind the search for verbal precision lies the compelling need for control, so that, if these authors are impelled to verbal deflation by more publicly moral, even political, notions, they want also, and perhaps with an even greater urgency, to exercise a more private dominion over themselves. (The distinction is a real one for them, though the areas of attention inevitably overlap.) The impetus for control is, in short, more consciously and concentratedly psychological and necessarily complicates the relatively simpler matter of socially defined ethical imperatives.

In theory at least, the method of achieving control follows the usual pattern of depth psychology: to bring to light, by conscious expression, the secrets and fears of the personality—"the woman in dark glasses and the humpbacked surgeons / And the scissor man" (Dog, p. 8)—and thus to exorcise them; to expose and, in the process, to cure the sense of guilt or impotence or distance the decade rehearses in its endless litany of unworthiness. So Auden proposes, in his version of the thirties' favorite Conradian metaphor, that the exile "with prolonged drowning shall develop gills."[18] But the intimations of depth, of immersion in the destructive element, are misleading. Not descent but travel, with its suggestions of linear movement, expresses their actual strategies; becomes in fact their most pervasive emblem or metaphor—and their most engrossing avocation as well. No doubt Isherwood and most of the other New Countrymen felt, as Keith Aldritt says in speaking of Orwell, that their "deepest concern was with the remaking of the self,"[19] but the fact remains that in The Berlin Stories Isherwood typically substitutes for an exploration of that divided, haunted, and estranged self (the self, in this case, of his narrators) a ramble through the crowded and exotic country of "The Lost" (p. v).

Furthermore, as he does so, he compromises in some sense the integrity of his narrators. Presenting William and Christopher as fluent, detached observers is undoubtedly meant to suggest, in terms of character, the appearance of surface but not to exclude the notion of depth. Unlike

Arthur or Sally, who do exist only in terms of linguistic surface, Isherwood's narrators are, it seems clear, meant to be seen as responding psychologically to the sense of an inner void, the perception of a space of negation, an emptiness waiting to fill and fulfill itself through contact with the world. Thus, if there is no investigation of the inner life in the manner of earlier novelists, there is nonetheless the assumption of a self: a self which, though habitually looking outward at others as mirrors, though dispersed into endless fragments, still seeks, as Woolf said, "to be whole; to be human" (p. 176).

Yet the fact that so many critics have taken these narrators at their own valuation—as reporters, cameras, and so on—has some significance, even if the judgments are mistaken.[20] We are, it should be noted, back to the question, mooted earlier, of the linguistic cart and the conceptual horse. No doubt Spender speaks for others of his generation in describing his attempt "to turn the reader's and writer's attention outwards from himself to the world";[21] and no doubt there is conscious intention involved not only in avoiding the direct presentation of sexuality (or homosexuality) but also in the effort to move beyond (or ignore) the metaphysical concerns of the twenties: "the experience," in Spender's words again, "of an all-pervading Present, which is a world without belief" (p. 14). But the tactical by-passing of the inner life is a more complicated matter. It is curious, for example, that for all its allegiance to Freud, the decade's psychological model is more behavioristic than genetic; and it seems legitimate to ask whether in this area it is not a question of the cart pulling the horse. Is it not the case, in short, that Isherwood and a good many of his contemporaries, intent on linguistic deflation and precision, narrow, even as they sharpen, their own range of expressiveness and, in turn, diminish the concept of character and of the surrounding world? Admirably successful in diagnosing the sickness of their age, especially as it manifests itself in the corruption and laxness of language, they fall victim, in some measure, to their own program of linguistic hygiene, with its compulsive concern for the spare and the understated.

What I am suggesting is that excluding the microcosm of the inner life and the macrocosm of the universe exacts the payment of a high, perhaps an excessive, price in perception and in the verbal forms that shape and embody it. This is nowhere more apparent than in the repeated attempts by writers of the period to suggest directly the shape and dimensions of New Country, the thirties' collective version of the anironic—or indeed to portray its likely inhabitants. Typically, given Spender's injunction to turn outward, the desired process of personal transformation goes hand in hand, is in fact defined by, the attempt to establish or reestablish the sense of social and linguistic compact—personal integrity being seen in terms of, even subsumed to, the authenticity of the group: "Yes," C. Day

Lewis writes, "we learn to speak for all / Whose hearts are not at home, / All who march to a better time."[22] But it is exactly here that the thirties writers most conspicuously fall short, not simply because they were, as Orwell[23] and, in a different way, Woolf (p. 175) suggested, too theoretical (Orwell's own repeated references to "common decency" are hardly clearer or more expressively adequate than Auden's to "light" and "love" or Isherwood's to "the genuine forms of life") but because language, once restricted and curtailed, will not, without a major shift in its user's perceptual framework (Isherwood's religious conversion, for example) easily stretch to encompass merely abstract and ideated forms. The fact of the matter is that the language of the thirties is suited to discrimination and exclusion, but in its severity, its addiction to parataxis, and its reductiveness, it lacks the lexical, syntactic, and rhetorical resources needed to embody the ideal future. Writing after the fact and deploring his and his contemporaries' inability to make use of "the old grand manner"—or at any rate to do so successfully—Auden noted:

> All words like Peace and Love,
> All sane affirmative speech,
> Had been soiled, profaned, debased
> To a horrid mechanical screech.[24]

But however pertinent Auden's lines are to establishing a conscious reaction to the general "pandaemonium" of the times, they overlook what is at least equally the case: that during the thirties the landscape of depth was effectively subverted (from within, so to speak) by a language devoted to recording the appearances of surface.

If Isherwood stumbles less often than most into the marshes of conceptual inflation and verbal legerdemain, it is not because his footing is surer but because he is, among his contemporaries, the most modest in his aims, the most chary—except in his collaborations with Auden—of "affirmative speech," the most resolute, along with Orwell, in what is, in his case, a strategic adherence to "the sounds, the smells and the surfaces of things."[25] There are, to be sure, exceptions to this general rule. The presence in almost all of the prewar novels of some more or less "ideal" figure to whom it is difficult to determine one's responses—Allen in *All the Conspirators*, Anne in *The Memorial*, Bayer and Natalia in *The Berlin Stories*—indicates that Isherwood was no more able than others to negotiate the terrain of New Country. But Isherwood in the years before his final departure from England is above all a novelist of limits; and his language, astringent, circumscribed, inevitably, if variously, ironic, suggests the "Lords of Limit" invoked by Auden:

> But to your discipline the heart
> Submits when we have fallen apart
> Into the isolated dishonest life.[26]

Not New Country but the dishonest life is the genuine subject of thirties writing, the effective determinant of its language at its most skillful. And it is precisely in his recognition of the decade's self-imposed linguistic restrictions, its necessarily narrowed range of options—its *discipline*—that Isherwood's success locates itself.

But that success is, in another sense, a measure of the decade's failure (and of Isherwood's as well) in achieving its primary goal. At their best, the writers of the thirties do approximate the ideal of transparency; the world as a mirror of self-concern is at times at least disenchanted. But it is important to recognize that the shift from reflectiveness to transparency, while it restores independence to the observed world, leaves it nonetheless merely and precisely an object of observation. Sharpened to a fine point of negation, the decade's language is, in the final analysis, incapable of effecting the interaction between self and world that is its primary desideratum. And the self, though hardly a neutral, unfeeling recorder, may be a camera after all, apprehending the world as phenomenon but failing to achieve the precarious and ongoing synthesis of phenomenological perception. At most, what is accomplished is the registration of an irrecoverable distance. Division remains, in spite (or because) of awareness, to undermine the decade's ideal of complete and total involvement.

There is, of course, nothing unusual about this particular failure in the literature of the first two-thirds of this century, though the thirties, with its political and social rhetoric, raises the question in a less clear-cut but acuter form. But more is at stake: not only the inability to carry through a connection with external reality but also the incapacity to convey unambiguously what that reality is. Current theories of postmodern writing, basing themselves on a contrast between early modernist explorations of inner and outer depth and contemporary rejections of it, tend to adhere to a belief in radical, unmediated change. But the school of apocalyptic leaps and irrational flights overlooks or ignores the logical, if unintended, link Isherwood and his contemporaries provide between the two periods, thanks to their personal discretion and technical reserve.

It would probably be an exaggeration to suggest that Isherwood's moral aims—or those of the thirties—simply fall captive to an overdetermined sense of control. Yet, once one has acknowledged the implicit and even, at times, the explicit moral tendency of *The Berlin Stories*, there remains something unresolved in the atmosphere the novels generate, which calls into question the exact nature of Isherwood's irony. Having said so much about irony in the previous section, I don't want to be overly insistent here. Nevertheless, it is important to recognize as precisely as possible, and the more so because they are not his alone, the problems implied by Isherwood's practice. Whatever the intention of *Mr. Norris* and *Goodbye to Berlin*, they, like so much other writing of the time, ultimately reveal an attitude very close to an acceptance of what they presumably mean to reject. Or, more accurately, they expose the divided loyalties of a decade impelled into public positions while continuing to struggle with the still vivid complexities (a legacy from the previous generation) of the private life—and caught besides between the early modernists' despair over life's disjunctions and their own guilty pleasure in what some of them at least perceived as "the drunkenness of things being various": "incorrigibly plural."[27] The problem, then, is not simply one of a language that, chosen to articulate a moral purpose, works instead to undermine and blur it, but, as I've insisted from the start, of the psychological choices which relate to and inform that language.

Thus, in his preface to *The Berlin Stories* (dated 1954) Isherwood writes: "Only a very young and frivolous foreigner, I thought, could have lived in such a place and found it amusing. Hadn't there been something youthfully heartless in my enjoyment of the spectacle of Berlin in the early thirties, with its poverty, its political hatred and its despair?" (p. x). So much, then, for morality, if one is to trust Isherwood's retrospective estimate of his narrators—and of himself (note the subtly revealing shift from the third-person comment on his characters to the first-person "my"); and so much, if one is to take at his word the still later Isherwood of *Christopher and His Kind*, for political concern: "To Christopher, Berlin meant boys."*[28] My interest, however, is not in autobiography as such, and there is no point in speculating further on the etiology of the problem, that is to say, on the nature of the bond that ties the historical Isherwood to the characters who equivocally project and stabilize in fiction the irresolutions and contradictions of his own life. The novels themselves demonstrate clearly enough the consequences of his compulsive but evasive self-concern. One hardly needs Isherwood's preface or *Christopher and His Kind* to recognize that William and Christopher, imperfect moral instruments that they are, respond, not unlike their author, with a sort of passive enthusiasm to the "spectacle" they are meant to deplore or to understand that in their near acceptance of life in Berlin they betray something oddly inconsistent in the irony by which Isherwood measures his narrators and which they in turn direct at the men and women whose paths they cross. The result of this imperfectly judgmental scrutiny, as irony deliquesces from the normative to the indecisive, is, paradoxically, not an enlarging but a flattening of the mysteries and resonance, of the self certainly, but also of the perceived world. That Isherwood and his surrogates are inextricably part of that world, *in* it, so many additional particles of its random ebb and flow,

*I don't mean to suggest that this "frank and factual" autobiography (p. 1) is devoid of social concerns, but the book does seem to me to flatten out the rich political implications that, on one level, the novels suggest.

hints more emphatically still at the ways in which the novels prefigure the ethos of a later time.

To say all this is, of course, to ignore the larger design of the two books: history remains determinative in *The Berlin Stories*, and at the end of the second novel Christopher leaves Berlin, responsive to the crisis without and perhaps to an equally urgent one within. But we cannot be sure of that. And we can hardly overlook Christopher's remarks as he takes his final walk in the city: "I catch sight of my face in the mirror of a shop, and am shocked to see that I am smiling. You can't help smiling in such beautiful weather. . . . No. Even now I can't altogether believe that any of this has really happened. . . ." (*G*, p. 207). But the last word, however we are meant to respond to it, does not, after all, belong to Christopher. Held in check by Isherwood's directing hand, he and William yield the foreground to Sally and Arthur (and others of "The Lost") and so diminish still further the novels' too covert intimations of depth. More vivid than the observant Bradshaw, Norris, patron saint of linguistic surface, gestures (like Forster in *The Life to Come* and, as will become apparent, like late modernism in general) beyond the "committed" thirties toward one aspect of postmodernism and of the suspensive irony that negotiates its transactions with the world: a two-dimensional space without character, without interiority or transcendence, and, finally, without ulterior significance. And though Isherwood himself (more complex, in any case, and more divided than his single-minded character) comes to reject that world in his postwar novels, the ambiguously ironic restraint of *The Berlin Stories* helps no less surely to bring it into being.

FOUR

The Epistemology of Late Modernism

"I daresay many people are not what they are thought to be."
"Most of them are what they are known to be," said Naomi.
  —Ivy Compton-Burnett, *A Heritage and Its History*

Writing to Isherwood after he had twice read *Mr. Norris Changes Trains*, Forster expressed, along with "much admiration and enjoyment," a slight hesitancy, a hint of polite discomfort. It was not, he suggested, "altogether [his] sort of book," because, as he went on to explain, it "dwells on the contradictions rather than the complexities of character, and seems to reveal people facet by facet whereas The Memorial if my memory serves tackled strata."[1] The reservation illuminates a fundamental difference between the practice and conceptions of Forster's generation and Isherwood's—or, to adopt now somewhat broader, more flexible categories, between those of modernism (early modernism, as it will henceforth be convenient to call it in this chapter) and late modernism. And it does something besides. Read today, the comment seems prescient of a still more radical change: the replacement of "well-made-characters who carry with them a fixed identity, a stable set of social and psychological attributes—a name, a situation, a profession, a condition, etc." (characters like Forster's, presumably) by what Raymond Federman, speaking for one group of postmodern writers, calls "word-beings," fictional creatures who "will be as changeable, as unstable, as illusory, as nameless, as unnamable, as fraudulent, as unpredictable as the discourse that makes them."[2]

The postmodern attitude, along with the full force of its disintegrations, may be left until later. Forster's own position is clarified in *Aspects of the Novel*, where, in the discussion of flat and round characters, he reveals his preference for those who, growing and changing, are "capable of surprising in a convincing way" (p. 54) and who, because of their roundness or complexity, their comprehensible depth, make more vivid what Forster sees as the major consolation of fiction, its ability to provide us with "a reality of a kind we can never get in daily life" (p. 44). The contrast between the unsatisfactoriness of life, in which "we never understand each other" (p. 32), and the power of art to create a structured space of belief, or desire, and thus to "solace us" (p. 44) runs throughout *Aspects* (and through most of modernism): a gloomy leitmotif which, by way of its insistence on the integrity of the fictional self at least, simultaneously expresses Forster's rearguard action against the instabilities of his world and reveals the nostalgia that underlies his aesthetic theories.

How legitimate it is to generalize from those theories is another matter, however, since in the treatment of character in his own fiction Forster is probably the least innovative of the early modernists. Virginia Woolf's celebrated announcement of a change in human character "in or about December, 1910"[3] sounds a bolder, if chronologically debatable, note. And the boldness is, of course, justified by her indefatigable experimentation. There is no need here to dwell on her various techniques of interiorization, on the ways in which the recesses of consciousness are made, ever more obliquely, available to the reader's inspection in order to demonstrate how significantly she alters the presentation of character. The question is whether in her work—or Joyce's or Conrad's or Ford's—the consequences of that change manifest themselves in a conception of character that is substantively different from Forster's.

Consider *Jacob's Room.* "It is no use trying to sum people up," her narrator writes. "One must follow hints, not exactly what is said, nor yet entirely what is done."[4] And later: "It seems that a profound, impartial, and absolutely just opinion of our fellow-creatures is utterly unknown" (p. 70). But we will misread the book badly if we assume that Woolf—or her narrator—simply throws up her hands in despair at the mystery of Jacob. Undoubtedly character has become a good deal more fluid and shifting, more elusive than Forster suggests, but what is at issue is the same epistemology of the hidden. For Woolf, and other early modernists, the tracking down of a character's (or for that matter, the world's) unity or truth, its essence, proceeds through more covert levels of being and demands from the reader more strenuous efforts at comprehension. But however speculative and inferential knowledge has become, the center —Jacob, "a young man alone in his room" (p. 94)—holds; and we are enjoined "to penetrate" (p. 92) the reality behind phenomena: "the skeleton [that] is wrapped in flesh" (p. 162). Character has not been dissolved, nor has the self been lost; though both have become manifestly more problematic. Indeed, the faith in some central core of being not only persists, as in Forster's theory, it is deepened by the mystery of that core's recessive presence; and the passion of the quest for dozens of Jacobs in the early decades of the century, translated into an almost obsessive concern with depth, is validated by just that underlying belief that, at some level, character remains intact.

With the thirties, as I've already argued, there is a noticeable, if somewhat ambiguous, shift to surface and along with it, inevitably perhaps, a change in attitudes toward character and characterization. If for no other purpose than to avoid a too tidy mapping of developments and movements, it should be recalled that there are proponents of surface throughout the century—Pound, Hulme, the imagists, Wyndham Lewis, Isherwood, Orwell, Waugh, to choose names almost at random and to stop for the moment with its fourth decade—but it is only toward the end of the twenties that one can begin to identify the rise of something like a new sensibility. The qualification of "something like" is deliberate: we are dealing with a reaction against modernism by writers who retain a good many modernist presuppositions and strategies and who, in a variety of ways, differ from one another as much as they do from the early modernists. The common thread, I suggested a moment ago as well as in chapter 3, is a new attention to surface, and that concern implies something still more interesting: a reversal—dramatic even when incomplete or unintended—in epistemological assumptions, which (rather than the attractions of political commitment, say, or the attempt to escape the confinements of the ivory tower) defines in the most basic way both the moral program of late modernism and the aesthetic retrenchments of its writers.

The reversal is fundamental. The early modernist tendency to connect truth with depth, and at times to sacrifice the phenomenal for the reality that is presumed to underlie it, gives way to a counterassertion that truth inheres in the visible. Thus the repeated announcements that things *are* what they seem—provided, of course, that the seeing eye is clear, unclouded by the mists of convention and tradition, free from the deliberate evasions and sentimentalities of the past and from the still more insidious deceptions of the self. The trick, then, is to see not more deeply but differently. The interrelated problems of knowing and evaluating present themselves less as inherent than accidental: matters not of necessarily limited but of correctably faulty perception. Auden's prewar poems, with their repeated injunctions to look, see, consider, and watch are relevant here: a repeated summons to attention or, more accurately, to attentiveness. And so too, to press into service again Auden's and Isherwood's usefully revealing play, is *The Dog Beneath the Skin*, that brash, mordant contribution to the ideology of the thirties, in which Alan Norman undertakes a circular journey that describes a movement not toward complexity (Alan is in all essentials unchanged) but toward "disenchantment." He learns, in other words, to recognize what was always there, obvious and unconcealed: the genteel corruption of his native village, which only a fatuously naive reading of appearances keeps him from recognizing at the start.

Reading appearances correctly is, in fact, the project of late modernism, its enemy not a failure to penetrate to some more authentic reality but a sort of cultural or psychological dyslexia, which blurs vision itself. Sifting appearances rather than plumbing depths: that is the nature of the enterprise and the central clue to its redefinition of character in terms of the "facets" and "contradictions" Forster found in *Mr. Norris*. But to limit oneself to Isherwood, even to take into account other members of the Auden circle, is to construct too narrow a base for the change I've been describing. And there is, I think, no need to. Taking as central an epistemology of surfaces brings into the fold of late modernism other writers, some of the thirties, some not, whose relation to Auden and his friends is tangential at best and in some cases nonexistent, but whose inclusion actually establishes the validity of the category. My test case will be the highly individual, even eccentric Ivy Compton-Burnett; my evidence, the two leading characters of what is probably her finest novel, *Manservant and Maidservant*.[5] No doubt one needs to construct a net with remarkably fine meshes to catch and hold so elusive a writer. As one of her critics writes: "Attempts to find [her novels] a literary ancestor or some relation in a modern movement have always proved abortive. Dame Ivy herself would have none of it."[6] Naturally, one feels daunted by Dame Ivy's veto, and rebuked. But not sufficiently, as this essay reveals, to keep from casting one's net.

. . .

To begin, then, at the beginning. We enter *Manservant and Maidservant*, appropriately, by way of dialogue, interrogation, and conflict:

"Is that fire smoking?" said Horace Lamb.

"Yes, it appears to be, my dear boy."

"I am not asking what it appears to be doing. I asked if it was smoking."

"Appearances are not held to be a clue to the truth," said his cousin. "But we seem to have no other."

Horace advanced into the room as though his attention were withdrawn from his surroundings.

"Good morning," he said in a preoccupied tone, that changed as his eyes resumed their direction. "It does seem that the fire is smoking."

"It is in the stage when smoke is produced. So it is hard to see what it can do."

"Did you really not understand me?"

"Yes, yes, my dear boy. It is giving out some smoke. We must say that it is."

There follows a passage of exposition, mainly a description of Horace, only the end of which need be quoted. Commenting on Lamb's "habit of looking aside in apparent abstraction," the narrator continues: "This was a punishment to people for the nervous exasperation that they produced in him, and must expiate."[7]

The most extraordinary, if not the most obvious quality of the passage is that, taken as a whole, it forces the reader to enact precisely those contradictory responses to the characters that are dramatized by the characters themselves as they react to the smoking fire. Which is to say that we apprehend them alternately as at least possibly complex and then as opaque, conceivably contradictory beings. It is Compton-Burnett's technique, of course, that enforces the alternation. As we enter Horace's mind at the end of the section quoted, brief and unelaborated though the narrator's remark is, the dimension of depth adds itself to our way of perceiving the character, establishing the expectation that we are to have access to his inner life and therefore to whatever clues we need to understand him and his actions. The expectation is a reasonable one, and familiar to any reader of fiction. But the effect of the dialogue, here and elsewhere in the novel, is completely different. The stress of language in these sections, so patently self-conscious and artificial, is such as to activate a kind of fictional circuit breaker, which, impeding the flow of current needed to sustain the reader's sense of the characters' verisimilitude, flattens them out, making of them, if not quite "word-beings," still unmistakably verbal constructs. In other words, the foregrounding of language makes the novel (in a new and more insistent way than among various early modernist works I've discussed) reflexive rather than referential, drawing our attention above all to the designing hand of its creator and inhibiting our surrender to illusion.*[8]

It isn't immediately apparent, however, why our awareness of Compton-Burnett's manipulation and control should cause her characters to become not only less self-contained and independent but, unlike Sterne's or Joyce's (in *Ulysses*), for example, less intelligible as well. But the explanation, surely, is that the confinement of characters to the surface of the page and their consequent exile from the depths of autonomous "worlds" in the novels of Compton-Burnett and later writers reflects not simply a playing with generic conventions and readers' expectations but a dissolution (uneven and irregular, to be sure) of the assumptions—causality, say, or psychological integrity—that create those worlds. It should help to make this point clearer if we return now to Horace Lamb and his cousin Mortimer, who, I've already suggested, replicate in their conversation the problem we experience in adjusting to them as characters. But

---

*If it seems illogical or arbitrary to single out language in the face of a general tolerance for what seem such equally unverisimilar tactics on the part of novelists as melodramatic plots or authorial intrusions, it can only be said that the resistance to high stylistic finish persists even today, notwithstanding the example of writers like Joyce and Woolf and the general insistence of twentieth-century criticism on the language of fiction.

what problem exactly? Though the interchange is strange enough, the reader is probably not altogether prepared for philosophy in the dining room. Nevertheless, it is what he gets or what he begins to recognize as he adapts his comprehension to the implications of the domestic scene and its apparent banalities: an epistemological struggle that realizes itself not beneath but in the characters' words. In brief, the words and the problem are one. Horace's peremptory self-assurance, his irritable questions and equally irritable statements (his "seem" seems less a concession to Mortimer than a sarcastic riposte) reveal a belief in the possibility of absolute, verifiable knowledge; and his discourse strains toward certainty, toward the discovery or uncovering of truth. Mortimer, on the other hand, with his repetitions and *chevilles*, his penchant for elegant formulations and for indirection (things naturally seem and appear to him; and his final, emphatic "We must say that it is" appears less a concession to Horace than a gesture of exasperation), Mortimer represents an entirely more modest and relativist approach, which eventuates in a guarded, pragmatic trust in appearances. Indicative and subjunctive, the two cousins define between them what one would say were mutually exclusive faiths: Horace's in the ultimate comprehensibility of the hidden, Mortimer's in the limits and complications of the visible. And, to stress the point once again: as they see, so too do we. Thus, whether or not it is her intention, Compton-Burnett makes the psychology of her characters—and, since they are effectively the same, our interpretative readings of them—a variable function of linguistic surface and illusionistic depth. From the reader's point of view, then, Horace, Mortimer, and the rest appear to inhabit two different world of fictional conventions and so to invite, even demand, what we may not be able to supply: an impossibly bifocal vision or an equally self-defeating squint.

Both Horace and Mortimer, in different ways, put these generalizations to the proof, and it will be helpful to look more closely now at each of them, examining Mortimer, as the (slightly) less problematic, first. Any attempt to make total sense of Mortimer immediately runs into problems. How, for example, are we to reconcile his somewhat mysterious love for Horace ("We cannot account for these things," the butler, Bullivant, says to him, "and perhaps it would lessen their meaning" [p. 222]) with his plan to run away with his cousin's wife? Or his gratuitous kindliness to the somewhat peripheral Miss Buchanan with his unpleasant treatment of his unwanted but devoted fiancée, Magdalen Doubleday? Or either, with his characteristic distance and detachment from others, from life itself? The list of attitudes, feelings, and actions is obviously not exhaustive, but it is long enough (and its details are sufficiently representative) to justify the questions I've been asking, and these further, summary ones as well, namely, how shall we comprehend and combine these data so as to understand by means of them a single unified character—or should we? Certainly it is at any rate possible to resolve contradictions and antinomies by hypothesizing some deeper level of character, and it is the habit of twentieth-century criticism to do just that. So, to choose an especially subtle and interesting example of this sometimes uneasy process, Jacques Rivière, whose insistence on depth might have been cited above in my remarks on early modernism, writes in an essay "On Dostoevsky and the Creation of Character": "In the end, the human being, however unusual he may be (if he is not mad, and perhaps even if he is), never escapes from a certain deep-rooted logic."[9] The essay, it should be noted, begins as an attack on the integrating, simplifying tendency of the French mind, but it ends, ironically enough, by exemplifying that famous Cartesian spirit. In other words, though Rivière at first stresses the claims of the unresolved (Dostoevsky) over those of coherence (the French tradition)—"We feel that Dostoevsky was most impressed by something to which he wanted to remain faithful throughout his work: the cohabitation, in every consciousness, of instincts that are contradictory as well as irreducible" (p. 246)—he comes at last to a definition of the novelist's task as one of "search[ing] out the law that governs" his character (p. 248). His responsibility is to explore the depths, to recognize their complexities, and finally to discover in them "a single tendency" (p. 248).

Is there a law that governs Mortimer's character? No doubt one can be found, or enacted. Thus, we might construct a coherent portrait of him as a fundamentally intelligent, self-aware, and, above all, loving man, forced out of his natural concern for others by his role as financial dependent and psychological subordinate in the Lamb household; forced instead into defensiveness and withdrawal, and into acute self-consciousness as well; and even, on occasion, driven, as in his surprisingly nasty rejection of Magdalen, on whom he does not depend, to devious expressions of his generally suppressed or verbally sublimated antagonism and resentment. A study, then, in frustration: the making of an esthete and an ironist. Other interpetations, some of them even less flattering to Mortimer, are possible, and very likely richer than the one I have sketched; but would they be, any more than mine, justified? The answer, I've already suggested, is ambiguous. Whatever in the book's technique approximates the traditional novel, if only in a residual way, supports or at least allows the reader's descent into depth and his search there for some explanatory "single tendency."[10] But as I've also noted, the bulk of the novel, its dialogic axis, not only fails to encourage, it quite specifically discourages the quest for complexity, that entwining into unity of only apparently discordant elements, which promises—unlike Compton-Burnett's narrator, who announces: "It can seldom be said that there is a key to a human personality" (p. 96)—to solve the most intransigent of mysteries.

The concentration on lingustic surfaces invites, rather, a view of character as discontinuous and, if not incoherent, still no more than an assemblage of surface contiguities.

I don't want, for the sake of dramatic effect, to push this argument too far. There is no need to invoke Federman's "new fictitious creature," who, we are told, "will be irrational, irresponsible, irrepressive, amoral, and unconcerned with the real world" (p. 13), no need, that is, to confuse Compton-Burnett's practice with postmodern theory—though it would be equally wrong to overlook in a novel like *Manservant and Maidservant* the seeds of Federman's "surfiction." In any case, his description is well in advance (to speak only in descriptive and not in evaluative terms) of anything one can fairly attribute, except by way of adumbration, to Compton-Burnett, whose novels hardly suggest so radical a dispersal of the unity of character. Her characters are, in fact, recognizably if not consistently themselves, hybrids of older and newer psychological formulations, simultaneously reinforcing and disrupting the reader's traditional modes of perception.[11] The effect, needless to say, is vertiginous; the problem, a matter of adjudicating between these different ways of responding and establishing a convincing perspective on character. For what we have here, I want to emphasize, is not the equivocal poise of opposites that characterizes so much of early modernist literature, the fierce balance of unreconciled and contradictory attitudes I earlier called absolute irony. Certainly there is a tension in the conception and construction of Compton-Burnett's novels—it is what I have been attempting to describe—but the effect on the reader is hardly the same. Granted the rival claims of depth and surface in *Manservant and Maidservant*, the book, I would suggest, opts finally, like late modernism in general, for surface, thus pushing away (and pushing us away) from the equipoise, the focused, steadied irresolutions of books like *A Portrait of the Artist*, *A Passage to India*, or *The Waves* and toward a more unsettling, ambiguous asymmetry. So, to return to Mortimer and to Forster's comments on Isherwood, it seems to me that we come closer to a satisfactory reading of Compton-Burnett's character when we view him totally from the outside, substituting for the notion of complexity the category of contradiction and for the suggestion of depth (or Rivière's governing law) the metaphor, hard, bright, separate, and inorganic, of facets.

I can imagine at this point the objection that Mortimer is in some sense special, that Compton-Burnett asks us to regard him (and only him) as he regards others, that is, with a view to the necessary self-sufficiency of appearances. But if Horace, the seeker of truth (Mortimer is a quite different creature, a teller of truth)—if he too demands to be seen as contradictory, it becomes legitimate to generalize about the novel as a whole. For Horace is the focus of its plot, the character most responsible for, as well as the potential object of, most of its exiguous if violent action. More importantly, he changes, and the idea of change immediately, inevitably, suggests "roundness" and complexity and the possibility, for us, of investing him with depth. Of that possibility, more in a moment. First, however, to underline the central fact. That Horace does change, and then on a number of occasions in the course of the book relapses, is indisputable. What it means to change, however, is altogether less clear.[12] This is not to suggest that Compton-Burnett fails to provide reasons for the transformation in Horace. It's clear enough that his circuitous discovery of Mortimer's and his wife's plan to elope motivates his new attitude toward his children and toward the expenditure of money. But the reasons themselves are subject to interpretation; so that, if I'm right in what I've said about Compton-Burnett's techniques, we face again, in trying to evaluate the significance of the change, exactly the same problem we did with Mortimer: that of choosing between two different and incompatible sets of presuppositions about the nature of character. Do we, then, to specify the alternatives, credit a fundamental alteration of Horace's essential self, assuming that such a self can be said to exist, or are we to see instead modifications, conscious, willed, and therefore unstable, of surface personality: behavioral tropisms, as it were, activated by discrete and specific stimuli?* Must we, when thinking of Horace's relapses, suppose a stable, underlying identity that continues to assert and reassert itself or ought we simply to recognize the ineluctable persistencies and discontinuities of habit? Shall we, finally, believe, as Horace does, in the possibility of development (his own) or agree with Mortimer that "it is the same old Horace after all" (p. 123)?

A distinction without a difference? I think not. What I am reaching after is suggested in one of the novel's downstairs conversations:

> "We all act inconsistently with our natures at times," said Cook.
> "Or the natures themselves are inconsistent," said Miss Buchanan.
> "A profound remark," said Bullivant.
> "And one that explains why we sometimes surprise ourselves and others," said Cook. (pp. 153-54)

Cook's first remark assumes a stability of character, a core of identity, the substance of which remains unaltered by the accident of inconsistency but is, presumably, amenable to growth and change. Miss Buchanan, on the other hand, effectively dissolves identity as a coherent entity by making it not more than and different from the sum of its parts but

---

*There is a good deal of evidence in the book to suggest that the characters regard the change as conscious and willed. "I expect," one of his sons says to him, "you will sometimes forget to be different" (p. 113). His wife tells him bitterly: "It is an utter and sudden change" (p. 118).

precisely their sum: a view that, if it does not embrace, at least opens the door to Federman's notion of character. Once more, then, depending upon whom we side with, we confront the problem, which forces us to decide not whether Horace changes and lapses (not even whether there are different sides to his character) but rather whether either state or both are to be seen normatively or, on the contrary, to be regarded, equally and consecutively, as constitutive of what we may continue to call character only if we understand ourselves to mean the contingent coexistence of the actual and not the essential coherence of the virtual.

My own aim, obviously, is to support Miss Buchanan, and not only, as must be equally obvious by now, so as to make of Horace a creature of contradictions. For to read his character in the way I urged we read Mortimer's is to confront Compton-Burnett's vision of life as well: to see in and through her characters a belief not in discoverable and enduring truths but in the truth of appearances and of the moment.* Simply to assert this, however, will convince no one; and to prove it, it becomes necessary to consider not only the characters of *Manservant and Maidservant* but its plot, the evidence of which, I had better say straight off, is not without its ambiguities either. Thus, depending upon which aspects of the plot one chooses to emphasize, it is possible to assess its impact and meaning differently. Indeed, in some ways it makes sense to regard it as that element of the novel that best articulates the tension of late modernism. Nevertheless, I think it will help finally, in this balancing act we are engaged in, to tip the scales against the attraction of depth and depth psychology and in favor of the contingent world of surfaces and appearances.

To give complexity its due: considered linearly, the plot of *Manservant and Maidservant* could be said to provide a series of tests for Horace Lamb. Again and again his change is put to the proof as he faces—first in the partly inadvertent attempt at patricide by two of his sons, then in the

---

*I don't want to suggest that Compton-Burnett would have agreed with what I'm saying. In fact, one of her remarks, quoted by Burkhart, seems to indicate the reverse: "I think it's very difficult to alter people, very difficult either to corrupt or improve them. The essence of people remains what it is" (p. 66). My argument all along has been that Compton-Burnett's technique (reminiscent of, if not by any means identical with, Isherwood's in *The Berlin Stories*) largely effects a subversion of what is apparently her conscious belief in an essential stability of character. On the other hand, one could also argue that it is precisely those who adhere to a belief in the general unchangeability of character who, when pushed nevertheless to contemplate or describe change, conceive it cataclysmically and disjunctively (which means in Horace's case, as we've seen, inevitably to speak of inconsistency or contradiction). Thus to assert that "the essence of people remains what it is" may represent, paradoxically, not a confirmation but a denial of an essentialist view of human nature, an assertion, instead, of an automatic responsiveness to or a violent break from the persistence of social institutions and habits. If nothing is possible, then, to extend the paradox, anything is possible as well.

more concerted effort at domestic regicide by his footman, and finally in the near fatal illness that brings him closest to death—the consequences of his earlier actions and habits. The unfolding, in short, as in so many traditional novels, of a story of slow and difficult growth and the intimation of the goal's achievement. Confronted by a final lapse on Horace's part, Bullivant says to Lamb's aunt: "The master may be glad to be assisted back to his standard, ma'am, the normal one for him now, as it is fair to see it" (p. 222); and if we agree with Bullivant's assessment, we shall necessarily agree too to think of Horace as a round character and thus to accord him the dimension of depth.

The interpretation is feasible but not, I think, compelling; and to stress the melodramatic quality of the plot's incidents is immediately to invite less clear-cut judgments. Melodrama, emphasizing the sudden, the shocking, the unexpected in events, creates an atmosphere in which it is possible to accept as plausible sudden changes in character as well—and Horace's family makes a point of how precipitously he has become another man. But by the same token, melodrama removes much of the connective tissue that holds together the conventional plot and so tends to attenuate characters; tends, that is, to present us with effects at the expense of causes. (Though Horace's first and major change proceeds from causes we are aware of, the secondary ones, the lapses, come fitfully and without explanation.) Melodrama, in short, may energize authentic change, as it does in Forster's novels, or it may so emphasize spectacle over motivation as to make the reader's belief in change a matter of uncritical faith—faith, of course, in the authenticity and reliability of the spoken word or the accomplished deed.

But to the degree that we rely exclusively on what is said or seen we begin to move again from complexity to contradiction, which brings us, finally, to a third quality of the novel's narrative and to a still more unsettled view of character. For the most striking property of *Manservant and Maidservant*'s plot inheres neither in the nature of its incidents nor in their melodramatic structure but in its circularity; or, to put it differently, in the way plot contrives pattern. Pattern, as Forster says, "is an aesthetic aspect of the novel" (*AN*, p. 104), which risks as it strives after beauty "shut[ting] the doors on life" (*AN*, p. 112), a comment that may be interpreted to mean, among other things, sacrificing richness and complexity of character. In this sense, *Manservant and Maidservant* certainly fulfills Forster's definition. Indeed, the overall pattern (shapely but inconclusive) is in some ways the emblem and summation of those never finally resolved conversations that make up the dialogic part of the novel. But the circularity intimates something more. The final chapter opens with an echo of those earlier discussions of the cold that dominate the opening chapters, and it ends with a return to the fire, smoking again as it did on the book's first page. Bullivant's pronouncement: "The old days have returned" (p. 243)—he is referring literally to Horace's recovery and his reappearance in the dining room—can no doubt be translated, like the plot itself, in different ways; but it is difficult to resist the temptations of irony as we round back to the beginning, to avoid concluding if not that Horace is identical with what he was at the start then at least that he has not altered in any profound and final way. Or, to undermine our powers of evaluation still further, must we admit, at last, that we are not in a position to know the hidden life? For surely the circularity of the plot not only symbolizes the possible limits of change but, in providing the book with its final aesthetic and aestheticizing dimension, moves us, the readers, into a position where, distant and detached, we are able to evaluate only the surfaces of the novel's fictional life. From the reader's point of view there have been no revelations (there have not been many from the characters'; only the absolutist Horace is truly surprised), and certainly no resolution. To be sure, we realize, as the characters do, that things have become more precarious, in a special way. A greater self-consciousness informs everyone, ourselves included, as if we dwelt where an earthquake had shaken and weakened but not destroyed the foundations of the house. But the metaphor is misleading: we are not in the house but outside it, and its blinds are drawn. If the temptation remains to read complexly, with an eye to what is inner and concealed, it is less an active desire than a velleity, a residue of older habits. Despite the fact that *Manservant and Maidservant*—or segments of it—allow the notion of strata, it is at the last the radically external view that is in the ascendent, creating our sense that we can do no more than register the unaccountable and unpredictable vagaries (the word is Bullivant's, and he uses it as he tries to account, by reference to "some vagary of the wind" [p. 243], for the smoking fire) of character in all its contradictions.

· · ·

The distance and detachment I just attributed to the reader naturally mirror and respond to Compton-Burnett's own vision and to the techniques (which partly resemble, partly differ from Isherwood's) that embody it, not only the circular plot but, still more, the point of view: that invariable, implacable distance she (or her narrator) maintains from her characters, even when recording their thoughts or feelings. Since these qualities in particular define the perspective of early modernist irony and since Compton-Burnett is among the most complete ironists of her time, it may help to place her in relation to her actual contemporaries[13] if we can gauge the degree of her conformity to the dominant mode of their writing. Certainly she shares the ironic view of life as inherently fragmented and disjunctive that determines the recourse of so many of her contemporaries to distance and detachment and makes of these qualities an instrument not only of exploration but of disillusion and defense. So Wolfgang Iser, who is probably the most suggestive of her recent critics, writes of her: "For Ivy Compton-Burnett . . . the self is either a myth or simply a stylistic device to present not reality but the *disconnectedness* of reality" (p. 252). But the self, as I've argued, is something different from either of these alternatives; is, actually, the sum of its appearances in time. And so, like Isherwood's characters in *The Berlin Stories*, Compton-Burnett's are capable of secrets but not depths,[14] and Iser, overlooking the possibility that her characters are at once as disconnected and present, existent, as reality itself, seems to me precisely wrong in constantly seeking to uncover "the substrata of that reality" (p. 252), the "unplumbed depths of the human character," "the unfathomableness of their inner recesses" (p. 247), and so on.[15]

But why, if for most early modernists the view from on high in no sense precludes the exploration of depth—indeed seems to invite it —should distance in Compton-Burnett stop short at the opacity of surface? The answer, I suspect, is quite simply that what most troubles the major modernists, the psychological and moral implications of distance, she refuses to consider a problem. For writers like Conrad, Woolf, and Lawrence and still more for Joyce and Forster, the authorial distance created by such techniques as style, tone, point of view, and even characterization is itself thematized on the level of psychology and moral action. So, typically, their novels take as protagonist a character disabled by the aesthetic view of life.* Figures such as Axel Heyst, Philip Herriton, Rickie Elliot, Clarissa Dalloway, Gerald Crich, and Stephen Dedalus, all, to a lesser or greater extent, simultaneously desire and shrink from confrontation with a world they find too ironically disjunct to face or grasp directly. And thus they impose on it a form, a frame, that resembles the mediating order of art, thereby confirming their estrangement from the life they seek. Typically again, the novels oppose to their spectatorlike characters figures who, ranging from Forster's primitivist Gino and Stephen through Woolf's suicidal Septimus Smith to Joyce's humanely, luminously imperfect Bloom, suggest the possibilities of direct involvement, the various modes of closing the gap between self and world. But what makes these books so problematic—Joyce's and Forster's in particular—what leads finally to a crisis in modernist consciousness is not the complexity of the struggle they mean to present but the intimation of a more covert and unresolved warfare. In other words, exactly the attitudes Joyce and Forster embody and reject in the persons of their

---

*To recall briefly what I mean by this phrase, the aesthetic view of life suggests the need to remain detached from and in control of life—a need that translates itself into the desire to find in life the stability and repose of art.

outsiders they confirm through their own techniques: the aesthetic threatens to subvert the moral; and one is hard put at the last to say whether victory lies with the enclosed and enclosing world of art, implicitly articulating its ideal of transcendence and resolving unity, or with the dynamic, imperfect world of human activity it overtly dramatizes.

Compared with these works, Compton-Burnett's are serene (for all their melodrama), uncomplicated (for all their linguistic difficulties and dialogic intensities), and, if one can use the word for so bleak a vision, reassuring. Reassuring in that her novels invite, not necessarily an approval, but an acceptance of life as it is, thereby intimating, like Isherwood's but in their own highly individual fashion, the suspensiveness of a later age. People suffer and cause suffering, but there is, after all, not much to be done. "The one ethical standard which seems absolute," Burkhart writes, summing up Compton-Burnett's "ethos," ". . . is intelligence. . . . To see and interpret life, with whatever results of pessimism, is the better kind [of power]. It is this vision and this understanding that the novels invite us to share" (p. 94). That seems to me, if too respectful of Compton-Burnett's own view of herself and her work, still true at one level; and it explains both why her admirers are so fervent and why they are so few. Almost all modernist irony, as I've argued repeatedly, posits in opposition to its vision of disjunctiveness a complementary vision of inclusive order, thereby generating a hope that more often than not outstrips belief and creating characters sufficiently complex to entertain at least the possibility of fundamentally altering their lives in the pursuit of that ideal. In Compton-Burnett's novels, however, there is no such anironic vision (nor is there, of course, any suggestion of the more ambiguous ideal of New Country); and irony itself, undisturbed by pressures to transform or surpass the discontinuities it registers, loses something of its early modernist generosity and breadth—its desire to restore significance to a broken world—even as it gains in clarity and, linguistically at least, in a certain richness of surface.

Not that Compton-Burnett totally ignores this central modernist concern, but, as her treatment of Mortimer Lamb demonstrates, she truncates and neutralizes it. Mortimer is apart not only in his financial dependency and in his role as bachelor uncle—"I have no proper place" (p. 88), he tells Magdalen—he is, as he indicates in words that recall some of Philip Herriton's pronouncements, psychologically the outsider: "I cannot imagine anything happening to me anywhere else," he says, referring to the fact that he has lived his whole life in one house, "or anything happening to me at all. Not that I mean anything; I do not much like things to happen, or I should not much like it. I am content to live in other people's lives, content not to live at all. Whatever it is, I am content" (p. 9). Mortimer's speech, with all its ironic qualifications, is in one sense a gesture of acceptance, more overt and less compromised, it should be said, than any to be found in Isherwood's novels. (Compare his later statement: "I do not think my life has any meaning. And I find I do not want it to have any. I am one of those creatures who drag out a meaningless existence, and they are not so much to be pitied as people think" [p. 141].) And despite the plan to take from Horace his wife and children—or, to return to the metaphor of contradiction: in addition to it—he is the onlooker, the nonparticipant, kin to those with whom he shares the aesthetic view of life: a man whose eyes "held some humour and little hope" (p. 9). But for Compton-Burnett, who, one suspects, shares Mortimer's self-defensiveness and for whom, as for Mortimer, irony is, in another, more covert sense, an aggressive use of "power" (to use Burkhart's revealing word), power that promises invulnerability as well as understanding, the question is not one of failing oneself and others in the act (or nonact) of viewing life aesthetically. No one in the novel serves, like Forster's primitives or Joyce's always vulnerable Bloom, to provide a counterideal of activity and participation. In fact, Mortimer, who announces, not without pride: "I live on the surface, not in the depths" (p. 48), is the ideal: the truth-teller, the man of intelligence, able, without cant or self-deception, to see more clearly than most, certainly more than his cousin, the limitations and, ultimately, the reliability of appearances. Finally, then, he serves as our major clue to Compton-Burnett's reversal of the priorities of high modernist irony; and in light of his and her allegiance to surface and detachment over depth and involvement—an allegiance that is, we've seen, as much moral (or amoral)[16] as aesthetic—it becomes still clearer that, measured against the standard works of early modernism, her novels are, at the least, highly anomalous.

But if, to return to the argument I began to make in the early pages of this chapter, one sees them in terms of late modernism, the anomaly disappears. And it is worth repeating that what is at issue is less a particular group of years or writers than a state of mind: one in which it is possible to see, uneasily coexisting, elements of two different, unbalanced, often contradictory sensibilities. Thus *Manservant and Maidservant* joins hands not with the writings of Austen and Congreve and the Greek tragedians, as her critics are prone to maintain, thereby reinforcing her own claim to freedom from cultural specificity, but with such otherwise unlikely (since in other respects such different) works as *The Berlin Stories, Keep the Aspidistra Flying,* or *After Leaving Mr. Mackenzie.* Indeed, the chief virtue of the category is perhaps that it militates against the too facile and common contrasts of modernism and postmodernism I've complained of, which do such scant justice to the jagged course of literary history. Late modernism interposes a space of transition, a necessary bridge between more spacious and self-conscious experimental movements, between, for example (thinking once more of character) Gide's and Rivière's preliminary attempts to legitimate impulses that dodge the conventional novelist's preconceptions—centrifugal and latent impulses that contradict one another or societal, and therefore literary, propriety—and Ionesco's *The Bald Soprano* or Pinter's *The Homecoming*, in which characters suddenly and discontinuously enact various alter egos, intemperately, absurdly reversing and disrupting the viewer's expectations, "surprising" him (to invert Forster's definition) "in a [totally un]convincing way."

Manservant and Maidservant, then, as emblem of another modernism, holding in doubtful check the pressures of established and emergent conventions, and of contrasting (disjunctive and suspensive) ironic modes of perceiving the world as well. But if it occupies an oblique position vis-à-vis early modernism, what of its relation to the phenomenon of postmodernism? It seems clear enough, self-evident in fact, that Compton-Burnett adumbrates in a variety of ways, and more manifestly so than Isherwood for the most part, the features we now see as characteristic of the movement. The attention to surface and the concern with language and, still more, the acceptance of a radically disordered world all provide common points of reference with postmodern irony. But here too there are limits to the connections that can legitimately be made; and as soon as one recalls the enormous distance Compton-Burnett establishes between herself and her characters—a distance, moreover, that defines itself along a rigidly vertical axis—it becomes impossible to overlook substantial, all-important differences. For postmodern ironists, however unlike one another in other respects, are agreed at least in acknowledging the inevitability of their situation in the world they describe. Whether or not they are involved with that world, they are *of* it, their perspective conditioned by a view from within reality itself. As we've seen, Compton-Burnett retains instead, like the early modernists (but unlike Isherwood and other writers of the thirties, whose subversions of modernist depth have different sources and whose practice is in this instance more prescient of what is to come), the Flaubertian-Joycean privileges of the godlike observer, though her god has become, to a degree, myopic, more attentive to the outermost layer of his creation than to its recesses—so that, finally, we doubt whether those recesses exist. To be sure, for Nathalie Sarraute Compton-Burnett's "méthode se contente . . . de faire soupçonner à chaque instant au lecteur l'existence, la complexité et la variété des mouvements intérieurs."[17] And it is hard to deny that these suspicions may exist, hard even to call them illegitimate, since I have acknowledged that Compton-Burnett uses the privileges of her omniscience to dip directly, if relatively rarely, into her characters' minds. Nevertheless, to assert it one final time, these soundings seem to me vestigial and misleading; it is Compton-Burnett's surfacings that are instructive and predictive.

But predictive of what exactly? To ask the question is not to suggest influences but to see whether recent developments, once identified, cast light back, intertextually, on the value and scope of Compton-Burnett's writing and, though we cannot take her as totally representative, on those of the late modernist enterprise as well. It is, however, only when we perceive postmodernism as no more monolithic than modernism that it becomes possible to recognize the significance of Compton-Burnett's premonitory approach to surface. For in surveying postmodernism's different tendencies, one comes to see that her novels are most congruent with its frequently reflexive, always reductive, and generally antireferential wing. They suggest, that is, the works of ironists like Federman (with his fragmented "grammatical being[s]" [p. 13]), Gass (with his "world of words"),[18] Sukenick (with his notion of personality as "a mere locus for our experience"),[19] and possibly, as Sarraute seems to imply, those of the *nouveaux romanciers* as well, not to mention Sarraute's own earlier "tropismes." Which is to say that, in rigorously pursuing the implications of the collapse of depth and in developing them, as those other writers do, into an epistemology based on the necessary legitimacy of appearances ("If you imagine," one of Muriel Spark's recent characters says, though hardly with her endorsement, ". . . that appearances may belie the reality, then you are wrong. Appearances *are* reality."),[20] Compton-Burnett provides for her readers discriminations that are clarifying but ultimately static. Static in that her books fail, as *Between the Acts* does not, to move in any way beyond their bleak acceptance to generate out of a vision of absence—the absence of depth and all that implies by way of lost coherencies and connections—new meanings, new modes of being. The failure is hardly surprising. Compton-Burnett's particular conventions, especially the morally and psychologically claustrophobic ambience within which her characters are made to move, work generally not to open up but to narrow the range of human possibility, so that it is all too easy for her and her readers to agree with one of Horace's daughters when she says: "The nature of man must be left-handed" (p. 169).

Like Mortimer, Compton-Burnett does "not [have] a high opinion of human nature" (p. 178). That is clear enough, but as one draws comparisons with postmodernism, the implications of that belief become more momentous. If her novels help to effect a revolution in the psychology of character, the revolution is finally and oddly sterile. Deprived of complexity, her characters, like Forster's in *The Life to Come*, are denied as well the consolations of authentic change. Notwithstanding their participation in still recognizable plots and other elements of the traditional, verisimilar novel, they are creatures of language, caught reflexively in a web of words; peculiarly of their time, for all their Victorian trappings; and unable to bring about what Compton-Burnett herself cannot imagine: the projection of even uncentered consciousness beyond itself and outward toward the world into a sphere of existential self-creation. Thus her inescapable difference from postmodernism's other major group of ironists, those like Barthelme, Coover, and Apple, who, while accepting the primacy of surface, nevertheless find in it (sometimes at least) the possibility of genuine if limited affirmation. Not content, as Compton-Burnett is, simply to question relentlessly what transpires on the surface, they interrogate surface itself, reinventing in their pop-inspired fictions new worlds of precarious, creative and generative referentiality. Compton-Burnett's reading of surface is, as I have been urging, more aesthetic, reductive, and self-enclosed. In the acid bath of her irony, the steady core of character dissolves, and we are left, as a token of late modernism's ambiguities, only with those curiously faceted, endlessly talking contradictions whose identity is their mere progress (in *Manservant and Maidservant* their circular movement) through events. As such, they represent perhaps the final challenge to early modernism's rage for order, at the same time that they announce themselves as forerunners of those attenuated word-beings who, unsteadied even by their author's distanced control over their destinies, perform in the pages of so much contemporary fiction their hectic, skeletal dance.[21]

 PART III

The Recovery of Depth

FIVE

A Map of Suspensiveness: Irony
in the Postmodern Age

CONNOISSEURS OF CHAOS

It [the mythical method] is simply a way of controlling, of
ordering, of giving a shape and a significance to the immense pano-
rama of futility and anarchy which is contemporary history.
   —T. S. Eliot, "*Ulysses*, Order, and Myth"

Phlebas the Phoenician, a fortnight dead,
Forgot the cry of gulls, and the deep sea swell
And the profit and loss.
   —T. S. Eliot, *The Waste Land*

Apparently implying extremes of experience, my two epigraphs in fact
signal the same message. Obverse and reverse of an identical, now suspect
coin, control and surrender spell out the nature of the modernist sensibility
(early modernism's especially); and that sensibility, as no one who has
followed its recent fortunes needs to be reminded, is currently at a discount, its imperatives the small change of a too well-worn and by now
devalued currency. My concern here, however, is not, as in the first
chapter, to rescue modernism from its detractors but to suggest those
qualities to which, rightly or wrongly, postmodernism reacts in its
multiple and at times contradictory attempts to define the character of its
own still nascent enterprise.* And at this point both the mythical method

*It's probably wise to stress here the phrase "rightly or wrongly." My intention is neither to
devalue the modernists' achievement, my respect for which I've tried to make clear, nor to
imply that postmodernism represents any necessary aesthetic improvement over its predecessor. And although I *am* suggesting that at least some postmodernists appear to have
discovered, or are in the process of discovering, various solutions to the modernist crisis,
that is another matter and no guarantee of superiority. Obviously, in the most fundamental

(Eliot's as well as Joyce's) and Phlebas become paradigmatic. The famous essay on *Ulysses*, to begin with that, focuses less on Eliot's gloomy sense of his age's dislocations than on the artist's ability to impose on futility and anarchy the aesthetically achieved reflex of an imperative need for order. Order indeed is nothing less than the age's talisman, its heroic response to "the incertitude of the void"[1] and, less metaphysically, to the inadequacies of human relationships and the frustration of human hopes. But for what they will into being—those heterocosms of the imagination in which fragmentation is overcome, discontinuity transcended—the modernists demonstrably pay a price, namely, the need to suffer the distance and detachment that are the inevitable corollary of an overly exigent sense of control and the special stigmata of modernist irony; or, to put it differently, to endure unwillingly the estrangement of the self from the world it seeks too urgently to shape and endow with meaning.

That the modernists yearn at the same time to overcome their detachment, their aesthetically determined and determining view of life, that they long to bridge the gap they themselves originate between the hovering self and the distant world, simply demonstrates, within its own terms, the insolubility of the problem; and, not surprisingly, the problem, suggestively, often brilliantly thematized into the opposition of the self-conscious outsider and the more fluid, instinctive participant, provides modernism with its most incessant, obsessive subject. Or half of it. For if modernist art pushes, on the one hand, toward an increasingly coercive and alienating control, leading at the very least to the kind of immobilizing strain embodied in the image that opens the fourth of Eliot's "Preludes": "His soul stretched tight across the skies"[2] and resulting finally in a total paralysis, absolute irony's poised stasis of irresolution; if this in fact describes one direction in which modernist art moves, then on the other hand we need to take account of Phlebas and all he represents: the imperial self reversed, hollowed out, emptied of all activity and will.

But if the reversal appears extreme—Eliot's tightly stretched soul become, as it were, Mrs. Ramsay's "wedge-shaped core of darkness"[3]—the truth of the matter, already suggested, is more complex. "Losing personality," as she sinks down, away from the surface, Mrs. Ramsay

---

sense what is at issue is a matter of differences, not of relative worth; and the judgmental aspects of my descriptions are to be seen, at least to a degree, as part of the attempt to present modernist assumptions *as they appear* to postmodern writers. My concern, I should add, is once more largely with early or high modernism, since, whatever the discriminations I've tried to make and whatever transitions I've tried to demonstrate in examining late modernism, it is, for the most part, to the general and generalized idea of modernism as a whole and as represented more specifically by writers like Eliot and others of his generation that postmodernism consciously attends and responds. I am, in short, returning here to the modernist crisis that is the subject of chapter 1, and will again refer simply to modernism by way of establishing contrasts with postmodern attitudes and practices.

intimates the abandonment of command in an ecstasy of selflessness; but what is at issue may be a yet more supreme egoism: "It was odd, she thought, how if one was alone, one leant to things, inanimate things; trees, streams, flowers; felt they expressed one; felt they became one; felt they knew one, in a sense were one; felt an irrational tenderness thus . . . as for oneself" (pp. 100, 101). This loss of the self, which is at the same time "a summoning together, a resting on a platform of stability" (p. 100) is also its recuperation, a rescue effort engineered by a physics of diffusion that, far from effacing the core of her identity, imprints it throughout a supple, yielding world. *The Waste Land*, to be sure, proposes in its final echo of the Phlebas section a less ambiguous response to the problem of the rampant ego: "your heart would have responded / Gaily, when invited, beating obedient / To controlling hands" (pp. 49-50); but the invitation to surrender, couched still in the language of control, merely ratifies the dynamics of the modernist imagination, itself obedient, even when it means to negate it, to the integrity of the self and to the principles of manipulation and arrangement that are, whatever its indisputable aesthetic triumphs, its inescapable confirmation.

Postmodernism (postmodern irony especially) has both less and more hope. Chary of comprehensive solutions, doubtful of the self's integrity, it confronts a world more chaotic (if chaos admits of gradations) than any imagined by its predecessors and, refusing the modernist dialectic, interrogating both distance and depth, opens itself to the randomness and contingency of unmediated experience. Or at any rate intends to. I'm confounding here, I know, the theory of postmodern irony with its practice: proclamations of necessary and willing participation in the problematic with (in the case of some contemporary writers) lapses into forms of order as constricting as, and less productive than, any proclaimed or exemplified by the modernists. In any case, all generalizations about a movement in progress are necessarily suspect, and it may be best for now to postpone any further ones and to proceed instead more inductively by looking first at the works themselves, beginning with two—Stanley Elkin's hilarious and frightening novella *The Bailbondsman* and Max Apple's genial story "Free Agents"—that open the door to the postmodern workshop and, in these instances at least, to the persuasive buzz of theory in action.

Whether or not it does so by intention, Elkin's novella provides, a half-century after the fact, a critique of Eliot's mythical method, a sardonic evaluation of its motive force and of its inadequacy in the face of the contemporary world.[4] More Mr. Eugenides perhaps than Phlebas (though the need to surrender his not inconsiderable abilities, his passion for life, and even his ego afflicts him sporadically), Alexander Main, the Phoenician bailbondsman of Elkin's story, is, however, less the intended conveyor of hieratic mysteries than victim of life's unfathomable meaning and of his own passionate need to know: "Mystery kept him going and curiosity killed him."[5] As Main recognizes, he is caught—a middleman in this as in everything else—between the world of Cincinnati courts and criminals, which he manipulates all too easily (a good Brooksian, he requires tension and tires of "his slick contempt, his ability to win which had never left him, his knack of topping the other guy" [p. 105]) and a universe that, as if with malevolent will, frustrates his desires and exceeds his powers to make sense of it ("How can I cross-examine the universe when it jumps my bond?" [p. 120]). And the recognition leads him, shrewdly if insanely, in Elkin's magnificent parody of the modernist aesthetic, to transform the "punks, [and] losers" (p. 105), the bail-jumping fugitives of his ordinary, daily life into mysterious, overdetermined symbols of the universal enigma, thereby establishing not only his "power to middleman, to doodle people's destiny" (p. 105) but his control, in the mythic drama he enacts, over destiny itself.

But Main, even in his plausible madness, is too aware and too self-aware—and too much the artist as well—not to tire of his characters; as he wearies even and finally of the extravagating Oyp and Glyp, the most romantically conceived of "his Diaspora'd enemies [his fugitive clients] drifting outward like the universe" (p. 29). *Like* the universe: the phrase tells the story. Oyp and Glyp (and the others) are the middleman's middlemen ("Crime was the single mystery he could get close to" [p. 106]), clues to the nature of the bail-jumping universe; but they are too, and after all, only its arbitrary signifiers, disposable, expendable, part of the world's recyclable trash. And so, after exalting them in a dream of extravagant crime, the climax of his long, unsuccessful pursuit ("Why, they *were* exalted! Mystery. Mystery. The reason he was a bondsman. The meaning of his life. The way he came to terms with what engined it. Mystery" [p. 106]), Main, impatient with his puppets, stages their oneiric dismissal and thereby opens himself, in what may be *The Bailbondsman's* most impressive episode, to a rampageous encounter with existential dread. Unhoused, destitute for the moment of his sheltering myth, Alexander Main confronts the inscrutable with a passion that kindles outrageous intensities of rhetoric: "*Au courant* I am as a deb with my nose for trend and influence and my insider's thousand knowledges. What does it mean? Everything I don't know and will never know leans on me like a mountain range. It creams me, Crainpool. It potches my brains and rattles my teeth" (p. 120). Onetime bail jumper, now assistant to the bailbondsman, who has already half transformed him into his image of a Dickensian clerk, Crainpool serves in this scene both as Main's after-hours auditor and as the victim of Main's impulse—another symbolic gesture—to silence the unanswering voice of the universe by killing his altogether tractable clerk.

The finality of murder is not, however, what the bailbondsman most wants or needs, and in the story's final turn Crainpool is forced out into the night, fugitive, unwilling successor to Oyp and Glyp, while his employer and now pursuer, once more full of wonder and delight, a zestful detective at a new boundary,[6] follows him into the dark: main man again, an Alexander who has found another world to conquer. For if Main finds it impossible to replay the same scene endlessly, he is still less able to endure, between the acts, the limiting reality of his situation: "His limited detective heart made him a Cincinnatian, kept him in this city of exactly the right size. And *still* he bit off more than he could chew, a tapeworm working in his brains" (p. 107). And so *The Bailbondsman* describes the endless, requisite reconstitution of the myth. But it does something more: it reveals the limitations of modernist irony (as well as the frustrated, impressive humanity of its constraining strength) and suggests at least the outlines of its postmodern successor. Like the modernist artist, Alexander Main is in pursuit of order or, failing that perhaps too exalted goal, of an orderliness capable of encompassing visions of extreme disorder in structures of formal perfection.[7] What matters obviously (to invoke Eliot once more) is the sense of control, but control for the modernists, New Critical theory notwithstanding, is always precarious —more a temporary mitigation of crisis (and its form) than a resolution of that crisis into unity. Here again the bailbondsman provides the model. As readers we recognize that the quest for Crainpool will be no more successful, no more final than those for his predecessors. That is, even if one imagines Crainpool brought down, there is clearly no assuaging Main's hunger for certainty; and for good reason: mirroring the universe, as we have seen, Oyp and Glyp are at the last "fugitives from fugitiveness itself, and because they were, there were limits to his power and his own precious freedom" (p. 105).

Freedom then is the key: the freedom, as Kierkegaard recognized, that is the ironist's goal. But though Alexander Main is exemplary of modernist (and of Romantic) irony in the strategies he brings to bear on the world, the world he confronts has changed. How exactly, it is worth pausing to consider by recalling what has been said about irony in earlier chapters. If, as I've several times suggested, the defining feature of modernism is its ironic vision of disconnection and disjunction, postmodernism, more radical in its perceptions, derives instead from a vision of randomness, multiplicity, and contingency: in short, a world in need of mending is superseded by one beyond repair. Modernism, spurred by an anxiety to recuperate a lost wholeness in self-sustaining orders of art or in the unselfconscious depths of the self (control and surrender again), reaches toward the heroic in the intensity of its desire and of its disillusion. Postmodernism, skeptical of such efforts, presents itself as deliberately, consciously antiheroic. Confronted with the world's randomness and diversity, it enacts (*urbi et orbi*) that attitude of suspensiveness which, as we've frequently seen, implies the tolerance of a fundamental uncertainty about the meanings and relations of things in the world and in the universe.[8] In these terms, Main's failure is a failure of suspensiveness. Unlike Barthelme's Thomas, he cannot "tolerate the anxiety" (*TDF*, p. 93); and since he cannot have his certainties, his freedom, he must be forever in pursuit of them: a modernist, as Elkin portrays him in his boisterous, mock-heroic fable, amuck in a postmodern world.

Elkin, however, addresses directly only part of the problem of suspensiveness. The remainder is the major subject of Max Apple's buoyant tale, which, though far briefer than Elkin's work, is, at least in its range of implied reference, more ambitious still. As a parable of the mind-body split, a humorous but serious treatment of the recurring problem that runs with particular insistence and intensity from the seventeenth century through modernism, "Free Agents" takes on Descartes specifically; and as a criticism of the mind's hegemony ("Now it's the body's turn to step into the twentieth century," the narrator's spleen tells him)[9] it reaches back into the entire Western tradition, represented by, among others, Socrates and Shakespeare. Narrating the revolt of the body's organs—or most of them: the brain, its soverignty ended, remains, later to become prosecutor in the trial that follows; and so too the eyes, modernism's privileged sense—against "Max Apple," the story's antiheroic everyman ("All important decisions," the spleen announces, "are tested on nobodies" [p. 43]), "Free Agents" moves to a resolution that may stand as emblem of postmodernism at its most lively and adventurous. As he waits for the jury's verdict, having at the trial's end declared himself dispersed, the narrator undergoes a rapid shift of moods. Paralysis (the image of the modernist crisis) gives way to indifference, indifference to memory ("The memory of fleeting sensuality. The taste of vanilla ice cream. The sound of the national anthem and Rice Krispies" [p. 50]), and memory to an acceptance of himself: "'I am what I am,' I whisper" (p. 50). At which point, no longer constrained, free agents at last, his organs voluntarily return to his body, and "Apple," reversing the Cartesian *cogito*, announces: "I shift gears. I rise. I walk. I spit. I think" (p. 51). "Full of myself," the story ends, as the suspensiveness imaged in the hung jury is augmented and completed by an energetic and joyous acceptance of uncertainty, "on tiptoes I bounce on the grass ready for everything" (p. 51). (Descartes, who couldn't endure an irritable doubt, preferred another gait: "marcher avec assurance," and another, less springy ground—"le roc ou l'argile"—to walk on.)

Acceptance is the key to the story's postmodern and ironic vision; and the final, sweet irony of "Free Agents" (to adopt the adjective reviewers are fondest of applying to Apple) is that, in and by accepting his situation, the narrator himself becomes a free agent, *hors de combat:* liberated in a world now and newly available to him. But if Apple's story defines the indispensable components of suspensive irony—the perception and acceptance of a world whose disarray exceeds and defies resolution—and if, moreover, it intimates the anironic vision of participation in the world (or in some part of it) that complements suspensive irony, still it can hardly be taken as totally representative of all postmodern views, which, as one might and should expect, vary both in their sense of disorder and, especially, in their response to it. Compared, for example, with the self-conscious, complexly unhappy artist-protagonist of Barthelme's "The Abduction from the Seraglio," Apple's narrator seems, for all his judicial anxiety, extraordinarily straightforward. Barthelme's, unable to rescue, or rather win back, his Constanze, sums up his relationship with her as follows: "We adventured. That's not bad"; but he then goes on in a choric afterthought to negate his not wholly uncheerful resignation and to reveal his ambivalence instead: "How I miss you / How I miss you."[10] "Things," as the hero of *The Dead Father* says, "are not simple" (p. 93); and acceptance may be, as it is here, reluctant at best. But no single example will suggest the range of options within the suspensive mode; and at the risk of muddying the waters I'm trying to fathom, it seems to me most useful to allow a cross section of postmodern artists and writers (or, for the most part, their characters and their often thinly disguised autobiographical narrators) to speak for themselves. As a sampling, then, a baker's dozen of quotations:

[1]   Well let me tell you, me I prefer discontinuity, me I adore discontinuity, I wallow in disorder, my whole existence for that matter has been a JOURNEY TO CHAOS (U.C. Press, 1965)! (Raymond Federman, *Take It or Leave It*)

[2]   Architects can no longer afford to be intimidated by the puritanically moral language of orthodox Modern architecture. I like elements which are hybrid rather than "pure," compromising rather than "clean," distorted rather than "straightforward," ambiguous rather than "articulated," perverse as well as impersonal, boring as well as "interesting," conventional rather than "designed," accommodating rather than excluding, redundant rather than simple, vestigial as well as innovating, inconsistent and equivocal rather than direct and clear. I am for messy vitality over obvious unity. I include the non sequitur and proclaim the duality. (Robert Venturi, *Complexity and Contradiction in Architecture*)

[3]   If all seems uncertain . . . if we come to survey emptiness without and emptiness within—I need not despair: we can always create a new role, initiate a new performance, conduct a renewed transformance, amid the endless series. The weary existential *angst* of the modern is transformed/performed by the spirited free play of the postmodern. (Campbell Tatham, "Mythotherapy and Postmodern Fictions: Magic is Afoot")

[4]   Interruption. Discontinuity. Imperfection. It can't be helped. This very instant as I write as you read a hundred things. . . . This novel is based on The Mosaic Law the law of mosaics or how to deal with parts in the absence of wholes. (Ronald Sukenick, 98.6)

[5]   Criticism is the production of more thread to embroider the texture or textile already there. This thread is like the filament of ink which flows from the pen of the writer, keeping him in the web but suspending him also over the chasm, the blank page that thin line hides. . . . Deconstruction is not a dismantling of the structure of a text but a demonstration that it has already dismantled itself. Its apparently solid ground is no rock but thin air. (J. Hillis Miller, "Stevens' Rock and Criticism as Cure, II")

[6]   [Randomness is] the sort of visual disorder that occurs in reality. . . . I believe in a kind of random order in the way reality has put itself together—a functional arrangement rather than a visual arrangement. (From an interview with Ralph Goings)

[7]   There is no order in the world around us . . . we must adapt ourselves to the requirements of chaos instead.
          It is hard to adapt to chaos, but it can be done. I am living proof of that: It can be done. (Kurt Vonnegut, Jr., Breakfast of Champions)

[8]   Finally, he simply gave in to it, dumped it in with the rest of life's inscrutable absurdities, and from that time on began to improve almost daily. (Robert Coover, "J's Marriage," in Pricksongs and Descants)

[9]   Somebody was nudging my tray along the rail at the museum cafeteria. I was trying to keep my tray from bumping the tray ahead. I held my fingers firmly on the tray top, hooked my thumbs underneath the steel bar. The pressure of the nudging tray increased. I gave in to the superior determination. Doubtless, the tray pusher had had an awful day. I let go. My tray slid into the next tray, which slid into the next, which crashed into another. At the cashier's corner, there was a pileup. Tea bags, jello, trays all over everything. (Renata Adler, Speedboat)

[10]   —Yes, success is everything. Failure is more common. Most achieve a sort of middling thing, but fortunately one's situation is always blurred, you never know absolutely quite where you are. This allows, if not peace of mind, ongoing attention to other aspects of existence. (Donald Barthelme, "The Crisis," in Great Days)

[11]   Quite simply then, he drowns. A random event, one that I imagine, considering the world as a whole, is quite common. (T. Coraghessan Boyle, "Drowning," in Descent of Man)

[12]   She hated her life. It was a minor thing, though, a small bother. She tended to forget about it. When she recalled what it was that had been on her mind, she felt satisfied at having remembered and relieved that it was nothing worse. (Don DeLillo, Players)

[13]   One thing in my defense, not that it matters . . . I know what "nothing" means, and keep on playing.

Why, BZ would say.
Why not, I say. (Joan Didion, Play It as It Lays)[11]

That there is a spirit common to these various passages is, I think, incontestable. All of the speakers are, in one way or another, connoisseurs of chaos: the vocabulary of disorder is both copious and insistent; the expectation of irresolution pervasive; the syntax of parataxis overwhelming. All welcome or at any rate subscribe to an aesthetic of openness and an ethic of improvisation or adaptation. And all, reacting to the desired control or freedom that modernist distance implies, locate themselves, however great their actual psychological remoteness from their surroundings, within the messiness and contingency of the real world. Their perspective consequently is limited and unprivileged: a recognition of the need "to deal with parts in the absence of wholes." Performance and play are the rule, and for those with less zest for the game there are at least the meager consolations of inevitability. My concern for the moment, however, is with differences, with the discrete though related attitudes that together subtend the arc of suspensiveness. Roughly speaking, my first six quotations express a positive, my last six a negative, tropism toward the notion of chaos (Vonnegut, urgent and worried in his effort at adapting, providing a transition of sorts); and the kinds of acceptance these responses generate, it follows, span a not inconsiderable distance. Between the almost manically exuberant, centrifugal (though still reflexive) energy of Federman's narrator, and the low-keyed, Beckettian, near catatonic endurance of Didion's; between the Whitmanesque ardor of Venturi's manifesto and the dull acquiescence of DeLillo's Pammy; even between Tatham's transformative/performative response to existential angst and the flat, blasé recording by Boyle's *nouveau roman*-inspired speaker of tragedy as "random event"—between all of them there is an affective chasm so large as to contest the inclusion of these different pairs within the same conceptual framework. Nevertheless, if instead of straddling extremes, one moves through the passages sequentially, it becomes apparent both that the differences are real and that they describe a continuum: a series of diacritically linked steps descending in an order of diminished enthusiasm—from Federman's amplitude to Sukenick's puzzled but still punning shrug; downward to the Coover and Adler passages with their resignation to the greater or smaller absurdities ("gave in to" is the crucial phrase in each); and ending finally, at basement level, so to speak, with the grudging complicity of the final quotations.

Suspensiveness, then, embracing chaos at all conceivable levels—universal and mundane, cosmic and quotidian—engenders modes of acceptance that equally run the gamut of possibility from the most expansive to the most shrunken and shriveled. But while it is necessary to recognize and keep in mind these differences, which in some ways are real enough, it is important as well to understand that they are after all perhaps too superficial—not simply because I've based them on a series of decontextualized bits and pieces of longer works but, more importantly, because in many cases they represent statements of intention rather than reflections of a more profound intentionality. In the long run one needs broader and more fundamental categories to determine the underlying, frequently unrecognized motive forces of postmodern irony. And to formulate these categories one needs to ask how exactly the ironist, given his awareness and acceptance of the fact of disorder, that is, of his incapacity to alter in any fundamental way the nature of things, situates himself in the world and at the same time (as he just as inevitably must) confers meaning on it.

THE SQUAMOUS MIND

The squirming facts exceed the squamous mind,
If one may say so.
   —Wallace Stevens, "Connoisseur of Chaos"

After awhile they lose their voices. "The real world is the last dream
left us," my father says hoarsely, embracing me at the door.
    &&&&&&
Mother exits. Father exits.
   —Jonathan Baumbach, *Reruns*

Reality, already dizzyingly problematic for the modernists, has become for one group of postmodern writers simply and finally unreal. So, in the latest of what promises to be an endless series of statements on the same subject, Raymond Federman writes of "the new novel" (elsewhere "Surfiction") that "it abolishes absolute knowledge and what passes for reality; it even states, defiantly, that reality *as such* does not exist."[12] The italics, as the formula goes, are mine and are meant to expose both the slipperiness and the equivocal effect of the formulation. The difficulty lies in determining whether reality for Federman is confusing, incoherent, without meaning, subjective, or, at its semiotic extreme, something that forever exists outside the enclosed space of intertextual sign systems. A strong temptation exists to see in such pronouncements, as Gerald Graff does, "little more than the obligatory hyperbole of avant-garde self-promotion"[13] or to regard them as familiar, if extreme, salvos against the traditional novel, whose "prime allegiance . . . is to verisimilitude" and which "merely confirms us in our conventional ways of seeing and talking."[14] Nevertheless, if there is little to be hoped for by way of new critical insights from Federman and his Surfictional colleagues, their brand of antirealism does help to illuminate the ways in which some postmodernists effectively modify and undermine the integrity of their apparent suspensiveness. So, in the essay from which I've just quoted, Federman proclaims that "the new novel invents its own reality, cuts itself off from referential points with the external world" (p. 122); and Ronald Sukenick, riding the same rails, advances still farther into the landscape of imagination, where "fiction adds itself to the world, creating a meaningful 'reality' that did not previously exist."[15] In short, even as they revel in the world's chaos, these writers deny the world its specificity and provocations. "The real world," to quote Federman again, "is somewhere else. . . . A world no longer to be known, but to be imagined, to be invented" (p. 124).

What is at work—and it is hardly possible at this point not to be reminded of the modernists—is clearly a process of substitution, of replacement. But of this metamorphic tendency more later. First, we need to note that the antirealism of the Surfictionists is directed inward as well as outward: against the self, the ego, fully as much as against the phenomenal world. Having announced that "Reality doesn't exist, time doesn't exist, personality doesn't exist" (though, fearless in his capacity to confound our expectations, he has just referred to "the contemporary writer—the writer who is acutely in touch with the life of which he is part"), Sukenick goes on near the beginning of "The Death of the Novel" —the work is fictional but the passage from which I'm quoting is indistinguishable from Sukenick's more discursive writings—to maintain that "Reality is, simply, our experience, and objectivity is, of course, an illusion. Personality, after passing through a phase of awkward self-consciousness [so much, presumably, for modernism], has become, quite minimally, a mere locus for our experience."[16] Whether one can distinguish as easily as all that, Nietzsche and his deconstructionist followers notwithstanding, between "an irreducible individual psyche" and personality as "a mere locus for our experience" is not a matter that demands resolution at this point. The intention of the remarks, namely, to subvert the modernist exploration of depth (the attempt to uncover a more essential reality and plumb its recesses) is apparent; and so too are the results: "If art is not reflection of reality," Sukenick writes in one of his essays, "then the last reflection to get rid of is self-reflection. The fate of Narcissus is to drown in contemplation of himself. The way out of the dilemma of Narcissus lies in the work of art as artifice. As artifice the work of art is a conscious tautology in which there is always an implicit (and sometimes explicit) reference to its own nature as artifact—self-reflexive, not self-reflective. It is not an imitation but a new thing in its own right, an invention" (TD, pp. 98-99).

To this ultraformalist, antireferential credo (masquerading as an antiformalist defense of "the disruptive energy of art" [TD, p. 90]), one wants to respond as Robert Scholes does in his eminently commonsensical critique of French semiotics: "Even semioticians eat and perform their other bodily functions just as if the world existed solidly around them."[17] And so too, Surfictionists. But more is at stake in Sukenick's argument, specifically the question of whether even the most tautological work of art can be other than emblematic of its maker's relationship to the life of which he is, as Sukenick acknowledges, inevitably part; and the additional question of whether the reader can or should avert his glance from the quality of that relationship. "Much of literary competence," Scholes rightly says, "is based upon our ability to connect the worlds of fiction and experience" (p. 117)—a statement that leads in the context I'm pursuing to a consideration of the dynamics of reflexivity: the goal of both Federman's and Sukenick's poetics of "invention." According to Robert Alter, the self-conscious novel (Alter's term is deliberately broader than but encompasses the notion of reflexivity) "is a novel that systematically flaunts its own condition of artifice and that by so doing probes into the problematic relationship between real-seeming artifice and reality."[18] What is essential is "the dialectic between fiction and 'reality' . . . a play of competing ontologies" (p. 182), since "the self-conscious novelists are always simultaneously aware of the supreme power of the literary imagination within its own sphere of creation and its painful or tragicomic powerlessness outside that sphere" (p. 98). Now, in the light of Alter's definition, it can be said that any fiction that over-privileges invention on the one hand and on the other "cuts itself off from referential points with the external world" dooms itself at a minimum to the self-indulgence he warns against (p. 182) and in all probability to a self-defeating devitalization of the world's substantiality.

And indeed those dangers are apparent in the fictional works of the writers whose essays I've been discussing, although it's also true that those works, Federman's especially, exceed and in some ways contradict the theories they are presumably meant to illustrate. *Take It or Leave It*, for example, though on one level, in its enormous, gargantuan energy, it celebrates discontinuity, disorder, and chaos; though it manages, in its Shandean digressiveness, its ultra-Shandean typographical games, and its insistent antimimetic, antireferential strategies, to frustrate the reader's narrative expectations and, more, to parody in its minimal, iterative story the specifically American myth of the Quest: "The Big Crossing," "The Great Journey," "The Discovery of America"; and though, finally, by handing over to an intrusive, "second-hand teller" the job of recording the misadventures of the book's subject, it seeks to undermine the notion of psychology—despite all this, the novel incontrovertibly establishes a set of circumstances that both situates and stabilizes the characters of its generally indistinguishable narrators. In his fine essay on the Fiction Collective, Larry McCaffery writes: "As the narrator constantly spews forth words in the form of stories, anecdotes, and digressions, we also realize that he is attempting to avoid a confrontation with his own frightening past." But when McCaffery goes on to assert that thanks to its various reflexive contrivances "the book never allows the reader to 'learn' anything or believe in it—in effect, it destroys or cancels itself as it proceeds,"[19] he demonstrates, I think, a willingness to take Federman too much at his own word: "I want to tell a story that cancels itself as it goes."[20] Avoiding the past certainly—the extermination of his parents in the concentration camps, his own escape, and perhaps even his down-and-out life in America—the narrator is just as surely (and as a consequence) in flight from "the despair, terror and boredom of existence." Shandean in this too, *Take It or Leave It* describes the attempt to escape time, death, and the problematics of identity (to acknowledge identity is to risk its destruction); and in context the by now familiar dictum of the essays—"TO CREATE FICTION IS, IN FACT, A WAY TO ABOLISH REALITY"—takes on another and more significant dimension. Narrated "on the edge of a precipice," the original teller's tale becomes, as it is retold and embroidered by the second-hand teller, "the game I'm playing now out of despair."

Federman's novel does, in short, something more than exemplify the theories that are expounded in the essays and in the novel itself. Less nonreferential than it believes itself to be, *Take It or Leave It* reluctantly gives phenomenal reality its due as the shaping, provocative force of its narrator's angry, defiant, despairing life. (Denying psychology, Federman nevertheless provides psychological explanations.) Or *almost* its due. For if one can detect in the book a "dialectic between fiction and 'reality'" and even explain its reflexiveness as the product of an impossible need to rise above, to cancel or annul reality, to deny it its "truth," still there is some question as to whether the novel finally recognizes that impossibility, whether in its attempt "to improve reality" it doesn't after all undo the dialectic and, rising to distances that leave far behind the most aesthetically detached of the modernists, assert, for all its willed fluidity, the desire for a familiar Cartesian control that would "rebâtir le logis," thereby reducing if not quite erasing the world.

Sukenick's work, more self-conscious and in some ways more extreme, diminishes this tension, the "play of competing ontologies," further still. The opening of "The Death of the Novel," parts of which I've already quoted, mounts the usual attack on an earlier discredited tradition: "Realistic fiction presupposed chronological time as the medium of a plotted narrative, an irreducible individual psyche as the subject of its characterization, and, above all, the ultimate, concrete reality of things as the object and rationale of its description" (p. 41). The story that follows attempts, most successfully in its treatment of narrative, to fictionalize theory and establish the claims of "the contemporary post-realistic novel."

As we might expect by now, this is not to say that theory disappears; and in fact the story comments copiously on itself as it proceeds: "Reality has become a literal chaos. . . . If reality exists, it doesn't do so *a priori*, but only to be put together. . . . The world is real because it is imagined" (p. 47). To substantiate these claims, the story employs what Sukenick, or his narrator "Sukenick," calls "the principle of simultaneous multiplicity" (p. 53), a loosely associative method that fractures continuity, parodies the ideal of structure, and, through devices such as montage and parataxis, suggests a mildly absurdist view of existence. (Beckett lurks and at moments obtrudes.) Not that reality—ultimate, concrete reality—is altogether absent. With an irony that he nicely turns against himself, Sukenick acknowledges the inescapability of "a series of overwhelming social dislocations" (p. 41)—the war, civil disobedience, and so on: "The long dirty finger of my country pokes its way into my life" (p. 43). Nevertheless, the major effort is one of subversion, and there are a number of arch efforts to undermine both the status of reality and the expectations of readers ("John Johnson was a short, slight fellow, tall and portly" [p. 57]). In any case, even if reality cannot be totally eliminated it can be randomized; and that is precisely what, in the name of invention, play, imagination, freedom, spontaneity, and improvisation, Sukenick strenuously works to achieve.

But that is where his problem begins: "The Death of the Novel" illustrates all too well the paradox of deliberate freedom, of self-conscious improvisation, of tendentious play. Despite Sukenick's description of it as "this unprecedented example of formlessness" (p. 49), the story is the very image of premeditation. The apparently freewheeling form ("We improvise our art as we improvise our lives" [p. 42]), "invented" to express suspensiveness ("I'm at my best when everything explodes," the narrator boasts, and anticipating Federman, goes on: "I thrive on chaos" [p. 100]), this form in fact conceals—and without too much prying reveals—a more fundamental principle of abstraction. Which is to say that the supposedly aleatory, shapeless, self-destroying story (Sukenick invokes Tinguely and, as so often, recalls the avant-garde of several decades earlier) exists within the inhibiting grip of the idea to which it relentlessly refers, just as we, as readers, are finally locked into the confines of a still more limiting structure: the structure of the narrator's consciousness, which, memorializing itself, renders almost totally unmemorable (and I use the word primarily in a neutral, descriptive sense) the substance of everything it records. Too facile, too rigid, too intellectual, consciousness, intent on itself and its workings, drains the world and inadvertently reveals that what passes for process is after all the somewhat meager product of its own circumscribing subjectivity. "The thing is, how does this fit in?" Sukenick asks rhetorically at one point apropos of an apparently irrelevant episode. The answer to the question, offered with some complacency, follows: "That's it, it doesn't" (p. 74). But in fact it does. Everything fits because everything refers back to the narrator, that mere locus of experience who, presuming to invent the world anew, merely appropriates it, substituting for the potential richness of experience the power of the constituting but insufficiently tensive imagination.

In a word, as compared with *Take It or Leave It*, "The Death of the Novel" is more reductive still: not simply a distancing of phenomenal reality but, as the world becomes less resistant, a displacement of it. And as these fictions demonstrate (to offer an initial definition of one of postmodern irony's two major types: the lesser half of my proposed map of suspensiveness), reductiveness names a number of interrelated strategies, or rather—since, as here, they are not necessarily purposed—tendencies: tendencies, in particular, to abstract the world's density (as Forster does in *The Life to Come*) into a more compassable form; to convert life's substantiality (again the example of Forster is relevant) into a concept or a set of ideas; and, finally, to submit phenomenal reality to the subjectivizing, idealistic transformations of consciousness. Not, it needs to be said at once, that all reflexive fiction is reductive: that is not an equation I intend. Barthelme's work, though often reflexive, rarely operates in the manner of the Surfictionists; even if, as is often the case, the texture of his stories inclines to verbal rather than sensuous intricacy. "It's all," as he says of his Balloon Man, "in the gesture—the precise, reunpremeditated right move."[21] So, in the story called "And Then," art is presented as an enchantment of the hostile, demanding world—an attempt "to get away from despair and over to ease and bliss" (*Am*, p. 109). But however fantasticated, the world is there: an undeniable pressure exerting itself against the story's reflexiveness, filling and overflowing the "gap" that follows the narrator's "and then." The story recognizes, in other words, that consciousness is implicated in the world, is intentional, and that reflexivity, however ingenious, can never abrogate the relationship; so that even the narrator's final desperate and extravagant decision—"I will reenter the first room, cheerfully, confidently, even gaily, and throw chicken livers *flambé* all over the predicament. . . . That will 'open up' the situation successfully. I will resolve these terrible contradictions with flaming chicken parts and then sing the song of how I contrived the ruin of my anaconda" (*Am*, p. 112)—even that hilarious gesture acknowledges, in and through its flamboyant buffoonery, the intractability of "the situation," which is, after all, the writer's need to keep the reader and himself interested not only in his own inventiveness but in the world that impinges on him.

Barthelme, then, confronts reality in a way that neither Sukenick nor Federman does, as one can see still more clearly in a totally felicitous parable called "The Great Hug." One of his several portraits of the artist—and in this case apparently of himself as artist—the story conjoins the Balloon Man and the Pin Lady as emblems of imagination and truth or, better, of art and reality: "Pin Lady tells the truth. Balloon Man doesn't lie, exactly. How can the Quibbling Balloon be called a lie? Pin Lady is more straightforward. Balloon Man is less straightforward. Their stances are semiantireprophetical" (*Am*, p. 48). The final word suggests, if it doesn't explain, the adversarial but inextricable relation of the two and predicts the apocalyptic great hug: "The embrace of Balloon Man and Pin Lady will be something to see. They'll roll down the hill together, someday. Balloon Man's arms will be wrapped around Pin Lady's pins and Pin Lady's embrangle will be wrapped around Balloon Man's balloons" (p. 47). But the encounter to come (or has it by the time the story ends already passed?) simply dramatizes the dialectic that already exists; and the Balloon Man's final words—"The Balloon of Perhaps. My best balloon" (p. 48)—contrive both an affirmation of fiction (more broadly, of art) and a recognition of its fictive status. The balloons themselves, like the Pin Lady's pins, are endless in their variety—"Balloon Man sells the Balloon of Fatigue and the Balloon of Ora Pro Nobis . . ." (p. 46)—but all, even the most optative of them, relate somehow to "the plain canvas gravy of the thing" (p. 45). And that of course is the point. "Not every balloon can make you happy," the Balloon Man says. "Not every balloon can trigger glee. *But I insist that these balloons have a right to be heard!*" (p. 48). In Barthelme's parable art adds itself to the world without, as in the works of the Surfictionists, substituting itself for it, thereby making reality, and art as well, not less but more various. "When he created our butter-colored balloon, we felt better," the story's speaker says. "A little better" (p. 48). The afterthought specifies the tone. Reflexiveness in Barthelme becomes (usually) expansive but not a cause for undue cheer. As the narrator of "And Then" remarks: "Goals incapable of attainment have driven many a man to despair, but despair is easier to get to than that—one need merely look out of the window, for example" (p. 109). Barthelme's fictional window remains open to the world—that is his strength—and art manages no more (but also no less) than to generate and register on its surface its own limited and local affirmation.

I'm beginning, however, to anticipate and trespass on my second category; and in returning now to the first I want to note that just as not all reflexive writing is reductive so not all reductive literature participates in the unintended negations of the Surfictionists. In *Play It as It Lays*, to cite one example, the near refusal of the world by the principal character is altogether deliberate, as is her rejection of causality and connection; and Didion's attitude, if it doesn't endorse Maria's withdrawal (there is some difficulty in fact in determining exactly what Didion's attitude is), seems at any rate not to contest too strongly the fundamental outlines of her protagonist's vision. And Charles Simmons's far more impressive novel *Wrinkles* brings into the open even more strongly what writers like Federman and Sukenick only inadvertently reveal: the diminished scale of contemporary life or, more accurately, a pinched and meager estimate of life's capacities. Eschatological and scatological—and in this, if not in its gray, glacial, and lapidary prose, reminiscent of Isherwood's *A Single Man*—the book relentlessly and effectively repeats in its succession of miniature chapters the arc of growth and degeneration that finally describes a broken circle and demonstrates the transciency of life and flesh: a quiet, sardonic study in entropy, whose unobtrusively reflexive technique manages, while referentially miming its protagonist's consciousness, to mirror its narrator's as well. At this point, however, it needs to be recognized that by introducing into this discussion books like Didion's and Simmons's I have in effect broadened the concept of reductiveness and raised a different though not unrelated problem, which challenges nothing less than the validity of the suspensive vision itself. So, in an enormously suggestive critique of Beckett, Allan Rodway writes: "This [Beckett's view of the human situation] is the stance of the metaphysical pessimist who assumes that all is for the worst in the worst of all possible worlds"; and he concludes: "Beckett, in short, springs a typically symbolist trap: making a part stand for the whole, but choosing an unrepresentative part. . . . Paradoxical to the end, he exaggerates by *minifying* reality."[22] The observation is an important one and, following Rodway's lead, one could observe of all the writers dealt with in this section (Barthelme excepted) that they too "minify" reality and that in this more radical sense Didion and Simmons are at one with the others in their subjectivizing abstraction of reality.

But having taken note of Rodway's highly normative approach, which, to repeat, means to call into doubt the very notion of suspensiveness, or at least its legitimacy (and thus raises philosophical questions beyond the scope of this chapter), I want to focus instead and again on the more oblique, because less conscious, sort of reductiveness I've imputed to Federman and Sukenick—and through them, it is to be understood, to other postmodern writers: many of the Fiction Collectivists of course but also, if only in some of their work or aspects of it, writers like Vonnegut, Coover, and Barth. Fictions like *Take It or Leave It* and "The Death of the Novel," then, reveal an irony beyond the irony—or ironic vision —they mean to disclose. Which is to say that reductiveness in the final analysis is less a form of suspensiveness than a contravention of its most vaunted claims (as, in another way and from an opposite direction, Vonnegut's angry, at times cranky, moral, satiric impulse contravenes it too). To be sure, these works intend suspensiveness, indeed proclaim their acceptance of contingency and absurdity ("I wallow in disorder"), but their implicit message, I've been arguing, bespeaks a need for order that outreaches that of the most chaos-ridden of the modernists. (Suspensiveness in Federman is, to borrow Derrida's useful term, *sous rature;* in Sukenick it is, more simply, negated.) The comparison with modernism is instructive, for as one comes more and more to realize, postmodernists of the Surfictional kind "reproduce," Barthelme notes with grim and comic awareness in *The Dead Father,* "every one of the enormities [of the fathers] . . . but in attenuated form" (p. 145). "Attenuated" is the word: unlovingly reactive, transforming paradox from the sign of crisis to a cause for play (while creating, all unwittingly, paradoxes of their own), discarding and scorning the modernists' urgent desire to recover an original wholeness but nevertheless imposing on unpatterned reality the squamousness of the abstracting mind, they are modernism's lineal descendents (or perhaps its illegitimate sons), patricides manqués.

In fact, in the covert, substitutive orders they create, the Surfictionists recall ("in attentuated form") nothing so much as the aesthetic manifestos of the early decades of the century; and aestheticism may provide as good a clue to the underlying impulses of these writers as reductiveness does. Or perhaps one should say that aestheticism is the master sign under which much that is reductive in contemporary culture coalesces. In which case, William Gass will serve as patron saint of Surfiction and, as we shall see, of a good deal else. Gass's relation to these writers, though real, is, however, oblique, tangential. The mood and attitude of suspensiveness, for example, certainly announce themselves in his work: "Our world," he comments in *Fiction and the Figures of Life,* ". . . lacks significance; it lacks connection"[23] and again, in *The World Within the Word:* "Irony, ambiguity, skepticism—these aren't attitudes any more which come and go like moods, but parts of our anatomy."[24] But one wonders nevertheless whether the world (or reality) is for Gass so much chaotic and unknowable as it is simply superfluous and unpleasant. Thus: "the object of art is to make more beautiful that which is, and . . . that which is is rarely beautiful, often awkward and ugly and ill-arranged"; and, in the same essay: "every successful work supersedes its model and renders the world superfluous to it" ("Gertrude Stein and the Geography of the Sentence," *WWW,* pp. 105 and 80). Furthermore, though pervasively antirealistic, antimimetic, and still more, in the manner of Bloomsbury, antiutilitarian, Gass's writing deflects on occasion away from art and toward the world it is intended to supersede, as in the final section of *On Being Blue,* where we are told that "every loving act of definition reverses the retreat of attention to the word and returns it to the world" (p. 87). The lapse is momentary—within a few pages "the wretched writer" is advised to "give up the blue things of this world in favor of the words which say them" (pp. 89-90)—but it is enough to suggest, by Surfictional standards, an impurity of sorts; and in "Thirteen Digressions," Sukenick, though not apropos of this particular work, takes note of the heresy and of its implications: "William Gass talks about fiction as an addition to reality, [but] Gass [also] thinks of fiction as a model of the world. . . . This is basically a subtler kind of imitation theory in which continuity between art and experience is broken because art is seen as a mode essentially different from experience" (*TD*, p. 94).

The observation is acute but its importance for us lies elsewhere. Sukenick's refusal of a distinction between art and experience is, once again, a claim to suspensiveness, a willingness to live with messiness. Gass, consciously celebrating the aesthetic, meets Sukenick then not on the level of the latter's theory but where, in practice, in "The Death of the Novel," say, consciousness comes willy-nilly to dominate the world. Sukenick, in other words, betrays an allegiance that Gass gladly avows: to the mind that, working through language, constitutes reality. For Gass's major concern, as he repeatedly stresses, is with the structures of consciousness and with relations within the work: "fragrant petals of pure relation" ("Upright Among Staring Fish," *WWW*, p. 207); and as is abundantly clear by now the major tendency of his work is aesthetic in the most extreme sense of the word. Speaking of *Remembrance of Things Past*, Gass writes: "this work, like all truly great ones, spits life out of time like the pit from a fruit. Out of the architecture of the word, the great work rises, but its reading requires a similar commitment, a similar elevation of the soul above mere living, mere mortal concerns" ("Proust at 100," *WWW*, p. 157). How at this point not to recall Clive Bell discoursing on "the austere and thrilling raptures of those who have climbed the cold, white peaks of art"[25] or to avoid applying to Gass his own comment about Malcolm Lowry: "Redemption through art was his real creed" ("Malcolm Lowry," *WWW*, p. 26)? And not only because of his ideas. As the books from which I've been quoting demonstrate, the proliferating ideas, endlessly spun out, transform themselves, dissolve, into words, phrases, images and analogies, tropes and figures, until, dizzy and surfeited, the reader is aware only of a voice and of the consciousness behind it, languorously energizing the world by infusing it with the self. The world is indeed within the word, for "the poet," we are told, "struggles to keep his words from saying something, and as artists we all struggle to be poets" ("Carrots, Noses, Snow, Rose, Roses," *WWW*, p. 301).

And the effect—on us? on the world? One final quotation will provide the clue: "Such are the sentences we should like to love—the ones which love us and themselves as well—incestuous sentences—sentences which make an imaginary speaker speak the imagination loudly to the reading eye; that have a kind of orality transmogrified: not the tongue touching

the genital tip, but the idea of the tongue, the thought of the tongue . . .
we subside through sentences like these, the risk of senselessness like this,
to float like leaves on the restful surface of that world of words to come
. . ." (*OBB*, pp. 57-58). The effect is reductive of course, as we move cen-
tripetally toward the centering self—the onanistic self made onanistic
word. More is at issue, however. All postmodern irony, all postmodern
art in fact, proclaims itself, in its rejection of the metaphysical and psychological abysses of modernist depth, an art of surfaces. But the metaphor
demands and deserves qualification. Against the ultimately self-enclosed,
self-referential world of words that Gass puts forth as his ideal one needs
to set a different ideal of surface—or perhaps one ought to say, keeping
in mind the reaction to modernism, an ideal of shallow depth, "the
surface of a depth," as Merleau-Ponty says, describing man caught up
in a world of shifting horizons: "What we call a visible is . . . a quality
pregnant with a texture, the surface of a depth," so that "things themselves, which are themselves not flat beings but beings in depth, inac-
cessible to a subject that would survey them from above, open to him
alone that, if it be possible, would coexist with them in the same world."[26]
Situating itself far more firmly *in* the world, seeking in place of the
unresonant flatness of the page a human, lateral, horizontal depth or
textured surface, this other form of suspensive irony, which Merleau-
Ponty predicts, defines the limits of Gass's aestheticism and, with it, of
whatever else, to the exclusion of the world, reduces itself to abstraction
and idea. Like its apparent opposite, pornography, the new aestheticism
(masquerading as the energy of imagination, as the other does of sexuality)
is finally the reflex of self-consciousness. And, too, like paranoia (the
energy of detection), that favorite subject of contemporary writers.

Pynchon's Oedipa Maas, caught to begin with in a typically modernist
dilemma—the solipsism (*"Shall I project a world?"*)[27] that expresses itself
in the characteristic image of the circular tower of the self—reveals the
typically modernist desire to find connections. But *The Crying of Lot 49*
is no *Howards End*, and there are no wych-elms and no Mrs. Wilcoxes to
promise redemption. The loss Oedipa feels for "the direct, epileptic Word,
the cry that might abolish the night" (p. 87) is the condition of *all* irony
—the original fall into disunity of which modernism, with its hope if not
to recover the original wholeness then at least to recreate it in worlds
elsewhere, is the final desperate phase. In Pynchon's America, however,
we are in a doubly fallen world. Modernist paradox gives way to postmodern quandary, to suspensiveness, and, for those who cannot accept
chaos, to the need for an order far more limited than any imagined by the
modernists—specifically, for Oedipa, the state of "the true paranoid for
whom all is organized in spheres joyful or threatening about the central
pulse of himself" (p. 95). But though she is tempted, Oedipa opts at the

last for "waiting": "at the very least, waiting for a symmetry of choices [an intensification of modernism's absolute irony?] to break down, to go skew" (p. 136); and her final question (which, ironically enough, does echo *Howards End*, with its plea for "Differences—eternal differences" [*HE*, p. 336]) is surely Pynchon's too: "how had it ever happened here, with the chances once so good for diversity?" (p. 136).[28] Whatever Pynchon's success or failure in dramatizing those chances, the question and the hope that pulses behind it remain emblematic: a counterassertion to the theory or practice of the writers I've been discussing, and a movement toward a state of genuine acceptance. For if the diversity of suspensiveness falls hostage among some contemporary ironists to a more imperious need for order—whether deliberately, as in Gass's case, or not, as in those of Federman and Sukenick—still that reductiveness, as we shall see, is only a possible response to, not the necessary condition of, postmodern irony.

THE SQUIRMING FACTS

To keep the emblems and tokens of North Pargiter . . . but at the
same time spread out, make a new ripple in human consciousness,
be the bubble and the stream, the stream and the bubble—myself
and the world together.
    —Virginia Woolf, *The Years*

Is Disneyland really necessary?
    —Ronald Sukenick, "The New Tradition in Fiction"

Main Street is almost all right.
    —Robert Venturi, *Complexity and Contradiction in Architecture*

There is something instructive about Sukenick's repeated attacks on pop art (something that goes beyond his simple failure to understand the movement, which is, as he defines it, "the desperate reintroduction of realism as media realism, stereotype. . . . As if the only thing we can make of our experience is the ultimate mirror image—a photograph, a negative, a cliché" [*TD*, p. 95]). For pop art and the other arts on which, directly or indirectly, it has had some impact are in fact, though superficially more shapely than works like Sukenick's, finally less reductive, more relational —the relation being one not, as in Gass, of an echoing intertextuality ("Against what do the great lines of poetry reverberate, if not the resoundings of other lines?" ["Carrots, Noses, Snow, Rose, Roses," *WWW*, p. 301]) but of consciousness and what is outside it. Two correlative points are at issue here, and it is worth pausing for a moment over the less central, if more paradoxical, of them: namely, that pop and pop-inspired art effect a more genuinely suspensive vision than do chaos-drunk writers like Federman and Sukenick without forgoing altogether a sense of the possibilities (loose and flexible to be sure) of order. One chapter of Venturi's *Complexity and Contradiction in Architecture*, for example, is called "The Obligation toward the Difficult Whole"; and speaking of Robert Rauschenberg's work, Lawrence Alloway writes: "Thus instead of an iconography in which each part is tightly related, we have an iconography of divergent episodes and simultaneous events, though . . . *within certain parameters*" (my italics). But Alloway continues, and this brings me to my second point: "The subject [of Rauschenberg's Inferno drawings], as Cage has put it, is 'a situation involving multiplicity' and the multiplicity, not its reduction, is the subject of definition."[29] The emphasis, in other words, remains on multiplicity, randomness, contingency; and order presents itself not as a solution to or a resolution of suspensiveness but as a modification, limited and partial, of it. (We are once more touching, that is to say, on the question of the anironic.) What matters, again quoting Alloway, who is here speaking of pop art as part of a larger cultural phenomenon, is "the impulse towards open-ended as opposed to formal descriptions of events and to a speculative rather than to a contemplative esthetics" (p. 122). Adhered to with consistency and integrity, that impulse offers instead of the reductiveness of the Surfictionists what I propose (in filling in the other, greener half of my map of suspensiveness, the second of its subdivisions or territories) to call generativeness or generative irony: the attempt, inspired by the negotiations of self and world, to create, tentatively and provisionally, anironic enclaves of value in the face of—but not in place of—a meaningless universe.

The world, in short, is accepted as a given and *in its essentials* as beyond change or understanding. But that recognition is not meant to imply either stoic resignation or suicidal despair. Even Venturi, accepting and proclaiming the necessary diversity of a pluralist society, acknowledges limits, in *Learning from Las Vegas*, to his robust vision.[30] The analogy with architecture has, however, worn out its usefulness for our purposes. Venturi's concern is rightly with the visible and concrete (the minimum obligation of his buildings, one might say, is not to fall down); the concern of the writers I mean to deal with is less pragmatic, more metaphysical. But not for that reason less immediate. The comparison with pop art at least will hold for a while longer and helps to suggest that generative irony means to replace Eliot's notion of myth as control with a questioning of the meaning of myth itself—or, as Alloway says about Jasper Johns's subjects, "pre-existing signs and systems of signs" (p. 136). This is not to enclose generative irony within the claustrophobic confines of a narrowly conceived semiotics but to recognize that things being

what they are, American culture being what it is, most writers who are in
pursuit of otherness or of their relationship to it are constrained to take
as their initial project not some Heideggerian discovery of Being but a
more mundane investigation of the man-made world: the impermanent,
bewildering, rubbishy environment that Barthelme calls "City Life."

Myth then changes not only its status (subject rather than instrument)
but its nature. Crammed with figures like King Kong, the Phantom of the
Opera, and Robert Kennedy (Barthelme); Castro and J. Edgar Hoover
and Norman Mailer (Apple); Lassie and Idi Amin (Boyle), contemporary
fiction makes even the most potentially heroic of its iconographic characters—historical as well as fictional—quintessentially *ordinary*. In the
spirit of Barthelme's "A Manual for Sons"—"'small' is one of the concepts
you should shoot for" (*TDF*, p. 145)—and of Venturi's praise for the
"ugly and ordinary" (*Learning from Las Vegas*, passim), generative ironists
puzzle over the legacy of the modernist heroic and contrive in its place a
syntax of interrogation. "Pop is a re-enlistment in the world," Robert
Indiana said in 1963,[31] and the statement will serve, if qualified with a
question mark or some other sign that bespeaks a less martial sense of
certainty. At any rate, the tendency of the remark is important, and it is
because of what it suggests that I have adopted pop art as my other
master sign to stand, in its openness, its inclusiveness, and its speculative,
comic impulses, in opposition to Gass's aestheticism and, perhaps one
should say as well, to the kind of simple, equally restrictive morality of
life-affirmation propounded by John Gardner in *On Moral Fiction*, which
is after all, like Gass's world of words, a residue of older orders: a
hankering, thinly disguised, for the comforts of the extraordinary.

Generative irony is in fact, along with its anironic complement, precisely the reverse: an effort to comprehend or, more accurately, to enter
into a relationship with the ordinary. Barthelme, much concerned with
the connection between the ordinary and the extraordinary, comes to
hand again with an example.[32] "The Death of Edward Lear" describes just
that, or rather Lear's remarkably low-keyed, matter-of-fact preparations
for his death, which Barthelme, matching his subject's intentions with his
own technique, recounts in a level and unemphatic way. The death itself,
occurring exactly at the time stipulated on the invitations that have been
sent out and after Lear's symbolic reenactment of the themes of his life, is
recorded with the utmost neutrality. There is nothing neutral, however,
about the story's intention, which Barthelme reveals as follows: "People
who had attended the death of Edward Lear agreed that, all in all, it had
been a somewhat tedious performance. . . . Then something was understood: that Mr. Lear had been doing what he had always done and therefore, not doing anything extraordinary. Mr. Lear had transformed the
extraordinary into its opposite. He had, in point of fact, created a gentle,

genial misunderstanding" (*GD*, p. 103). Quietly daring in its treatment of death, Barthelme's story itself intends a misunderstanding or rather a clarification about the way in which death and life are understood and misunderstood. And the story does not stop here. Describing the subsequent staged versions of Lear's death, it ends: "One modification is curious; no one knows how it came about. The supporting company plays in the traditional way, but Lear himself appears shouting, shaking, vibrant with rage" (*GD*, p. 104). The epilogue, it seems clear, broadens out to encompass within its statement art as well; and the moral, for this is unabashedly a moral story, comments on the human inability to emulate the original Lear: to accept as ordinary, whether in life or art, the condition of being human. Making death ordinary, reducing its portentousness, Barthelme obliquely, paradoxically affirms the value of living; and his story emerges as both antiheroic and suspensive: a celebration of Lear's deliberate, undramatic stand against the irrational claims of life and art (which is to say, humanity's contrivance of and connivance in those claims) to a final meaning that in its ordering sweep annuls the smaller pleasures and pains of life itself.

The attitudes that "Edward Lear" presents by way of lucid understatement emerge too, but only partially, reluctantly, and obscurely, in Robert Coover's *Pricksongs and Descants*, a book that, precisely because of its internecine conflicts, reveals better than Coover's novels the particular tensions of his fictional world. Certainly the collection makes clear the postmodern impulse to demystify (evident in the treatment of Noah, Joseph, and others) that is everywhere in Coover's work and that is addressed, presumably, in the somewhat overblown "Dedicatoria y Prólogo" to the "Seven Exemplary Tales": "They struggled," he says of Cervantes's stories and surely of his own, "against the unconscious mythic residue in human life and sought to synthesize the unsynthesizable, sallied forth against adolescent thought-modes and exhausted art forms, and returned home with new complexities" (p. 77). In Coover's case, the new complexities depend upon the recognition that life in a "universe [that] is closing in on us again" (p. 78) is ordinary, humdrum, banal, and absurd.[33] But the acceptance of life's dailiness is, except at moments, less complete than in Barthelme's work. The desire to endow life with a kind of intensity persists ("Maybe," the narrator of one of the stories speculates, "it's just that we've lost a taste for the simple in a world perplexingly simple" [p. 147]) and helps to explain the preternatural emphasis on sex and violence that is ubiquitous in *Pricksongs and Descants*. But one must push further still into the tangled underbrush of Coover's aesthetic. Sex as well as violence are in his mind intimately related to death, and death more often than not precipitates in turn the consoling powers that art confers, so that the extraordinary, promising initially to heighten, threatens at last to destroy the ordinary: to remystify and stabilize "the flux and tedium" (p. 16) through an art that, as Coover repeatedly insists, invents life. That, at any rate, is the tendency of the most critically praised of the fictions—"The Magic Poker," "The Elevator," and "The Babysitter"[34]—the deliberately and often archly reflexive works that, while purporting to articulate a vision of suspensiveness and while denying "the futile artifices of imposed order" (p. 28), in fact set consciousness in defiance of death. The aestheticizing consciousness of course, asserting its freedom, playing with sex and violence, submitting their potential for death and annihilation to the safely invulnerable dominion of art.

My concern, however, is not with these stories, which, though both more restrained in their form and more explosive in their content, still recall the works of the Surfictionists (there is, Alter rightly says, "a certain aridness" about them [p. 222]), but with those others that call into question the absolute autonomy of art over the ordinary disruptions of life and the final fracture of death. Less typical of the collection as a whole, these fictions are not for that reason anomalous; and it may well be because his imagination is so violent that Coover's art must finally acknowledge death and thus the ultimate futility of its own enterprise, must accept reality not only as material to be aesthetically shaped and not only as mere absurdity but as a source of potential meaning. To say this is not to propose an incompatibility between reflexivity and generative irony, a point I've already made in connection with some of Barthelme's stories and could make again with the example of John Irving's *The World According to Garp*. Indeed, Coover himself demonstrates the inadequacy of the opposition in "The Hat Act," a parable (anticipating Barthelme's "The Flight of Pigeons from the Palace") of the artist and his relation to his audience, which reflects not only on itself but back over the collection whose final story it is. Pushed to produce greater and greater marvels until he at last commits murder, the magician of the tale figures the artist as overreacher and dramatizes Coover's critique of an aestheticism seeking to dominate a reality (the magician's assistant) that will be subjugated only so far. But "dramatizes" may be the wrong word for so self-conscious and thinly textured a tale. "The Leper's Helix" confronts the same problem more suggestively if also more opaquely. The last of a group of three stories called "The Sentient Lens," "The Leper's Helix" tips the paradox of the collective title toward the necessary risks of feeling, and for the first time the impersonal "we" of the earlier tales gives way, hesitantly and imperfectly, to the first-person singular. Horrified but also oddly attracted, the narrator awaits the approach of the leper, the encounter (this much at least seems clear) of the artist with "brute reality" (p. 181), with his material, and finally with death. But even more is at stake: controlled as much as controlling, the narrator first acknowledges the leper's movement, the "staggering . . . jerking, twisting" (p. 179) helix he describes on the desert, as "less true perhaps than our perfect circle, yet for that the more beautiful" (p. 180); and then, confronting the fact of what he has heretofore only imagined, embraces his destiny: "There is in us that conditions acceptance" (p. 181). But as must be the case, if I am reading the story's symbolism aright, there is no resolution. Sitting beside the unburied leper, the narrator waits, for his own death presumably. But the acceptance has been registered, the high aesthetic claim (the perfect circle) abandoned in favor of an art that takes brute reality as "its counterpart" (p. 180) and, if as its subject, then also as its master.

"What terrible game will *you* play with *us?* me" (p. 182), "The Leper's Helix" ends; and the story that follows it in the volume is in some ways an answer to that question. "Paul stepped off the curb and got hit by a truck" (p. 183), "The Pedestrian Accident" begins, and for most of its length the tale records, in a triumph of grotesque comedy, Paul's observations and his reactions to the crowd that gathers around him as he lies mutely under the truck. "The world was an ephemeral place," he thinks plausibly, "it could get away from you in a minute" (p. 184); but for the most part he inclines to accept with a kind of bemused detachment the spectacle of which he is the squashed and expiring center: "Strange, thought Paul," as he watches the antics of the egregious Mrs. Grundy, "how much I'm enjoying this" (p. 189). To be sure, one can detect something savage in Coover's attitude, a grudge against the insensate universe and against the indifference of the motley crowd. But the anger is held in check by the careful neutrality of the presentation and more importantly by what it represents: the overwhelming sense of inevitability Coover suggests through the doctor's central speech on process and change. "'I know it's not easy to accept death,' the doctor was saying. . . . 'We all struggle against it, boy, it's part and parcel of being alive, this brawl, this meaningless gutterfight with death. In fact, let me tell you, son, it's *all* there is to life. . . . But death begets life, there's *that*, my boy, and don't you ever forget it! Survival and murder are synonyms, son, first flaw of the universe! . . . New life burgeons out of rot, new mouths consume old organisms . . . only old Dame Mass with her twin dugs of Stuff and Tickle persists, suffering her long slow split into pure light and pure carbon!'" (p. 202). In the last paragraphs of the story, however, as Paul lies, Christ-like, in the rain, a dog gnawing at his entrails, the mood shifts abruptly, and Coover's implicit anger spills over, to the story's detriment, into pathos and horror: a revealing sign of the tension (contradiction rather) in his work between aggrieved, awestruck acceptance and revulsion, which explains on the one hand his grimly comedic energy and on the other his more characteristic retreat (in this volume anyhow) to the domination of the aesthetic.

In short, Coover's suspensiveness, such as it is, is hard won; and perhaps in only two of the fictions of *Pricksongs and Descants* can one discover an acceptance not only of the absurdity of the universe but of the need to respond to it, to take it in his stride and move beyond an ever-present outrage toward a more encompassing and exhilarating horizon. Or perhaps only in one. "J's Marriage," from which I've already quoted ("Finally, he simply gave in to it [that is, the mystery of Mary's pregnancy], dumped it in with the rest of life's inscrutable absurdities" [p. 117]), is rather dour in its acquiescence; and Joseph's summation just before his death is something less than joyous: "Separately or additively [he] could make no sense of any day of his life . . . but . . . in spite of everything there was nothing tragic about it, no, nothing there to get wrought up about, on the contrary" (p. 119). "Romance of the Thin Man and the Fat Lady," on the other hand, manages an affirmation that, thanks to the story's inventive exuberance, rings true even as (or because) it grounds itself in a condition of absurdity more palpable, pervasive, and ordinary than anything suggested by the miracle that blights poor Joseph's existence. Concerned in part, like "The Hat Act," with problems of art, the story encompasses a good deal more: "The much recounted mating of the Thin Man with the Fat Lady is a circus legend full of truth. In fact, it is hardly more or less than the ultimate image of all our common everday romances, which are also, let us confess, somehow comic. We are all Thin Men. You are all Fat Ladies" (p. 138). And more still. Coover's allegorical circus of life and love meditates as well on the elusiveness of metaphor, the complexities of awareness and self-consciousness, and the vanity of desire. Desire is what sets the inner story going, as the Thin Man attempts to build muscles, the Fat Lady to reduce, each to please the other; and the narrative, which we needn't pursue here, details their separation and eventual reconciliation. But it is just at this point, the moment when they accept themselves, their relationship, and their situation, that the narrator, whose own reflections are concentric to the story he has just told, is seized by the irony of the accomplishment (theirs and his)—"we have . . . held fast to our precious metaphor. Yet, somehow, strangely, it has lost some of its old charm" (p. 147)—and is forced to recapitulate for himself the struggle of his characters: the fiction of life imitating, in this superbly vertiginous *mise en abyme*, an art that is the allegorical image of life. But the recaputlation is of necessity an abandonment, an assertion, first, of diversity ("For remember: these two, magic metaphor or no, are not the whole circus. Nor—to borrow from the hoariest spiel of them all—in this matter of circuses, is life one. There are three rings—" [p. 147]) and then, more urgently, of mortality: "Who can grasp it all? And who, grasping, can hold it! No, we have lost many things, go on losing, and must yet lose more. Even the Thin Man will grow old and bent, the Fat Lady will shrivel and die. We can hang on to nothing. Least of all the simple" (p. 148). But with nothing to hang on to, faced with the multiplicity of life and its finality, with its vanity and senselessness, the narrator wins through to his own tenuous but genuine affirmation: "But listen! the losses! these too are ludicrous, aren't they? these too are part of the comedy, right? a ring around the rings! So, damn it, let us hoot and holler and thrill" (p. 148).

The affirmation, limited, local, and temporary, has been earned, earned not only by the honesty and capaciousness of the vision but, equally or more, by its embodiment: art's paradoxical tribute to the squirming facts of life that exceed it. The point is an important one and serves to explain why, instead of concentrating on this story alone, I've dealt with others that less fully and (to come to what is central) less successfully articulate the kind of suspensiveness I'm now concerned with. The question involves the conditions that define the matter of artistic success; and to begin with one needs to state the obvious, that no more than in any other literary work is success here to be gauged simply in terms of the statement of a position (the moral or rather the moralistic view). Coover's "Romance" is a better story than "The Hat Act" not because—or not only because—its vision is more comprehensive, less "minifying," but because it contrives a density of presentation that exposes the abstract meagerness of the other tales. Though they are less wary of story, character, chronology, and so on than the Surfictionists, generative ironists, like postmodern writers in general, remain suspicious of the neat and orderly structures one associates with modernism. And so the faithful translation of their vision, which, I've indicated, both speaks to the fact of a bewildering universe and allows at the same time for the possibility of small gestures of difficult, hard won assent, requires not the external shape of Forster's "pattern" nor even the elaborate interconnections of his "rhythms" but rather a richness of observed and invented detail that neither overmasters nor is overmastered by the artist's tentative, flexible control. In short, the imagining and rendering of their world is for generative ironists a matter of texture and tone. Thus, if modernism privileges sight (and so structures that are, however subtle, determinate) and reductive irony a kind of internalized sight, a hectic and fevered imagination that, in opposition to its proclaimed intentions, imposes an order of abstraction and idea, generative irony attempts to activate consciousness as a whole, making of its relationship with the world something dynamic, kinetic, and reciprocal. It responds, that is, not to a concept of the world but to its texture, embodying that texture—or its impact on consciousness—in the shifting but ultimately unified modulations of attitude and voice. Tone then becomes an instrument of discovery, open like the pop art that inspires so much of this irony to a condition of "significative doubt"[35] and therefore to the exploration and creation of tentative, even momentary meanings or values in the world.

Seen in these terms, Coover's stories, apart from "Romance of the Thin Man and the Fat Lady," are less an expression of than a groping toward generative irony—when they are not more directly a contravention of it. In fact, Coover's work in general (*The Universal Baseball Association, Inc.* is the splendid exception) tends to vacillate between an excess of energy (*The Public Burning*) and an excess of control (the self-consciously aesthetic stories of *Pricksongs and Descants*), between diffuseness and thinness; and we may leave him now, representative of a transitional stage in our investigation, to move on (before arriving at more exemplary figures) to some final difficulties that beset postmodern irony and threaten in particular its potential for a generative response to the conditions it depicts. To come to the matter directly, the principal risk of suspensiveness, evident in Adler's elegant and stylish *Speedboat*, is passivity: a state of mind or being that replaces modernism's passionate desire to lose the self, "to sink deeper and deeper, away from the surface,"[36] with a willingness to float aimlessly in an ocean of urban flotsam and technological junk. The danger is one to which Adler's protagonist is particularly prone—"I have lost my sense of the whole," she says. "I wait for events to take a form" (p. 6)—and the novel renders with considerable success the quality of her consciousness. The question, however, is whether *Speedboat* itself doesn't fall prey to the same kind of passivity. To put this another way, the central interpretative difficulty of the book (one is reminded of *Play It as It Lays*) concerns the attitude Adler, and therefore the reader, adopts toward Jan Fain. One can imagine certainly—the epigraph, from Evelyn Waugh's *Vile Bodies*, suggests it is the case—that the novel intends satire, of its protagonist especially; but if that is so, something has gone drastically wrong. The techniques that articulate Jan's self-conscious bafflement provide us with most of the clues we have to Adler's attitude as well, and their effect is not to enhance but to blunt our sense of a substantive difference between author and character. The constant qualifications of the style, the muted bewilderment and deliberate flatness of the tone, and above all the novel's artfully antiformal structure, the fragments related (or unrelated) by a too deliberate inconsequence —all have the effect of sinking the book's multitudinousness to a level of pale uniformity. Passivity as a moral quality or attitude translates aesthetically into a perilously monochromatic texture; and *Speedboat*, for all its cleverness and wit, finally lacks vividness and solidity.

Why this should be so becomes clearer if one sets the novel against Isherwood's protosuspensive *Goodbye to Berlin*, a book that Adler's recalls in a good many ways and most particularly in its choice of a first-person narrator who, as outsider in a perplexing metropolis that at the same time mirrors her inner life ("My own mind is a tenement" [p. 10], she says), becomes the alienated spectator both of herself and of the equally fragmented world in which, somewhat marginally, she exists. (One keeps expecting Jan Fain to announce that she too is a camera.) But the differences are more instructive and can be suggested, to begin with, by way of a minor but similar symbolic detail that crops up in both books in dissimilar ways. At one point in *Goodbye to Berlin* there is a reference to an old man, a cocaine addict, who "had a nervous tic and kept shaking his head all the time, as if saying to Life: No. No. No" (p. 125). The only reference, it is a significant one: the old man helps to define the atmosphere of negation and death that becomes increasingly menacing in Isherwood's Berlin. Adler's Watergate America is defined more bathetically: "'Far from it,' the man who cleans up this office after hours keeps muttering to himself. 'Far from it. Far from it'" (p. 147) and on other of his appearances: "Don't dwell on it . . . Don't dwell on it" (p. 155). The response is as illogical as any made by Dickens's Mr. F's Aunt, and it is an index to the irrationality of *Speedboat*'s postmodern world, in which the activity and metaphor of traveling (Isherwood's and the thirties') is transformed into a kind of purposeless browsing, and in which Isherwood's already ambiguous moral impulse is attenuated still more.

Not that either Adler or her narrator fails to stipulate a set of values. On the contrary, the small, unheroic, and difficult virtues of sanity and decency are proclaimed throughout; but for reasons that are revealing and instructive, they are nevertheless curiously unresonant. In the first place, there is deep in the book's spirit a suspicion of the energy required to make these values effective. One inclines to take seriously in a book called *Speedboat* the single incident that refers to the title. The anecdote, which concerns an American woman "who had been overexcited about everything since dawn," tells of how "in her eagerness, [she] began to bounce with anticipation over every little wave. The boat scudded hard; she exaggerated every happy bounce. Until she broke her back" (p. 78). The lesson, which endorses discretion and understatement, is clear and is delivered, it seems, with some relish and not a little cruelty. In the second place and as the tone of the passage just quoted indicates, Adler's irony is not only vision but manner, and indeed a mannerism of sorts. Jan's assertion: "I think sanity . . . is the most profound moral option of our time" is followed almost immediately by the undermining generalization, "There doesn't seem to be a spirit of the times" (p. 4). We are dealing then, as I've been insisting, not only with the self-canceling perplexities of Jan's consciousness but with techniques that reflect and confirm them, and in such a way that we are at the very least in doubt about Adler's own perspective. To take one last example, a not untypical specimen of Jan's meditations: "What is the point. That is what must be borne in mind. Sometimes the point is really who wants what. Sometimes the point is what is right or kind. . . . The point changes and goes out. You cannot be forever watching for the point, or you lose the simplest thing: being a major character in your own life. . . . The point has never quite been entrusted to me" (pp. 55-56). Even in its truncated form the passage discloses a good deal. The ethical dilemma that Jan doggedly but abstractly pursues cancels itself out in an all too conscious gesture of self-deprecation, as if a wished for engagement with the world were prohibited, not as in Isherwood by a profoundly recalcitrant egoism, but by emotional fog or fatigue. Only the final, reductive decrescendo of the paragraph has impact, and that not because it resolves or even addresses the problem but because it so cleverly and cynically confirms through its characteristic registration and ironic dissolving of emotion the puzzled reader's sense that there is, after all, nothing to be done. Sanity, decency, and the rest are, along with all the oddities and quirks the book obviously relishes and delights in, absorbed into the sameness of its texture; and that may be the strangest of the novel's qualities. For if *Speedboat* acknowledges a passion for anything, it is, as in *The Berlin Stories*, for language—for its exactitude and correctness and for its capacity to communicate. The adjectives that describe the speedboat—"austere," "spare"—are relevant here, but they have more than a merely descriptive force. As for Isherwood, so for Adler austerity and spareness suggest both the strength and the limitation of their linguistic projects, since, to recall a point made earlier, the ascesis of language, if it makes for clarity and discipline, also (it is the Catch-22 of ironic understatement) narrows the range of expressiveness open to an author and diminishes his concept of the world. In Adler's novel, where the world's resistance is in any case less, technique tends at a minimum to call attention to itself and so to reveal the absence of that tension to which the book pretends. Language in *Speedboat* finally reflects and enacts (they are the same) a failure of courage; and the generative and generous vision the book promises founders as its supposititious passion for language becomes, in the narrowest sense, only a valorization of style.

Of course contemporary literature as a whole betrays a conspicuous awareness of its language and, given the critical climate, the fact hardly surprises. What matters in this context is the degree to which and for whatever reasons style becomes "mere style," that is, usurps the referential and more broadly creative functions of language and becomes completely its own excuse and end. Among works that more nearly express than *Speedboat* does the kind of generative irony I'm describing (Susan

Sontag's similarly structured "Debriefing" comes to mind and so too does
Irving's *Garp*—though each in its own way is flawed, the one by tenden-
tiousness, the other not by melodrama but by an excess of play), in works
like these, language retains, in Paul Ricoeur's terms, a dimension of
reference as well as of sense: "It goes beyond the mere function of pointing
out and showing what already exists. . . . Here showing is at the same
time creating a new mode of being."[37] The creation of new modes of
being seems a fair description of the works with which I want to close,
and since they are by Elkin and Apple, they will bring me back full circle
to my starting point.

There is nothing passive, certainly, about Elkin's work; but no more is
there, despite its exuberant linguistic inventiveness, any suggestion of
aesthetic self-sufficiency. In fact, Elkin's *The Living End*—an ironic
theodicy in which God, to no one's satisfaction, justifies or at least
reveals His ways to the throng He has assembled at His "gala," the last
"Levee at the Lord's,"[38] as it turns out—devotes itself to an investigation
and critique of precisely that attitude. "What do you make of Me," Elkin
has God ask toward the end of His long, extravagant explanation of
matters cosmic and trivial, "Who could have gotten it all right the first
time, saved everyone trouble and left Hell unstocked? . . . Why do I do it
then? Why?" The answers that come from the multitude: "'So we might
choose,' said one of the saved. . . . 'Goodness,' a saint shouted. 'You get
off on goodness'" (p. 143) are only, as the title of one of the novel's three
sections suggests, the conventional wisdom; and God's own answer when
it comes is both more brutal and more intelligible: "Is that what you
think? Were you born yesterday? You've been in the world. Is that how
you explain trial and error, history by increment, God's long Slap and
Tickle, his Indian-gift wrath? *Goodness?* No. It was Art! It was always
Art. I work by the contrasts and metrics, by beats and the silences. It was
all Art. *Because it makes a better story is why*" (p. 144).

Obviously there is nothing new in the notion of the Creator of the
universe as its supreme artist. But Elkin's God, petty and vindictive,
legalistic and sadistic, egocentric, "a sucker for worship" (p. 103) with a
"game show vision" (p. 137), is something else again: an emblem, like
Barthelme's Dead Father, of modernism, with "a thing for heights. . . . a
sort of majestic Fop posed on postcard and practicing His Law only
where there was a view" (pp. 141-42); a Bauhaus God, "a form-follows-
function sort of God" (p. 54), a devotee of structure for its own sake; in
short, less artist than aesthete, the reflexive Creator whose quirky design
exposes in Himself and in the world the absence of any moral center. It is
part of the book's power and a mark of its success that one is made to
revel in the magnificent energy of Elkin's amoral monster, this proto-
typical exponent of art for art's sake; but that is not to gainsay the novel's

anger nor to deny the countervision it offers to God's limited and severe aesthetic. No less conscious and no less episodic than God's (to judge by the world's history God is the prototype of the picaresque novelist as well), Elkin's art, even when its techniques are similar, has different aims. Myth serves, as the parodic use of *The Divine Comedy* demonstrates, not to order chaos (one is reminded again of Elkin's response to Eliot's "method") but to reveal it; and the unity of the book inheres finally in texture and style, in local effects that, in their referential, creative force, stubbornly refuse the peremptory justification of art as supreme order. More than God's contrasts and metrics, beats and silences (but all that too), Elkin's language, the source of the novel's colossal vitality, operates as well, like the language with which the dead are endowed, "to heighten perception" (p. 25). To that end words, active and dynamic, cascade in a nonstop movement of inventiveness ("Let them have the straight lines of their trade wind, trade route, through street, thrown stone vengeance" [p. 34]); and parts of speech metamorphose—nouns into adjectives, adjectives and nouns into verbs, verbs and adjectives into nouns—with dizzying exuberance: "'I was Pearl Harbor'd,' he might scream, 'December Seventh'd by the Lord'" (p. 108); "'Death softens the tongue,' Ladlehaus said, 'it kindly's us'" (p. 52); "And even *that* did not assuage the panic of his burning theater'd, air raid warning'd, red alert afterlife" (p. 35); "What can I do but go along if He in His infinite wisdom Abrahams me and Isaacs the kid" (p. 123).

But it is perhaps the book's imagery, its special idiom (which frequently recalls the bright, hard finish of pop art), the texture of pervasive, intentionally jarring contemporary reference, that most clearly discloses its intentions. "Hell was the ultimate inner city" (p. 30); "Heaven was pure light, its palaces and streets, its skies and landscapes primary as acrylic, lustered as lipstick" (p. 121). And The Virgin Mary thinks distastefully of her name: "the capital letters and epithet like something scrawled in phone booths or spray-painted in subways" (p. 110). At work thoughout the book is a reductiveness (to use that word now without its pejorative connotations) that transforms the cosmic and universal into the ordinary and quotidian: a reduction to the stubbornly human, which is exactly where Elkin's values are located. Cherishing the "ensnarement by the real" (p. 77) that he attributes to one of his characters; preferring to the cloudy solemnity of final things the sense of earth, "distance familiar again, volume, mass, and dimension restored, ordinary" (p. 25), Elkin, like Barthelme in this, strives to make the extraordinary ordinary and, more importantly, insists that the ordinary *is* extraordinary. Not surprisingly, the sentiment, manifested through Elkin's style, is shared by virtually all of his characters: "I loved it there," Jesus says of his time on earth. ". . . I loved being alive" (p. 107); and when last seen, Mary is described as "savoring the ordinary" (p. 148). Lesefario treasures his "last human contact" (p. 101), though it is of his murder; and Ladlehaus, affirmed by Elkin, meditates guiltily on his unquenchable curiosity and interest: "All those years dead, he thought, and still human. Nothing learned, death wasted on him" (p. 80). But the admirable Ellerbee is the character who most cogently voices the novel's mundane ethic and suggests its exact shape. Abandoning hope for the moment—he is in hell —"and with it memory, pity, pride, his projects, the sense he had of injustice—for a little while driving off, along with his sense of identity, even his broken recollections of glory," he thinks defiantly: "Let them have everything. Their pastels back and their blues and their greens, the recollection of gratified thirst, and the transient comfort of a sandwich and beer that had hit the spot, all the retrospective of good weather, a good night's sleep, a good joke, a good tune, a good time, the entire mosaic of small satisfactions that made up a life" (p. 34).

Random and yet not altogether accidental, since identity creates their value even as its own integrity is created by them, the satisfactions Ellerbee remembers are—these seem the key words—"transient" and "small." And that is the clue to Elkin's affirmation of life, an affirmation, if one can say so without sounding or making Elkin sound sentimental, of effort and concern, of caring and trying, and even of goodness. Elkin's deliberate assent to the occasional human possibilities of a senseless universe does nothing to deny that senselessness or to pretend that Ellerbee's "entire mosaic" has more than limited and personal force against the life and history that are the subject of God's absurdist "story." Or, for that matter, that art has. The point is made in the middle section of the novel in an episode that describes God's attendance· at a student concert, overheard as well by Ladlehouse, the central figure of Elkin's *Purgatorio*. As one would expect, the music is for God pure aesthetic pleasure, self-contained and final, a pleasure that leads Him to decree the death of one of the younger musicians whose performance makes Him "all smarmy" (p. 94). To Ladlehaus it is that—"He had forgotten about music, forgotten harmony, the grand actuality of the reconciled" (p. 92)—but it is something more: an enlarging of sympathies; a contact with, not a diminution of life; a harmony that includes without dissolving "distraction" and "displacements" (pp. 92, 93). It is, finally, one of "the ceremonies of innocence" (p. 95) that refreshes life without altering its fundamental nature—but that, to the extent of its limited power, alters it nonetheless, for "here was where the world dovetailed with self, where self tallied with sympathy and distraction alike" (p. 92).

"Here" is of course music. But it is also that sense, which God says His critics accuse Him of lacking, of "just ordinary earth" (p. 142), the locus of Elkin's attention and of the affirmations he makes, positively through his characters and the texture of his novel, negatively through his antimyth of the Supernal Creator. *The Living End*, then, satiric in its portrait of God (both as symbol of man's need for total meaning and as image of reflexivity and aesthetic control), proves suspensive in its acceptance of a stochastic universe—God's justification is ingenious but ultimately unsatisfactory—and generative in its call for a dynamic, freely willed but antiheroic response to it. "Everything was," Ellerbee thinks. "The self and what you did to protect it, learning the house odds, playing it safe" (p. 45). Like Barthelme, Elkin comes out finally for the "small satisfactions"; but unlike the Dead Father, Elkin's God triumphs—a sign, it may be, of residual *saeva indignatio*, of an incomplete exorcism of "the real McCoy Son of a Bitch God Whose memory Ellerbee would treasure and eternally repudiate forever" (p. 45)—triumphs, at any rate, by annihilating in His final Doomsday act all of creation. "Because," He explains, self-regarding to the last, "I never found My audience" (p. 148). The complaint is not unfamiliar in the records of contemporary literary discourse but had better be left anonymous. After all, the Creator's creator has the last word, and that word, appropriately, is *"everything."*

Elkin in his angry gusto and explosive humor is the full symphonic orchestra; Max Apple at his best, as in the title story of *The Oranging of America* and the slightly later "Disneyad," is all chamber music. Equally postmodern, Apple's prose is more intimate, its tone, at once affectionate and aware, more understated—full of a significative doubt directed at the contemporary world of goods and services and at the founding fathers of that world, chief among them the remarkable and comic Howard Johnson. In part God—"HJ raised his right arm and its shadow spread across the continent like a prophecy"; "he contemplated the map [with its dots signifying existing and projected "HJ houses"] and saw that it was good"[39] —he in no way resembles Elkin's autocratic bully-boy. The benign creator rather of twentieth-century pop America, Johnson represents the God of civilization or of "the civilizing instinct" (p. 8) in its most innocent and euphoric form. The innocence is insisted upon by the story's imagery, for if Howard Johnson is the patriarch of a commercial Manifest Destiny, he is also, with "his large pink head" (p. 4) and his "long pink jowls" (p. 13), a great oversized baby, "all pink" (p. 14), naively playing at children's games. But that isn't all there is to it: "they were more than businessmen," his associate Millie Bryce thinks, "they were pioneers" (p. 8); and Millie's notion transforms Johnson's buoyant capitalism into the experience of an American Adam, exploring and naming the untouched, uncircumscribed country with all the wonder of its original inhabitants: "Howard knew the land, Mildred thought, the way the Indians must have known it" (p. 7). And finally, most importantly, Howard Johnson, Adam and God, becomes too in Apple's complex vision a single-minded Quixote, setting his romantic vision of America against that "something alien" (p. 8), the flaw in paradise, which announces itself, in Millie's ulcerous intimations of mortality, as the inevitability of death. Johnson himself chooses to ignore or evade that inevitability: "Howard had once commented that never in all his experience did he have an intuition of a good location near a cemetery" (p. 16). Or it may be more accurate to see him, in his Quixotic assurance, as tilting at death, since the HJ houses are a deliberate attempt to displace "the old motel courts huddled like so many dark graves around the stone marking of the highway" (p. 16). The latter probably, since even death—it is the funny, touching, ironic climax of the story—proves no match for his redoubtable powers; and "The Oranging of America" ends with his gift to Millie of her immortality or, in the form of the portable cryonic freezer he attaches to his car, with a reasonable approximation of it, for "freezing her remains was the closest image she could conjure of eternal life" (p. 14).

How we are to react to all this and to the spectacle of the reunited pair, off on the road again, "ready now for the challenge of Disney World" (p. 19) emerges as the central problem of the story, but it is one I want to postpone for now. It will be easier, I think, to comprehend the remarkable achievement of "The Oranging of America" if we look first at some of the other stories, in which Howard Johnson's combination of qualities (energy and imagination, innocence and shrewdness, and so on) and the symbolic overlappings that in the story serve to unite them begin more and more, along with the fragile balance of Apple's irony, to separate out into opposition and conflict. As they do notably in "Disneyad," where the integralness of Howard Johnson dissolves and is replaced by the opposing visions of the brothers Disney. At first glance the opposition is simple and classic: between Walt, the artist, whose originating idea that "there is no stillness" (p. 195) becomes the source of all that follows and Will, the businessman, whose enterprise translates that idea first into cartoons and then into Disneyland and Disney World. But Walt, although he possesses an interesting enough aesthetic (a postmodernist ahead of his time, he is fascinated by surface and discontinuity, uninterested in thought, identity, and story), remains himself passive, colorless, unenterprising, and, curiously, for someone with a passion for "random motion" (p. 201), unchanging. Like Howard Johnson in his importunate vision, but only in that, Walt suggests a man almost without will—or rather (the pun is deliberate: in "The Oranging of America" his brother's name is given, correctly, as Roy), *Will*, adventurous and managerial, is his will: at once the realization and defeat of his obsession with the nonhuman. But paradoxes attend. If Will seems at times an unusually gross Sancho Panza who has gained the upper hand over a preternaturally melancholy and ineffectual Quixote, the fact remains that he, not Walt, is the idealist, bringing Disneyland to America as Howard Johnson does his restaurants and motels. Less innocent than his brother, more calculating and materialistic, even crass and self-interested, he has nevertheless the energy and imagination that orange America, while Walt mopes, gets airsick, and doubts the wisdom of everything his brother does.

And yet, without question, our sympathies are with Walt, and it is important to understand why. The synthetic powers of the Howard Johnson story notwithstanding, we're apt to discover in Apple's work, as both the "Disneyad" and *The Oranging of America* in general demonstrate, a more characteristic duality of vision—a primitivist vision of sorts that endorses the originating but not the implementing stages of modern individualism. "Will brought him ventures," Walt thinks, "but since Steamboat Willy there had been no 'adventures,' no risks of his talent, no taste of the world" (p. 202). Walt's residual taste for adventure and the world make him Apple's hero, albeit a rather pathetic one; and the crushing of his pioneering spirit endows the story with its comic pathos. Leaving aside again "The Oranging of America," one can't help discovering that Apple's sympathies are with the founders, the pioneers, the adventurers, the small-scale dreamers and against the moguls and entrepreneurs, the parodic but inevitable extensions of Howard Johnson, whose dreams, like Will's, are of immortality, or of something close to it. "'Man is only dust and time and spirit,' Will said, 'but Disneyland can make him strong as an angel.' He threw a strike scattering the pins deep into the abyss" (p. 210). Yet the story ends with Walt, who, though "powerless as usual before the brilliant energy of his brother," throws a strike himself, "aiming toward Anaheim" [i.e., toward Disneyland] (p. 212). Not a victory, to be sure, but a protest against the surrender of his will, which identifies Apple's more vigorous protest as well.

The protest, as I've suggested, can be found everywhere in *The Oranging of America*, complicated, however, by an awareness that the roots of the present extend into the past that Apple values. The Big Boss of "Gas Stations," owner of Oasis—the world's largest rest stop—is a onetime idealist, a dreamer of generous dreams, whose success is the ironic measure of his failure, while the Colonel of "My Real Estate," his vision realized in the commercial success of the Astrodome, dodders spitefully in a wheelchair, a still less attractive comment on Howard Johnsonism gone sour. And, finally, in "Noon," where the narrator murders Larry Love, the game-show host who is "the electric version of Horatio Alger" (p. 124), the American pop dream, hardened into unforeseen prosperity, becomes positively black. But the sardonic grimness of "Noon" isn't Apple's final comment. Most of the stories have in them, like Sancho at Quixote's deathbed, figures seeking to revive a dying dream. Unless they represent instead a new breed of Quixotes determined to overleap the inglorious present of the Colonels and Big Bosses and the satanic Larry Love and to restore the America that glows in Apple's fiction (though not without flickers of irony): the world of Howard Johnson and Walt Disney, of Kennedy and the Beats. Or at any rate, since that is impossible, the requisite innocence having been lost, to project the values of that world into a different, less stable and less expansive sort of future, as the admirable Ferguson does in "Vegetable Love" when he at last frees himself from the rigid, unbending, and appropriately named Annette Grim. Offering the hope of perfection and certainty, Annette mixes vegetarianism with a belief that everyone needs to locate his "spot," his center of consciousness, which she of course has discovered but which Ferguson, "seeking his center like a dog after its own tail" (p. 43) can't seem to find. And, as the simile suggests, for good reason. Recognizing finally that there are no absolutes, Ferguson abandons his search for Annette (and her simple, simplifying ideas), heads off, rather vaguely, south with the newly met Kathleen ("herself not completely vegetarian" [p. 44]), and opens himself to uncertainty, life, and, by implication, death: the specter that dominates and haunts Apple's collection of stories. In the face of that final fact and of the various absolutisms that, along with Annette's, seek to deny it, Ferguson proclaims his version of suspensiveness and thereby becomes the model for Apple's other antiheroic heroes (including the narrator of his novel *Zip*), who recognize too, as a character in another story says, that "it's a mean, impersonal world with everything always up for grabs. Alvarado knows it, and he accepts it" ("Understanding Alvarado," p. 91). So, searching like Ferguson for something outside the self, the narrator of "Gas Stations," a contemporary pioneer and small-scale idealist, pursues in the teeth of the Big Boss's melancholy scorn ("You're just a piss-call romantic mooning over the good old days of Rockefeller" [pp. 100-101]) his reconstituted dream of a purer America; Jack Spenser ("My Real Estate") affirms his equally small-scale and ancestral belief in property against the Colonel's monumental Astrodome; and the protagonist of "Selling Out" strikes against his possible stroke (the presence of death again), making off at the end with the girl, as in so many of these stories, toward an unspecified and indefinite future: the image precisely of suspensiveness and of the possibility of a generative reaction to it.

The most suspensive of the stories, however (to return to it now), is in fact "The Oranging of America," not because, as in the others, Apple thematizes his typical opposition and so locates his values within a single character—but because he doesn't. The figure of Howard Johnson is seamless, a composite of the pioneers and industrialists who elsewhere walk separate paths. Not that we read without irony in the more ordinary sense. Death will not be gainsaid, Johnson's ingenuity notwithstanding, and we recognize—it is what makes the story both more comic and more frightening than the rest—that he is after all not God but a lesser demi-urge, the architect, for good and for bad, of American popular culture. Nevertheless, the integrity of Howard Johnson within the pages of Apple's story is such that our questions and doubts are directed ultimately not at him but at ourselves, as they are when we stand in front of a canvas by, say, Lichtenstein or Johns or before one of Oldenberg's soft sculptures. In other words, "The Oranging of America" is above all about *our* response to Howard Johnson, the myth of Howard Johnson, finally about our response to our own myths and to their contradictory sources, which include the need for rest and comfort but for movement too and for the possibility of immortality above all: the power of those myths translated metonymically into a motel room—"Your friend, your one-night destiny" (p. 17). The question then is not so much of Howard Johnson's reality as it is of our perception of that reality and of the reality of the world we have made for ourselves.

Apple's triumph—nothing less expresses it—lies in his ability to keep the top spinning; which is to say that, reading the story, we acknowledge the authenticity of the myth-making process even as we interrogate the myth itself: the pink baby God, the sentimental genesis (part sunset, part Robert Frost) of the orange that covers America, the benign pioneering expansiveness, and, once more, the promise of immortality, the American denial of death. Accepting a different view of life, and death, a view like Elkin's of a universe without inherent meaning (which Howard Johnson implicitly denies), Apple forces us to speculate on the significance of the sign that, again in the manner of pop art, he doesn't so much create as re-create for us. Howard Johnson belongs to the reader first—part of what he brings to the story—the inevitable if not the right God for our times; and the reader is invited by Apple to recognize both the urgency and the hollowness of the myth, our myth, as he simultaneously subjects this particular formulation to his irony and nonetheless endorses, even applauds our ineradicable need to generate meaning and value. The implications of that generativeness, as they emerge from the story and from the whole of the collection, remind one of Barthelme's praise of the ordinary and Pynchon's of diversity; of Coover's "hoot and holler and thrill" and Elkin's "small satisfactions"; and of course of "Max Apple" himself in "Free Agents," "ready for everything." Taken together, the attitudes and responses recalled here recognize both the limits and the possibilities of suspensive irony and, in a larger sense, suggest the au-thentic shape of a distinctively postmodern art. Neither reductive nor, on the other hand, hopeful of reestablishing in art or in life an aesthetic of total order, endorsing modest pleasures in a world accepted as making no ultimate sense, it is a vision that lacks the heroism of the modernist enterprise but that, for a later and more disillusioned age, recovers its humanity.

SIX

Barthelme Unfair to Kierkegaard

No longer, like the early modernists, poised judicially above the world he surveys, the postmodern ironist is (to recall what is perhaps the central theme of this third part) typically involved *in*, though not necessarily *with*, that world: a part of, even though he may be apart from the other objects in, his own perceptual field. Moreover, and as one would expect, with a change in the angle of vision there comes a change in the vision itself.[1] The symmetry of modernist disorder gives way to an awareness of randomness and simple contingency; omniscience of understanding to an indecision about the very meanings and relations of things; Woolf's anguished cry—"Why is life so tragic; so like a little strip of pavement over an abyss?"[2]—to an attitude that takes for granted, more, naturalizes, the abyss as one constituent among others of the new prolific and dumb reality. Predicated, then, on the assumption of the ironist's immanence in the world he describes, suspensive irony positions itself differently from its predecessor vis-à-vis the objects of its perception and, rejecting modernism's transcendent heterocosms or vast inner depths, carries on and redefines the problem of the artist's relation to the world that surrounds him. "Surrounds" is the operative word here, as we move closer to the present. More alert, perhaps, but otherwise indistinguishable from his fellow browsers milling about in the technological clutter and confusion of the world-as-shopping-mall, the ironist today keeps his eyes and his options open. Not paralyzed but stupefied, it often seems, he staggers from store to store, counter to counter, his attitude one of slightly dazed and sometimes dazzled acceptance. So Paul, the victim of Coover's "A Pedestrian Accident," who, as we saw in the last chapter, is literally flattened to physical and mental numbness by a truck marked MAGIC KISS LIPSTICK IN 14 DIFFERENT SHADES scans the surrounding scene, collapsed, like him, to "Stuff and Tickle," with fascination and occasional aesthetic bemusement, and "[lets] himself be absorbed by it;

166

there was, after all, nothing else to do" (pp. 204, 202, 188). It is this kind of acceptance (in the sense that—to take a less dramatic example—one accepts the inevitability of his bad back going out from time to time) that both expresses and creates the shape of recent ironic fiction.

This is, in a manner of speaking, to take one's acceptance neat, undiluted—as some postmodern writers do and as still more purport to do (recall Federman's "I wallow in disorder"). But having, in the last chapter, concerned myself with more intricate responses to the world's disarray (as it presents itself to most serious contemporary writers); having, that is, dealt with irony in conjunction with the anironic, I want here to acknowledge the possibility at least of a more intransigent, unalloyed suspensiveness. I argued earlier that irony—all irony—usually engenders an ideal to complement and mitigate its harsher vision; and when I speak of irony, it is generally, if not inevitably, of the composite entity the two together create. No doubt others will disagree, but I had better make clear my own belief that irony achieves most complexity and suggestiveness when—as in *The Living End* or "The Oranging of America" or, indeed, as in "The Great Hug" and "Edward Lear"—it includes in its final vision the counterforces that are within its power to generate. But, to repeat, it need not, and in the stories I mean to deal with first in this assessment of Barthelme, it doesn't. Stringent and acerbic, these fictions articulate suspensiveness at its most radical and uncompromising, thereby revealing what underlies the compensatory gestures of reductive and generative ironists alike.

The notion of acceptance, at least during the last hundred years or so, inevitably conjures up a more or less bleak sense of the ordinary. From Laforgue's "Ah! que la vie est quotidienne" to Barthelme's "Critique de la Vie Quotidienne,"[3] by way of Neruda's "Walking Around," with its surrealist image of dailiness as random laundry on a line, weeping "lentas lágrimas sucias," the obstinate triviality of life increasingly impinges on the literary consciousness. But here again some discriminations need to be made. The modernist sensibility, haunted by a vision of pervasive grayness and (as in *Howards End*) of a creeping red rust, finds ultimate expression in one of Forster's comments in *A Passage to India*: "Most of life is so dull that there is nothing to be said about it . . . and a perfectly adjusted organism would be silent" (p. 125). But for all its flat and bitter finality, the remark heralds not silence but a dramatic exploration of metaphysical extremes; and if Forster fails in his quest for a redeeming order, it is not because of complacence or a willingness to accede to the dailiness of life. Barthelme's "Critique," on the other hand (reminiscent of Laforgue in its elegance and archness, though its bitterness is certainly more pedestrian and low-keyed), accommodates itself more easily to the banal horrors of *la vie quotidienne*. Not that the story is without incident (there is, notably, the moment when the narrator's former wife tries to "ventilate" him with a horse pistol [S, p. 12]), but if it is true, as Philip Stevick notes in his introduction to *Anti-Story*, that "to allow the middle range of experience to co-exist, in a single work, with the extremities of contemporary experience is to do strange things to that ordinariness, to deny it its solidity,"[4] it is equally the case that that coexistence may, as it does in Barthelme's fiction, serve to render extremity more ordinary—to deny *it*, and not the middle range of experience, a solidity of specification and response.

In any case, the "Critique," though it manages, characteristically, to combine the hilarious and the dismal, provides a rather too facile treatment of its subject, and its value is more representative than particular, supplying as it does a pattern for more successful examples (the Edward and Pia stories of *Unspeakable Practices*, among others) of Barthelme's relentless investigation of the humdrum. Of these, the best is probably the title story of *City Life*. More eccentric in incident and development, it expresses in a number of ways Barthelme's relation to *la vie quotidienne*. Speculating in the final section of the tale on "the most exquisite mysterious muck," which is the city she lives in and "which is itself the creation of that muck of mucks, human consciousness" (*CL*, pp., 178-79), Ramona goes on to contemplate the possible explanation of the virgin birth of her child: "Upon me, their glance has fallen," she thinks, reflecting on various of the men in her life. "The engendering force was, perhaps, the fused glance of all of them. From the millions of units crawling about on the surface of the city, their wavering desirous eye selected me. . . . *I accepted. What was the alternative?*" (*CL*, pp. 179-80; my italics). Ramona's last words sum up, mutatis mutandis, that is, allowing for a different level of awareness and for the artist's privileged sense of control, Barthelme's position as well. Implicated in the world he describes, Barthelme accepts —at least in this group of stories—not only the material that world offers him but the attitude of resignation his ironically suspensive mood seems, at this point, to entail. How else to react to "brain damage," when, as the narrator of the story by that name admits: "*I could describe it better if I weren't afflicted with it . . .*" (*CL*, p. 156)? Or, as Dan announces, in a much quoted passage from *Snow White*, apropos of the linguistic "trash phenomenon": "I hazard that we may very well soon reach a point where it's 100 percent. Now at such a point, you will agree, the question turns from a question of disposing of this 'trash' to a question of appreciating its qualities, because, after all, it's 100 percent, right?" (*SW*, p. 97).

There is a danger, however, of equating appreciation or even acceptance with the presence in these stories of a significative void—especially if one attempts to bring to bear on them the same analytic techniques regularly applied to the classics of modernist literature. But the lack of an easily paraphrasable theme or an extractable moral or, on the other hand, of a pattern of search and, if not resolution, then closure, doesn't necessarily imply the absence of human reference of one kind or another. Nevertheless, a number of recent critics seem bent on developing a good deal further than Forster would have accepted his definition of art as a "self-contained harmony." So, Sukenick, describing a particular elaboration of "the new tradition," writes, playfully perhaps but still seriously: "Needless to say the Bossa Nova has no plot, no story, no character, no chronological sequence, no verisimilitude, no imitation, no allegory, no symbolism, no subject matter, no 'meaning.' It resists interpretation. . . . The Bossa Nova is non-representational—it represents itself."[5] The main lines of Sukenick's argument, reminiscent of Robbe-Grillet's in *Pour un nouveau roman*, are familiar enough by now, but it is worth quoting further his remarks on "abstraction, improvisation, and opacity," which are the essential features of the bossanova style: "As abstraction frees fiction from the representational and the need to imitate some version of reality other than its own, so improvisation liberates it from any *a priori* order and allows it to discover new sequences and interconnections in the flow of experience. . . . Opacity implies that we should direct our attention to the surface of a work, and such techniques as graphics and typographical variations, in calling the reader's attention to the technological reality of the book, are useful in keeping his mind on that surface instead of undermining it with profundities" (pp. 44-45).

Although Barthelme provides Sukenick with one of his major examples, it isn't clear which exactly of his stories Sukenick has in mind, but the explorations of *la vie quotidienne* will serve as an initial test of whether or how fully Barthelme conforms to the ideal bossanova pattern. The major problem Sukenick raises has to do with "meaning," and it is one Barthelme deals with directly from time to time as well. So, in "Kierkegaard Unfair to Schlegel," the narrator notes disapprovingly that the philosopher "fastens upon Schlegel's novel [*Lucinde*] in its prescriptive aspect—in which it presents itself as a text telling us how to live—and neglects other aspects, its objecthood for one" (*CL*, p. 96). But Barthelme seems, generally, less dogmatic than Sukenick, and in an interview with Klinkowitz, elaborating on an earlier remark about collage, he hedges his bet on the question: "This new reality," he says, apropos of what is produced by the collage, "in the best case, may be or imply a comment on the other reality from which it came, and may be also much else. It's an *itself*, if it's successful."[6] In any case, if, in his emphasis on the self-referential quality of art, Sukenick meant to suggest that the principal intention of contemporary literature is not to re-present a stable, objective reality or if the suggestion was simply that the formal (even when disguised as the antiformal) takes precedence over the mimetic, there would be no need to quarrel. But more, as we know, is implied in the praise of Barthelme as "very bossanova"; and in the face of this denial of meaning, it is necessary to assert that the stories of daily life do "refer," that they refer most directly to the kind of inner life Barthelme (through his narrators) frequently denies his "characters." In other words, the stories are, in Susanne Langer's sense of the term, "presentational": the knowledge they provide is of the forms of feeling. Not to recognize this fact is to miss what may be most distinctive about Barthelme's work—the articulation not of the larger, more dramatic emotions to which modernist fiction is keyed but of an extraordinary range of minor, banal dissatisfactions. "Yours is not a modern problem," one character tells another in "City Life." "The problem today is not angst but lack of angst" (CL, p. 176). Barthelme's stories express not anomie or accidie or dread but a muted series of irritations, frustrations, and bafflements. The title of his fifth volume is exactly right. Even at its most funny or absurd, Barthelme's is a world of *Sadness*, sadness occasionally moderated by snatches after sexual satisfaction, by a persistent intellectual curiosity, and by the inventive pleasures of art—but never, especially in the stories of unmitigated acceptance, canceled by any of them.

The question of art brings us back to Sukenick's description and to another group of stories, which, to be fair, are probably more the kind of thing he had in mind in choosing Barthelme as one of his exemplars. The distinction between the two kinds of fiction is apparent in a piece called "The Balloon." The story ends (somewhat contradictorily, given its initial assertions) with the narrator's admission that the balloon "is a spontaneous autobiographical disclosure, having to do with the unease I felt at your absence, and with sexual deprivation . . ." (UP, p. 21). It is, in other words, in its fantastic way, an expression of the forms of feeling; and the story as a whole can be taken as one of Barthelme's most inventive descriptions of the presentational mode. Without its explanatory ending, however, the story suggests something different. Or at any rate the responses and reactions of the characters *within it* to the gigantic balloon that covers their city for some forty-five blocks point to less discursive meanings. (I emphasize for its paradigmatic value the anecdotal aspect of the story—quite simply what happens in it—because in the final analysis "The Balloon" is an exercise not *in* but *about* play, that is, a highly ideated, conceptualized work; but of that aspect of Barthelme's fiction, more later.) What is important for the moment are the narrator's assertions, first, that "it is wrong to speak of 'situations,' implying sets of circumstances leading to some resolution, some escape of tension; there were no situations, simply the balloon hanging there" (UP, pp. 15-16), and, then, that "we have learned not to insist on meanings, and they are rarely even looked for now, except in cases involving the simplest, safest phenomena" (*UP*, p. 16). In brief, the story tells how various New Yorkers respond to this curious presence that is "not limited, or defined" (*UP*, p. 20)—how they manage (or don't manage) to accept the "unmeaning" particularity of the balloon: its *thereness*.

Finally, then, "The Balloon" can be seen as a parable of reactions to reality as an irreducibly mysterious, varied, and changing surface; and as such, the story serves as prototype for those of Barthelme's fictions in which he and his narrators perceive the world as a kind of haphazard, endlessly organizable and reorganizable playground. Thus, whereas the presentational stories take as their recurrent starting point the inevitable flaws of human relations, the ludic ones (to borrow a word from Barthelme out of Huizinga) deal with the odd relationship between the individual mind and the humanized world of things and objects on which that mind has, collectively and precariously, left its imprint.

Predictably, the ludic fictions most obviously inspire Barthelme's technical innovations. The use of collage, of fragments,[7] of pictures and black spaces; the sudden irruption of large, capitalized remarks, which may or may not comment on the surrounding text; the reliance on what one critic (referring to his own "rhythms") calls "interval (with abrupt interface) & repeat/repeat of cliché (with slight variation)";[8] the constant experimentation with styles, ranging from the severely paratactic to the most involutedly subordinative: all function, of course, to call attention to the fact of writing (or *écriture*, as we are learning to say), to the medium in which Barthelme and his perceptual field intersect. Indeed, Sukenick's animus against depth makes a good deal of sense in connection with stories like "Sentence": one nine-page-long, remarkably resourceful experiment in syntax. The emphasis on surface has, of course, spatial, moral, and psychological implications, but the force of Sukenick's argument and of Barthelme's practice suggests that the question is, in the first instance, an aesthetic one; and we may start with that in coming again at the problem of meaning.

It's difficult to avoid the inference that a good deal of contemporary literature represents a belated response to the by now familiar imperatives of modern painting. So Clement Greenberg writes: "Realistic, illusionist art had dissembled the medium, using art to conceal art. Modernism used art to call attention to art. The limitations that constitute the medium of painting—the flat surface, the shape of the support, the properties of pigment—were treated by the Old Masters as negative factors that could be acknowledged only implicitly or indirectly. Modernist painting has come to regard these same limitations as positive factors that are to be acknowledged openly."[9] The translation of Greenberg's "limitations" into literary terms—the flat page, the technological shape of the book, the physical properties of words—provides the foundation on which ultra-formalists, advocates of the nonreferential, and antimimetic critics construct their minimalist or purely aesthetic theories. No doubt, Barthelme's most apparently experimental fictions, do, at their best, give something of the sense of art as gratuitous play and of life as unqualified suspensiveness (at their worst, they suggest "attempts to make complex the simple, so that we will not be bored" [*UP*, p. 133]); but whether even play is without meaning is another matter.

The apotheosis of play sounds in fact suspiciously like yet another affirmation of art for art's sake; and it should seem clear by now that that phrase, unsupported by some clarifying or defining context, is among the most perversely empty literary slogans ever invented. Not that there is any difficulty in understanding Woolf's animus against books that require that "the reader should finish them, actively and practically, for himself";[10] or Clive Bell's against paintings pandering to a taste for the anecdotal; or, in a different way, Forster's counterpointing of the order of art and the disorder of life. But what is invariably at issue in these and other cases is a refusal of the didactic and tendentious, an unwillingness to convert art into an instrument of immediate utility. There is, however, nothing contradictory between the service of art and the attribution to it of semantic or even moral force, provided one keeps one's terms of reference large and flexible. Surely, confronted with even the most homogeneously colored, unpainterly painting, one can argue (Barthelme is summarizing Huizinga) "that the play element in culture serves a civilizing function" (*GP*, p. 130), or, in a formulation I prefer, one can follow Merleau-Ponty: "What will be transmitted to the canvas," he writes, "will no longer be only a vital or sensual value. . . . There will also be the emblem of a way of inhabiting the world, of handling it, and of interpreting it . . . in short, the emblem of a certain relationship to being."[11]

The problems that accrue as one moves from pigments to words are familiar enough. And even if one chooses to regard words as being as devoid of fixed, inherent meaning as pigments; even if one maintains that the relation between signifiers and signifieds is arbitrary, that meaning is generated diacritically, that, above all, signifieds are overdetermined in relation to signifiers, so that ambiguity is not only potential but inevitable; even if, finally, as one of Barthelme's narrator's maintains, "signs are signs, and . . . some of them are lies" (*CB*, p. 109), still the difficulties remain. But what the semiotic vocabulary does suggest is that, if Barthelme's fictions are to be compared with painting, the comparison ought more properly to take as its point of reference not modernist but pop art. A number of reviewers have drawn the analogy casually, and in the last chapter I suggested the special relevance of pop art to the whole generative wing of suspensive irony; but it is worth pursuing the connection further, especially in relation to picture stories like "The Expedition." In his admirable study, Lawrence Alloway describes pop art as "essentially, an art about signs and sign systems":[12] "The attitude of the Pop artists toward the signs and objects they use," he writes, "is neither one of simple acclaim, celebrating consumer goods, nor of satirical condemnation of the system in favor of some humanistic norm of conduct. On the contrary, they use the objects of the man-made environment with a sense of meaning in process" (p. 47). The last phrase is particularly to the point, as are Alloway's comments on "the provisional nature of all communication," on "the mobility of signs" (p. 47), and on "the significative doubt of Pop art" (p. 21). Stories such as "The Joker's Greatest Triumph," which tackles the problem of reusing the cultural detritus of our times, or "A Nation of Wheels," with (to use another of Alloway's phrases) its combination of "high style and low subjects" (p. 19), express perfectly the ways in which supposedly self-referential play and an adherence to surface work not to deny but to create meaning. To be sure, the meanings are neither altogether stable nor completely clear. In fact, it is precisely the referential ambiguity that generates the suspensiveness of Barthelme's irony, as it does Lichtenstein's or Johns's.

Like the pop artists, Barthelme puts aside the central modernist preoccupation with epistemology, and it may well be the absence of questions about how we know that has operated most strongly to "defamiliarize" his (and their) work. Barthelme's concerns are, rather, ontological in their acceptance of a world that is, willy-nilly, a given of experience. Here, one can speak legitimately of surface in that there is not for Barthelme, as there is for Clive Bell, a potential awareness of 'essential reality, of the God in everything, of the universal in the particular, of the all-pervading rhythm . . . that which lies behind the appearance of all things—that which gives to all things their individual significance, the thing in itself, the ultimate reality."[13] But the absence of depth implies the lack not of meaning but of certainties. Life has become, for better or for worse, less mysterious but more puzzling, and beside Bell's cadenced, assured phrases one needs to juxtapose Ramona's laconic "I accepted. What was the alternative?" Not for Ramona—and not for Barthelme—"the ultimate reality." Over the past several decades the quest has become a futile, indeed an unreal, one. "We must not . . . wonder," Merleau-Ponty writes, "whether we really perceive a world, we must instead say: the world is what we perceive" (PhP, p. xvi). The question, then, is how exactly to live in that world (a largely humanized world in Barthelme's fiction), and Ramona's answer—a kind of grim-lipped hilarity in the face of the provisional—is emblematic of her author's in many ways as well. "The world in the evening seems fraught with the absence of promise" (S, pp. 3-4), the narrator of "Critique de la Vie Quotidienne" remarks; and so too do the days. The simpletons of Barthelme's fictions are those like

Perpetua, who, having left her husband, imagines that she sees a "new life
. . . spread out before her like a red velvet map" (S, p. 37). Wisdom, so it
seems, lies in a stoicism of sorts. At the end of "The Policemen's Ball," the
unspecified "horrors" that have waited for Horace throughout his evening-
long seduction of Margot "had moved outside Horace's apartment. Not
even policemen and their ladies are safe, the horrors thought. No one is
safe. Safety does not exist. Ha ha ha ha ha ha ha ha ha ha!" (CL, p. 62).
Barthelme is one up on Horace, being an intimate of the horrors and the
chronicler of their laugh. But by the same token, his is the more difficult
position to maintain. To be conscious and even to value, as he obviously
does, that "muck of mucks" called consciousness and at the same time to
acquiesce simply and completely in an attitude of suspensiveness toward
things as they are exacts a difficult balance. So it is hardly surprising that
from time to time, and increasingly, Barthelme's acceptance moves beyond
Ramona's resignation to explore alternatives both more affirmative and
more complex, creating in the process a more comprehensive and flexible
irony as well.

. . .

In one of the stories of Guilty Pleasures, Barthelme returns to the
problem of the quotidian in a baroque exhibition of play about play. The
fascination of the piece—apart from its pyrotechnical inventiveness—lies
in the fact that as Hector, an almost frighteningly prodigious game-freak,
and Amanda, his ever more weary and unconvinced protegée, play and
discuss games and game-theory, we become aware of the various impulses
that underlie Barthelme's different kinds of fictions. Amanda's briefly
enthusiastic response to Hector's inventions ("'These games are marvel-
lous,' Amanda said. 'I like them especially because they are so meaningless
and boring, and trivial'" [GP, p. 133]) underscores the presentational
element in the stories: the link between fictional form and the forms of
feeling; while Hector's final creation, "Ennui . . . the absence of games . . .
the modern world at its most vulnerable" (GP, p. 134), expresses the
Beckettian source and rationale for the ludic pieces. But another of
Amanda's comments, which supplies the story's title—"Games Are the
Enemies of Beauty, Truth, and Sleep, Amanda Said"—is more interesting
still and different in kind from the others. For what the comment does is
to embody a persistent reactive strain in Barthelme's work, which belies
still further the programmatic rejections of meaning in much postmodern
criticism. Not that Amanda is to be regarded transparently as a porte-
parole. One can hardly imagine Barthelme using in his own person, even
with the ironic qualification of "and Sleep," such high-flown words as
beauty and truth. Nonetheless, Amanda's rejection, as compared with

Ramona's acceptance, marks a difference: a refusal simply to acquiesce in cultural givens, which defines a number of Barthelme's stories too.

I don't want to make too much of poor, besotted Amanda. The point is simply that in her refusal of life as a game and of games as an adequate representation of life she gestures toward a more conceptual mode of apprehending and defining her situation; and this generalizing, reflective response to the experiential, to the immediately perceived, works better in some ways for Barthelme also, whose most successful, if not always his most obviously and dramatically innovative, fictions are of this kind. Furthermore, if Amanda's gesture is, despite its vocabulary, essentially negative, the same can be said of the force behind much of Barthelme's conceptual work. So much then for Amanda. Barthelme's rejections are the more interesting, and they are very much of a piece. Except in some of the more feeble parodies, however, they are *not*, as one might expect, rejections of the daily (though they do in fact lead ultimately to a reassessment of attitudes toward it) but of those who seek to stabilize and rationalize that world. In other words, Barthelme is, at his best, an anticonceptual conceptualizer, working inductively toward an understanding of the necessity but also of the limits of acceptance.

In a general way, what Barthelme takes his stand against are pretensions to certainty and the insistence on perfection; large demands and great expectations; dogmatisms and theories of all kinds. In "Kierkegaard Unfair to Schlegel," the enemy is religion, as it is in "The Rise of Capitalism," where the saints deliver "the same old message" (*S*, p. 146) of hope in the other-worldly; in "The Sandman," it is prescriptive, specifically psychological, change; in "Report," the technocratic mentality; in "Engineer-Private Paul Klee," war. "Me and Miss Mandible" takes on education and the reliability of signs; "Marie, Marie, Hold on Tight" (if I read that curious story correctly), the pedantically theoretical questioning of the pedantic. Two of the stories deserve closer attention. In "The Photographs," two English scientists, or a Bob and Ray version of them, discuss, against the background of one's revelation of his affair with the other's wife, what they are to do with the photographs the practical-minded Reggie has inadvertently taken of the human soul. Their central exchange on the subject goes as follows:

"It seems to me to boil down to this: Are we better off *with* souls, or just possibly *without* them?"

"Yes. I see what you mean. You prefer the uncertainty."

"Exactly. It's more creative. Take for example, my, ah, arrangement with your wife, Dorothea. Stippled with uncertainty. . . . The humdrum is defeated. Momentarily, of course."

"Yes, I can understand that. Gives the thing a bit of zest."

"Yes. You'd be taking away people's zest. They'd all have to go around being good and all that." (*GP*, pp. 158-59)

And so they decide to burn the photographs, proving in two senses that, as Barthelme says in his introduction: "Guilty pleasures are the best."

The attack on certainty, hidden meanings, and depth is carried still further in one of the most subtle and funny of the fictions, "The Glass Mountain." Divided neatly and parodically into a hundred sections, so as to subvert the fairytale or romance form it reductively imitates, the story describes the narrator's successful ascent of the mountain, with its "sparkling blue-white depths" (*CL*, p. 66), and his discovery at the top of "the beautiful enchanted symbol." "I approached the symbol, with its layers of meaning," he writes in section 97, "but when I touched it, it changed into only a beautiful princess," whom he disposes of in the next section by throwing her "headfirst down the mountain to my acquaintances" (*CL*, p. 71). The motive for the quest is explained earlier on:

57. A few questions thronged into my mind.
58. Does one climb a glass mountain, at considerable personal discomfort, simply to disenchant a symbol?
59. Do today's stronger egos still *need* symbols?
60. I decided that the answer to these questions was "yes." (*CL*, p. 68)

The project of the story, and of others like it, is in fact precisely one of demystifying, of disenchanting—not, as among English writers of the thirties, language and the world, but the cultural imperatives (scientific, religious, psychological, governmental, and aesthetic) of the present and the past: of everything, in short, from Batman to the American Dream. As compared with the enchanted symbol, the narrator's acquaintances, shouting throughout the climb a volley of obscene discouragements and standing on the sidewalks below—which the narrator sees with a curiously radiant intensity as "full of dogshit in brilliant colors: ocher, umber, Mars yellow, sienna, viridian, ivory black, rose madder" (*CL*, p. 66)—are pure, disenchanted, phenomenal reality, and, so the story implies, all the better for that.

Barthelme's irony becomes in these stories, or—an important reservation—in those aspects of them I've isolated, something more, or less, than suspensive—or, more accurately, becomes suspensive in a richer and more complex way. (Part of the total effect of "The Glass Mountain" derives, certainly, from the narrator's blandly accepting, mountain's eye view of such sights as "hundreds of young people shooting up in doorways, behind parked cars" [*CL*, p. 66].) The rejection of certainty, even if the ostensible goal is no more definite than an uncommitted openness to experience, implies a less provisional attitude than that discussed earlier in this chapter. Indeed, the ability to sustain indefinitely an attitude of total, unqualified acceptance—unless one effectively neutralizes reality by genuinely and intransigently pursuing the high aesthetic road, as some practitioners of the *nouveau nouveau roman* and some reductive ironists I've looked at purport to do—requires something like the bemusement of one of Barthelme's city dwellers or the indifference of one of Hardy's gods. Small wonder, then, that at the very least Barthelme does, from time to time, actively recreate his sense of the ordinary or obliquely redefines his attitude toward it by setting off against them the dogmatisms that menace their integrity. But under the pressure of a more transitive irony, the ordinary may itself become the source not of resigned contemplation but of positive irritation, as it does to the letter writer of "The Sandman," who angrily asks his girl friend's psychiatrist: "What do you do with a patient who finds the world unsatisfactory?" and answers peremptorily: "The world *is* unsatisfactory; only a fool would deny it" (*S*, p. 93).

The answer is important, symptomatically, since any assertion of judgment necessarily threatens that resignation, which, rather than its emotional by-products, sadness or dailiness or the muted "lack of angst," determines Barthelme's strategy of acceptance, as it has so far revealed itself. Furthermore, any deviation from simple acceptance opens the way still further to an irony mediated by the impulse to correct or improve or assert—or, alternately, to a desire to abandon completely the world as perceived by the ironic imagination. In either case, to a position which obviously contravenes the neutrality of the purely suspensive. So, to take the extreme case, a handful of Barthelme's stories (they are, for the most part, early ones) suggest, in Tony Tanner's words, "the countering instinct to get away from matter altogether."[14] The Baudelairean longing expressed by the old woman in "Florence Green is 81" *"to go somewhere where everything is different"* elicits from the narrator the statement: "A simple, perfect idea. The old babe demands nothing less than total otherness" (*CB*, p. 15)—and from Tanner the comment that "although the idea is mocked, like every other idea offered as idea in Barthelme, this note of yearning for an unknown somewhere else sounds throughout his work" (p. 404). (Tanner is discussing only the first three books.) The same note sounds again, and again ambiguously, at the end of "A Shower of Gold," where the protagonist, Peterson, asserts against the wildly absurd situation in which he is involved (an antic, existentialist television program) his own identification with Perseus and Hamlet, that is, with classical and Renaissance traditions. He "went on and on," we're told, "and although he was, in a sense, lying, in a sense he was not" (*CB*, p. 183). It is even tempting to imagine that in the title of the volume from which these two stories come (*Come Back, Dr. Caligari*) there lurks, though with an altogether conscious perversity, a comically nostalgic longing for a lost order.

In any case, although one could point to other examples of this typically *modernist* anironic yearning in Barthelme's fiction—in "The President," for example, or in the ambiguously utopian portrait of "Paraguay," or, perhaps, in the remarks on equanimity in *Snow White* (pp. 87-88)—the strain is not, after all, as dominant as Tanner suggests, and it is effectively mocked in "A City of Churches," where both the heroine of the story and the discontent of the town itself refuse the completeness of perfection. Barthelme is, then, less seriously attracted by an escape into the realm of total otherness than by the temptation to find *within* the ordinary possibilities of a more dynamic response. The distinction is important. Modernist irony, seeking in the anironic some release from its own perception of fragmentation, characteristically imagines, as I suggested earlier, an image of total order. Whether the image is frankly of another world (Yeats's Byzantium) or of some symbolically sufficient enclave in this one (Howards End; the greenwood to which Forster's lovers flee in *Maurice*) or even of an ideal still to be, or only temporarily realized (Lawrence's star-balance; Woolf's lighthouse; Forster's "Only connect . . ."), in all of these cases the emphasis falls on a unity in which all discontinuity is comprehended and dissolved. Postmodern ironists are less sanguine; and rightly so, for the anironic has come to suggest in recent times as one of its possible and extreme realizations not resolution but annihilation. Through the looking-glass of contemporary chaos, one glimpses, as in late Forster, death or the death of consciousness—which may explain the concern with the apocalyptic in much recent fiction or with the self-abnegations of the minimalist and the aleatory in painting and music.

Still, if the present surrounds the ironist with a different and less hopeful context and offers him fewer possibilities of reconstruction or escape, his problems are, nevertheless, in some sense the same as his predecessors'. The change in irony over the past two hundred years from technique to vision has had as probably its most interesting result the transformation of distance (then and still one of the main aesthetic conditions for the successful functioning of irony) into a metaphor for a series of psychological and moral problems. Briefly, among the German Romantics, a source of freedom, mastery, and joy, distance gradually becomes the symbol of estrangement and alienation; and by the beginning of the twentieth century, it is, as I've tried to demonstrate, the figure of the outsider, the uncommitted spectator, longing to overcome his self-consciousness and make contact with the world outside his limited and limiting ego, that dominates the literary landscape of writers such as Eliot, Joyce, and Forster. If Barthelme differs from these authors, it is not because he perceives the tension between distance and involvement any less intensely. Indeed, he is in many ways far more conscious of the nature and implications of his irony. His originality lies, rather, as we shall see, in his treatment of the problem and in his solution to it.

But first the problem itself, which undergoes its most extended and ingenious exploration in "Kierkegaard Unfair to Schlegel." Against the background of a dialogue about the ineffectiveness of his political activities, "A," the transparently authorial respondent, gradually begins a defense of his own irony in terms of the power and control it confers on him. The introduction of Kierkegaard's *The Concept of Irony*, however, with its familiar but brilliantly summarized arguments about the ironist's subjective freedom, his alienation of existence, and his infinite absolute negativity, leads finally to A's admission that "mostly I am trying to annihilate Kierkegaard in order to deal with his disapproval" (*CL*, p. 97). The ultimate failure to do so becomes apparent in a conversation toward the end of the story between A and his interlocutor, Q:

A: But I love my irony.
Q: Does it give you pleasure?
A: A poor . . . A rather unsatisfactory. . . .
Q: The unavoidable tendency of everything particular to emphasize its own particularity.
A: Yes.
. . . .
Q (aside): He has given away his gaiety, and now has nothing. (*CL*, p. 99)

But that is not quite all. If the story charts A's loss of his freedom and particularity, it confirms, in its construction (the abrupt and apparently illogical cuts from one section to another, the absurdist elements, the narrative and tonal shifts), the power that Barthelme as author and ironist retains. The fundamental tension of "Kierkegaard Unfair to Schlegel" inheres, then, not in A's unwilling fall from ironic grace but in the disparity between that internal drama and the authorial techniques used to articulate it. Of course, much modernist literature exhibits the same tension—but with an important difference. Whereas Forster's formalist aesthetic acts as a continuous counterforce to his assertions of spontaneity and freedom (except when he lapses into a desperate sentimentality), Barthelme's more open form allows with a greater frequency for the congruence of the aesthetic and the experiential. To a degree at least, structure becomes a window not a frame. I don't want to exaggerate this point: a good deal of twentieth-century literature, as Mark Schorer has taught us, uses technique as discovery; and there is no lack of artifice in the fictions of Barth or Coover or Gass, not to mention the *nouveau* and the *nouveau nouveau roman*. A number of Barthelme's pieces too verge on the precious and the contrived, but what one senses in the best of his work is an effort to use art to overcome art (as the modernists characteristically employ consciousness to move beyond consciousness)—or, better still, an attempt, parallel to that in "The Glass Mountain," to disenchant the aesthetic, to make of it something not less special but less extraordinary.

The desire to tame the extraordinary relates back, in turn, to the question of irony and distance. Unlike the classic modernists attempting to annex the world to the self or to lose the self in the world (compare the crazed cry of Flaubert's St. Antoine: "descendre jusqu'au fond de la matière,—être la matière!" or Lily Briscoe's craving in *To the Lighthouse* for "unity," "intimacy," some "device for becoming, like waters poured into one jar, inextricably the same, one with the object one adored"), Barthelme has more modest aims. If, indeed, he is, as ironist, already part of the world around him and not its distant observer, if that world is, furthermore, perceived not as object but as field, and if, finally, the phenomenal presents itself not as the veil of appearance but as multiform, irreducible reality, then the notion of involving himself with, or of encompassing, all of life is in any case an impossibility. But the suspensive no less than the equivocal involves its psychological and moral distances, and Barthelme seems of late less willing or able to abide at least their more drastic manifestations. Forced to deconstruct the monster he has built "to instruct [him] in complacency," the narrator of "Subpoena" ends his story on a note of mounting hysteria: "Without Charles, without his example, his exemplary quietude, I run the risk of acting, the risk of risk. I must participate, I must leave the house and walk about." The last sentence may well cut two ways, slicing away at the narrator's objectless compulsion to act as much as at his earlier complacency; and the lesson he learns in looking at Charles—"See, it is possible to live in the world and not change the world" (S, p. 114)—may be read in different ways as well: as an attack on those who seek to impose their certainties or as the refutation of the value of passive acceptance. It seems best, in fact, to let the ambiguities of the story stand and to see in it Barthelme's attempt to narrow (in the words of a pompous character of an earlier tale) "the distance between the potential knowers holding a commonsense view of the world and what is to be known, which escapes them as they pursue their mundane existences" (CB, pp. 119-20)—between, that is to say, activity and awareness: the mutually implying alternatives of all ironists of this century.

But how then, exactly, does Barthelme go about narrowing the gap? In two ways. First, by a further series of rejections, which come, interestingly, among his several portraits of the artist. Earlier examples of these, especially "The Dolt" and "See the Moon?" have been extensively mined by critics seeking statements of Barthelme's aesthetic (fragments, collage, the difficulties of writing, and so on), but more revealing for purposes of the present discussion are the group in *Sadness*. All four, in one form or another—and in a way typical of twentieth-century considerations of the artist—concern themselves with the problem of the extraordinary. "The Flight of Pigeons from the Palace," the simplest and most immediately amusing (it is one of the picture stories) is a parable of the artist in an age of the conspicuous consumption of schlock, in which "the public demands new wonders piled on new wonders." "Some of us," the narrator admits ruefully, suggesting all those essays on the obsolescence or death of fiction, "have even thought of folding the show—closing it down"; and in its last lines, the story both confirms and mocks the notion of ever new wonders, which, "when you become familiar with them, are not wonderful at all," as, on a low-keyed, naive note of hope resurgent, it introduces one last marvel: "The new volcano we have just placed under contract seems very promising . . ." (*S*, p. 137). The reader, observing it, violently smoking, in the illustration just below, is left to judge the likely efficacy of this and other wonders constructed or discovered for the salvation of art.

Coming at the problem of the remarkable from a different angle in "The Genius" (the protagonist is in fact a scientist, but the equation with the artist will hold, I think), Barthelme exposes his much admired, much honored figure as self-conscious, vain, insecure, and inauthentic. At issue in both these very unlike stories is what may be called a *critique de la vie extraordinaire*, which is carried further in the far more subtle "Daumier," a wild farrago of a fiction, whose point is that "the self cannot be escaped, but it can be, with ingenuity and hard work, distracted. There are always openings, if you can find them, there is always something to do" (*S*, p. 181). The distractions are, of course, from the quotidian; the openings, for the most part, the ingenious inventions of art. "Daumier" traces its artist-hero's attempt to escape "the original, authentic self, which is a dirty great villain" through "the construction of surrogates" (*S*, p. 161). The surrogates are the vehicles for the fictions within the fiction, which are in turn punctuated by the original Daumier's reflections on the lively-dismal life around him and on the psychology of self-salvation implicit in his artistic efforts. To complicate matters, the two surrogates illustrate, roughly (since even in the first "desire has been reduced . . . to a minimum" [*S*, p. 162]), the conflict between the active and the contemplative: a reechoing of the problem of the story itself. Further, the *mise en abyme* of "Daumier" outdoes even Gide and Huxley and Coover, as Celeste, a figure from the first surrogate's adventures, enters into the artist's "real" life—where she is last seen domestically preparing him a *daube*. But if, in this movement from fiction to life (or rather, from the secondary to the primary level of the fiction within Barthelme's story of Daumier), there seems to have been an accommodation of the aesthetically dramatic and the psychologically distant to the ordinary, nonetheless it is the second surrogate who, literally, has the last, unsettling word, as Daumier repeats verbatim his less than sanguine comment on the availability of "openings." And it is, finally, the second surrogate, "the second-person Daumier" (S, p. 180) who, talking to himself about his inability to sustain any attachments, recognizes that he is "a tourist of the emotions" (S, p. 177), thereby acknowledging both the price one pays for trafficking with the extraordinary and, too, the inescapability of that "dirty great villain," the self. Ultimately, "Daumier" is a stand-off: not a solution to but a dramatization of the mazelike interrelationships and the even more profoundly immiscible qualities of art and life, the uncommon and the ordinary, the distant and the still unsatisfactory. Even if one overlooks Daumier's avowal that "there would be a time when I would not be happy and content," the assertion that he now is, "temporarily" (S, p. 180), remains both fantastic (to the degree that it depends upon the doubly fictive Celeste) and suspect. "Daumier," even as it playfully seeks to disenchant earlier images of the artist, in some sort reenforces them, becoming, as it were, Barthelme's most suspensively ironic tribute to the equivocal: a boisterous assault on, but never quite a disruption of, modernist poise.

"The Temptation of St. Anthony," on the other hand, whatever its difficulties, does take a stand. The story seems at first sight a fairly straightforward contrast between the saint, who represents, according to the narrator, "something pure and mystical, from the realm of the extraordinary, as it were," and the townspeople he lives among for a time, who, in their dislike of the ineffable, feel, with varying degrees of belligerency, that "the things of this earth are good enough for them" (S, p. 150). As one becomes more aware of the narrator, however, things seem less simple. Seeing himself as "sort of like a friend" (S, p. 151) to St. Anthony, he is a reasonably intelligent man, tolerant, sympathetic, capable of appreciating, if not altogether of understanding, the phenomenon he finds himself faced with. Indeed, his open-mindedness, his attempts, marked by endless qualifications, to be fair to all sides eventually irritate and force the reader to question, if not exactly to distrust, his view of things. There is no reason, for example, to doubt his opinion of the community, or his assertion, apropos of his friend, that "in the world of mundanity in which he found himself, he *shone*" (S, p. 157). But it is not at all clear that he recognizes the judgment the story passes on the saint, even though it derives directly from his own central perception: that "St. Anthony's major temptation, in terms of his living here, was perhaps this: ordinary life" (S, p. 152). In short, "The Temptation of St. Anthony," although it is by no means an encomium to conformity,

asserts, in its sympathetically critical portrait, the need for the extraordinary to find its place amidst the quotidian. And the retreat back to
the desert, marking a failure to do just that, indicates another stage in
Barthelme's questioning of the distance and the inadequate suspensiveness
that Anthony—parabolically the saint as artist or the artist as saint
—represents.

.   .   .

But if escape is unacceptable and if acceptance, in the sense of Ramona's
acquiescence, is not enough, what then? The fact is that increasingly in
Barthelme's work, if not consistently, mere acceptance is modified by a
more positive, more affirmative anironic attitude of *assent*; at which
point the Barthelme of this chapter becomes congruous with the generative
ironists—including Barthelme himself—described in chapter 5. Some clari-
fications are needed at this point. In the first place, the objects of Barthelme's or his characters' assent are remarkable not by virtue of being
outside or substantially different from common life. It is not a question of
discovering Bell's "ultimate reality" but of agreeing with Wilde that "the
true mystery of the world is the visible, not the invisible." The extraordinary exists as part of the phenomenal world or it doesn't, effectively,
exist at all. In the second place, even the use of the word "discovery," as if
one were constantly scrutinizing sidewalks and gutters for lucky pennies,
is misleading. What is at issue is not an essentialist but an existential
quest: a subjective, though not for that reason a random or arbitrary,
conferring of value, based on a continuing sense of the nature of *la vie
quotidienne*. So the letter-writing lover of "The Sandman," after his
outburst at his girl friend's normalizing psychiatrist, goes on: "What I am
saying is that Susan is wonderful. *As is.* There are not so many things
around to which that word can be accurately applied" (*S*, p. 93). Susan
may stand as another of Barthelme's emblems, this time of all the good a
flawed world has to offer—*as is*, depressions and *chasmus hystericus*
included—to someone who approaches it not, like her psychiatrist, *ab
extra*, but like her lover, whose approach is, by contrast, radically intentional and direct.

Barthelme's assent, then, is, as compared with Forster's in *The Life to
Come*, dynamic, exploratory, ongoing, experiential: the supervenient
alternative Ramona was unable to imagine. In some sense, of course,
Barthelme's fictions are themselves the best examples of his own particular form of assent—the prevalence of short stories itself, perhaps (or
of so loosely structured a novel as *The Dead Father*), the sign of a
preference or an affinity for mixed and modest pleasures, as opposed to
the larger and more final satisfactions sought by an earlier time. "How
joyous," ends "Nothing: A Preliminary Account," "the notion that, try as

we may, we cannot do other than fail and fail absolutely [at the task of defining nothing] and that the task will remain always before us, like a meaning for our lives" (*GP*, p. 165). Less derivatively and archly and in a more upbeat way, Barthelme suggests the nature of assent in "Engineer-Private Paul Klee Misplaces an Aircraft between Milbertshofen and Cambrai, March 1916," one of the most amusing and successful of his works. The incident to which the title of the story refers is the pretext for a contrast between Klee, the artist or man naturally at home in the world, an instinctive inhabitant, unlike St. Anthony, of the *Lebenswelt*, and, on the other hand—or rather, at a considerable remove—the Secret Police, who watch him as he discovers the loss of his plane and then as he decides to "diddle the manifest" (*S*, p. 69) in order to cover the loss. The Police, melancholy and inept, hidden from the world it is their duty to observe but by which they "yearn to be known, acknowledged, admired even" (*S*, p. 66), are the very type of distance and disengagement: unhappy gods exiled from the fullness of the creation. "We are secret," they announce lugubriously, "we exist in the shadows, the pleasure of the comradely/brotherly embrace is one of the pleasures we are denied, in our dismal service" (*S*, p. 70). Klee, by contrast, is an adept at pleasure, modest pleasures. Moving, by order, through the absurdity of a world at war, he finds time for "bread and wurst and beer" (*S*, p. 65), for paintings and reading, and for meetings with his Lily. Having reached his destination, he says to himself: "I wait contentedly in the warm orderly room. The drawing I did of the collapsed canvas and ropes is really very good. I eat a piece of chocolate. I am sorry about the lost aircraft but not overmuch. The war is temporary. But drawings and chocolate go on forever" (*S*, p. 70). I don't want to burden so light and joyous a story with the ponderous vocabulary of existential analysis. Enough to note that if Klee is inexplicably thrown into an absurd world, he manages nonetheless to enjoy thoroughly the openness and fecundity he also finds (or creates) in it, agreeing apparently with Heidegger that "the ordinary is basically not ordinary; it is extra-ordinary." Neither a rebel nor an accomplice, he accepts what he must and assents to what he can: a totally ingratiating model of *Dasein*, the contingency of being-in-the-world.

As one of the most attractive and attractively rendered figures in the stories, Klee offers himself as an obvious antithesis to Barthelme's Kierkegaard, the two suggesting in some ways the oppositional archetypes of their author's fictional universe. Humanistic, tolerant, nondirective, Klee intimates the possibility of irony (irony completed by the anironic ideal it implies) as a graceful, even integrative gesture toward the world. Kierkegaard, on the other hand, religious and prescriptive, presents irony, disapprovingly, as we've seen, as an infinite absolute negativity. However, as one traces Barthelme's movement (admittedly a serpentine and by no means consistent movement) from passive acceptance, through the rejection of dogmatisms and certainties, to assent, Kierkegaard gradually takes on a less monolithic typological significance. Leaving aside the religious question—and that is a large omission, of course—one can see that, in fact, Kierkegaard pronounces what Klee, less magisterially, to be sure, enacts: "What is wanted, Kierkegaard says, is not a victory over the world but a reconciliation with the world" (*CL*, pp. 95-96). To put it another way, as the self-viewed antagonist of Barthelme's ironic distance, his defensiveness, his infinite absolute negativity, Kierkegaard (or, more accurately, I suppose, the tradition he in part initiates) supplies precisely that existential-phenomenological background out of which Barthelme operates, even as he, not infrequently, parodies it. "As to 'deeper cultural sources,'" Barthelme said in response to one of Jerome Klinkowitz's questions, "I have taken a certain degree of nourishment (or stolen a lot) from the phenomenologists: Sartre, Erwin Straus, etc." (*TNF*, p. 52).

My argument, then, is that the modification of Barthelme's suspensive irony is precipitated by exactly that current of thought which has supplied twentieth-century artists with their visions of dailiness, absurdity, and drift. And inevitably so. For the postmodern writer, at least for those who refuse the lure of a new, reductive ultraformalism, there is no consolation in the thought of other, more perfect worlds—those artful spaces that haunt the modernist imagination. There is only the open, temporal field of the phenomenal, with which, in Barthelme's case, "reconciliation" is achieved through the homeopathic agency of his critiques of *la vie quotidienne* and *la vie extraordinaire*. Not, it needs to be stressed again, that assent (still sporadic, in any case) *replaces* acceptance in Barthelme's later work. No; if Barthelme differs from not only Sukenick but from Jean Ricardou, Philippe Sollers, and *Tel Quel* in his refusal of a purely aesthetic surface, he differs no less from the Forster of *The Life to Come* in denying that what Forster calls "the smaller pleasures of life" constitute the whole of it. For Barthelme, assent is added to without canceling the more generalized attitude of acceptance, as stories like "The Sandman" and, of course, "Engineer-Private Paul Klee"—and too *The Dead Father* —make clear.

To speak once more in terms of irony: no doubt much of the explanation for Barthelme's characteristic suspensiveness is to be found, as among other of his contemporaries, in his response to the confusion and multiplicity of his world; but more striking, if more speculative, is his effort to resist the subject-object dichotomy we have learned to recognize, in man's metaphysical imperalism, as the baneful inheritance of Cartesian and Romantic dualism—an attempt, in other words, to remain open to the experience of (nonmetaphysical) otherness. But if, to quote Pierre Thévenaz, one of the less well-known phenomenologists, "the world gives itself to consciousness," it is also the case that, Thévenaz continues, consciousness "confers on it its meaning"[15]—gives it, in a movement of reciprocity, its value. With figures such as Klee, then, Barthelme helps to define what we have already seen in writers like Elkin and Apple: not just another but, in every sense of the word, the most generative stage in the development of modern irony—one in which the gaps and discontinuities of twentieth-century literature, heretofore the mark of absence or negation, become instead the sign of a not yet constituted presence. Thus, no longer the familiar cause of horror or paralysis, they are transformed rather (as they are already in Woolf's *Between the Acts*) into the source of a continuing activity predicated on the need to choose, to confer meaning: to add to the humility of acceptance (even, or especially, of those gaps in which future meaning lies latent) the irreducibly human fuction of assent.

Both modernist and postmodern literature are less homogeneous than some critics like to imagine. Within the modernist camp, even within the fortress of Bloomsbury, as many still see it, counterforces to the ruling orthodoxy are discernible, not least the phenomenological strain that overtakes Woolf's work after *The Waves*. And among postmodernists, it is equally clear that the ascendency of the subjective, the open, and the temporal is threatened by a contemporary and exotic version of a supposedly discredited aestheticism. Sharp distinctions, then, are difficult and suspect. What *has* changed, or become apparent, in the course of the century, from Gide to Cortázar, is our sense of the space in which art and literature operate, that is, more fundamentally, the nature of our perceptions; and the lesson—if one can use so old-fashioned a word—of Barthelme's work is that a writer can, rejecting illusionist and psychological depth in fiction, nonetheless avoid the all too frequent banality of flatness, not by reimposing a metaphysical perspective or a theologically schematic world view, but by recognizing in what ways the dynamics of surface (of moral as well as aesthetic surface) are determined by an acknowledgment of the "horizons of the flesh."[16] Surface, in other words, may generate a particular, complex dimensionality of its own—or a depth of a kind different from that of classical perspective. So, as Merleau-Ponty writes: "The perceived thing is not an ideal unity in the possession of the intellect, like a geometrical notion, for example; it is rather a totality open to a horizon of an indefinite number of perspectival views which blend with one another according to a given style, which defines the object in question" (*PP*, p. 16). In a novel like *A Passage to India*, it is precisely the geometrizing of the universe—or the inability any longer to retain a belief in the Newtonian cosmos—that leads to breakdown, to a corrosive view of infinity. But the horizon of the phenomenal world is not an objective thing or place "out there"; it is the subjective, but no less real, result of being in the world: the shifting boundary of *human* depth, the pledge of man's necessary interaction with a world of which he is not only part but partner.

Barthelme's assumption of that partnership is manifest precisely in the movement from the relative passivity of acquiescence to the activity of decision and judgment (however tentative or qualified), which is implied in the transvalued irony of his assent and which is nowhere better illustrated than in the immensely attractive story "Rebecca." Burdened by her "ugly, reptilian, thoroughly unacceptable last name" (*Am*, p. 139), Lizard, by a judge's refusal to change it, by her equally unchangeable greenish complexion, and by a series of less dramatic frustrations, Rebecca precipitates a quarrel with her lover, Hilda, watches her world collapse around her, and sees it reconstitute itself, provisionally, imperfectly, but lovingly, with Hilda's invitation: "Come, viridian friend, come and sup with me" (p. 144). Funny and sad, the vignette is in itself testimony to the fragile, dubious strength of human relationships and to an acceptance of life altogether different from Ramona's. But the story, despite the apparent centrality of the two women, belongs, in fact, to the narrator, the intrusive, playful, partisan figure whose comments manage to engage the reader's sympathy and whose digressions and reflections avert its spillover into the sentimental. It is the narrator, always letting the reader know that he is in charge of, indeed the creator of, his fiction, who reserves for himself the last, nicely balanced, astringent and affirmative remarks: "The story ends. It was written for several reasons. Nine of them are secrets. The tenth is that one should never cease considering human love. Which remains as grisly and golden as ever, no matter what is tattooed upon the warm tympanic page" (p. 144). The final sentence, with its reminder of the ambiguous relations, or disjunctions, between life and art, provides besides, in its image of mechanical process (the tympanic page) and its moderating suggestion of human response (the warm page), a comment on the complexity of surface: the warm tympanic page, which, whatever its "objecthood," is also the sign of a vital depth, or, better still, the horizon of Barthelme's assent.

Barthelme's tympanic page is about as different as one can imagine from Sukenick's ideal of opaque surface, and it seems clear that, especially in the more generative of his fictions, he is increasingly writing himself out of membership in the bossanova club. Not that his work lends itself to a division into discrete, sequential stages. Ramona, Amanda, and Klee, though in different degrees at different times, all populate the Barthelmean landscape, suggesting the varied, overlapping impulses to accept, to reject, and to affirm (and suggesting as well the variousness of postmodern literature). The ludic strain in his work persists, not as a denial of meaning, of referentiality, but as an assertion of the artist's privilege to create meaning. And so too does the suspensiveness, not least in the sense that his work refuses the epistemological quest for ultimates and absolutes. Barthelme remains part of the world he perceives, approaching it through a process of interrogation to which he opens himself as well. Furthermore, life, as he sees it, not only refuses to offer up assurances and answers; it continues to be in large part, for human beings trying to make their way through it, frustrating, disjointed, and drab. "Rebecca," like other works discussed in the last two chapters, acknowledges the smaller pleasures against the background of a life still *fort quotidienne*. But, with all of this said, it is no less true that there is, at the least, a change of emphasis in Barthelme's later work: a sense that, Ramona notwithstanding, an alternative, the possibility of assent, does exist. In the final analysis, the alternative presents itself, however malapropos or offensive the word sounds to many today, as a humanism of sorts—less anthropocentric, less hopeful, to be sure, than that of the modernists; based instead, like Sartre's or Merleau-Ponty's, on an ethic of subjectivity and risk. Thus, if the necessary incompleteness of Barthelme's world is in one sense the definition of its persisting sadness, it is, in another, the source of its pleasures. Still, no doubt, as the title of one of his collections suggests, guilty pleasures—but the signs too of an active presence forging, tentatively, a morality, an ideal at any rate, and an irony for postmodern (or, possibly, post-postmodern?) man.

NOTES

Introduction

1. I'm thinking, for one, of Ronald Sukenick, who, in "Thirteen Digressions," *Partisan Review* 43 (1976), writes: "Irony, highly valued [by the New Criticism] as a means of control, becomes a form of suppression that chokes off libido" (p. 90). For a discussion of Sukenick's own work, see chapter 5. The essay will be referred to hereafter as *TD*.

2. Geoffrey Thurley, *The Ironic Harvest: English Poetry in the Twentieth Century* (London: Edward Arnold, 1974), p. 36. The phrase in my next sentence is from the same paragraph.

3. See Leo Spitzer's essay called "Linguistics and Literary History," in *Linguistics and Literary History: Essays in Stylistics* (Princeton: Princeton University Press, 1948), pp. 1-38, and especially pp. 18-20. On Spitzer as a predecessor of phenomenological criticism, see Robert R. Magliola's *Phenomenology and Literature: An Introduction* (West Lafayette, Ind.: Purdue University Press, 1977), p. 37.

4. See, for example, David Couzens Hoy's *The Critical Circle: Literature and History in Contemporary Hermeneutics* (Berkeley and Los Angeles: University of California Press, 1978).

5. Magliola, *Phenomenology and Literature*, p. 15.

6. John Ashbery, "Self-Portrait in a Convex Mirror," in *Self-Portrait in a Convex Mirror: Poems* (New York: Penguin Books, 1977), p. 70.

7. D. C. Muecke has published two books on the subject of irony: *The Compass of Irony* (London: Methuen & Co., 1969) and a shorter version called *Irony* in the Critical Idiom series (London: Methuen & Co., 1970).

8. Wayne C. Booth, *A Rhetoric of Irony* (Chicago: University of Chicago Press, 1974). See especially for the point I'm making chapters 1, 8, and 9.

9. Norman Knox, *The Word Irony and Its Context, 1500-1755* (Durham, N.C.: Duke University Press, 1961), p. 188.

10. For a discussion of irony in Diderot, see Jack Undank's *Diderot: Inside, Outside, and In-Between* (Madison, Wis.: Coda Press, 1979). On the subject of Romantic irony, see Peter Conrad's lively *Shandyism: The Character of Romantic Irony* (New York: Barnes & Noble-Harper & Row, 1978), a virtuoso essay that manages to shed light on almost everything except irony, and David Simpson's *Irony and Authority in Romantic Poetry* (Totowa, N.J.: Rowman & Littlefield, 1979). The critical literature on Kierkegaard and Nietzsche is too gargantuan for me to offer even cursory suggestions here.

11. Northrop Frye, *Anatomy of Criticism: Four Essays* (Princeton: Princeton University Press, 1957), p. 42.

12. Hayden White, *Metahistory: The Historical Imagination in Nineteenth-Century Europe* (Baltimore: Johns Hopkins University Press, 1973), pp. 434 and xii. Subsequent references to this book and to all other works quoted will be given, after their first citation, parenthetically in the text throughout this study.

13. Daniel O'Hara, review of *Of Grammatology*, by Jacques Derrida, in *Journal of Aesthetics and Art Criticism* 36 (Fall 1977): 362. I am especially grateful to O'Hara for our discussions of some of the critics considered here. Among younger critics, O'Hara and Paul Bové demonstrate in their work fruitful and incisive ways of dealing with the subject of irony.

14. On the fundamental conservatism of J. Hillis Miller's deconstructive criticism see William E. Cain's acute and persuasive essay, "Deconstruction in America: The Recent Literary Criticism of J. Hillis Miller," *College English* 41 (December 1979): 367-82. Since writing this introduction, I've had the opportunity to read Denis Donoghue's review essay, "Deconstructing Deconstruction" (*New York Review of Books*, 12 June 1980, pp. 37-41) in which, with his usual cogency and lucidity, Donoghue makes the case against deconstructive criticism and especially against de Man's version of it.

15. Paul de Man, *Allegories of Reading: Figural Language in Rousseau, Nietzsche, Rilke, and Proust* (New Haven: Yale University Press, 1979), p. 300.

16. Jonathan Culler, *Flaubert: The Uses of Uncertainty* (Ithaca, N.Y.: Cornell University Press, 1974), p. 211.

17. Gustave Flaubert, *L'Education sentimentale*, ed. E. Maynial (Paris: Editions Garnier Frères, 1964), p. 327.

18. W. H. Auden, "September 1, 1939," in Edward Mendelson, ed., *The English Auden: Poems, Essays and Dramatic Writings, 1927-1939* (London: Faber & Faber, 1977), p. 247. Throughout this book I've quoted, wherever possible, from this edition, but I have retained the more familiar titles of *The Collected Poetry* of 1945 (New York: Random House). The collection will be referred to hereafter as *EA*.

19. William Empson, *Seven Types of Ambiguity: A Study of Its Effects in English Verse*, 3d ed. (New York: Meridian Books-Noonday Press, 1955).

20. E. M. Forster, *A Room with a View*, Abinger ed., edited by Oliver Stallybrass (London: Edward Arnold, 1977), p. 126.

21. Virginia Woolf, "A Summing Up," in *A Haunted House and Other Short Stories*, new ed. (London: Hogarth Press, 1953), p. 140.

22. The phrase is from "The Tower," in *The Collected Poems of W. B. Yeats* (New York: Macmillan Co., 1951), p. 196.

23. Daniel Cahill, "An Interview with Jerzy Kosinski on *Blind Date*," *Contemporary Literature* 19 (Spring 1978): 142.

24. See chapters 2 and 5 for a fuller discussion of these phrases and the ideals they imply.

25. John Ashbery, "Tenth Symphony," in *Self-Portrait in a Convex Mirror*, pp. 46-47.

26. At least in the English-speaking world. I have attempted, wherever possible, to refer to French analogues in literature and criticism.

27. See, on this last point, Gabriel Josipovici's splendid book, *The Lessons of Modernism and Other Essays* (Totowa, N.J.: Rowman & Littlefield, 1977). My remarks do not necessarily apply to English critics, as the examples of Frank Kermode and David Lodge make clear.

28. John Barth, "The Literature of Replenishment: Postmodernist Fiction," *Atlantic*, January 1980, p. 67.

29. Vincent Descombes, *Le Même et l'Autre: quarante-cinq ans de philosophie française (1933-1978)* (Paris: Editions de Minuit, 1979), p. 82.

30. Maurice Merleau-Ponty, *The Prose of the World*, ed. Claude Lefort, trans. John O'Neill (London: Heinemann, 1974), pp. 124-25.

Chapter One

1. Donald Barthelme, *The Dead Father* (New York: Farrar, Straus & Giroux, 1975), pp. 3 and 14. The book will be referred to hereafter as *TDF*.

2. William V. Spanos, "The Detective and the Boundary: Some Notes on the Postmodern Literary Imagination," *boundary 2* 1 (Fall 1972): 158.

3. Renata Adler, *Speedboat* (New York: Random House, 1976), pp. 72-73.

4. F. C. McGrath, "The Plan of *The Waste Land*," *Modern British Literature* 1 (Fall 1976): 23.

5. Cleanth Brooks, *Modern Poetry and the Tradition* (Chapel Hill: University of North Carolina Press, 1939), p. 167. The book will be referred to hereafter as *MPT*.

6. T. S. Eliot, *The Complete Poems and Plays, 1909-1950* (New York: Harcourt, Brace & Co., 1952), pp. 47 and 49.

7. See Paul de Man, "The Rhetoric of Temporality," in *Interpretation: Theory and Practice*, ed. Charles S. Singleton (Baltimore: Johns Hopkins University Press, 1969), pp. 173-209.

8. Maurice Beebe, "What Modernism Was," *Journal of Modern Literature* 3 (July 1974): 1073.

9. See T. S. Eliot, *"Ulysses*, Order, and Myth," in *Criticism: The Foundations of Modern Literary Judgment*, ed. Mark Schorer, Josephine Miles, and Gordon McKenzie (New York: Harcourt, Brace & World, 1948), p. 270.

10. Of Cleanth Brooks's work, besides *Modern Poetry and the Tradition*, I'll be discussing *The Well Wrought Urn* (New York: Harcourt, Brace & World-Harvest Books, 1975) and "Irony as a Principle of Structure" (1949), in *Twentieth Century Criticism: The Major Statements*, ed. William J. Handy and Max Westbrook (New York: Free Press, 1974), pp. 59-70. The book and the essay will be referred to, respectively, as *WWU* and *IPS*.

11. For a more extensive treatment of Brooks than mine, see Paul Bové's stimulating and thoughtful essay, "Cleanth Brooks and Modern Irony: A Kierkegaardian Critique," *boundary 2* 4 (Spring 1976): 727-59. My discussion overlaps with Bové's at a number of points, but his implies in many ways a different conception of modernism from the one I'm arguing for here.

12. Murray Krieger, *The New Apologists for Poetry* (Minneapolis: University of Minnesota Press, 1956), p. 132. The book will be referred to hereafter as *NAP*.

13. Some of I. A. Richards's formulations about the nature of irony in *Principles of Literary Criticism* (New York: Harcourt, Brace & World-Harvest Books, 1972) seem to come closer to what I'm describing. But the context in which they appear—psychological rather than formal—limits their value for my argument. See pp. 247-53. The quotation is from E. M. Forster, *A Passage to India*, Abinger ed., edited by Oliver Stallybrass (London: Edward Arnold, 1978), p. 72. The novel will be referred to hereafter as *PI*.

14. Virginia Woolf, *Jacob's Room*, new ed. (London: Hogarth Press, 1954), p. 95.

15. E. M. Forster, "Art for Art's Sake," in *Two Cheers for Democracy*, Abinger ed., edited by Oliver Stallybrass (London: Edward Arnold, 1972), pp. 88 and 90. See Thomas M. McLaughlin, "Approaches to Order in Bloomsbury Criticism" (Ph.D. dissertation, Temple University, 1976). Forster's collection of essays will be referred to hereafter as *TC*.

16. Compare Krieger's reading of this passage, *NAP*, p. 193.

17. Robert Venturi, *Complexity and Contradiction in Architecture* (New York: Museum of Modern Art, 1968), pp. 46-47.

18. D. C. Muecke, *The Compass of Irony* (London: Methuen & Co., 1969), p. 123. Hereafter, I'll be quoting from Muecke's briefer version of that book, *Irony*, referred to as *I*.

19. Citing Friedrich Schlegel ("Irony is a form of paradox") and Connop Thirlwall, Muecke raises the possibility of what I have been calling genuine paradox (*I*, p. 22), but he

goes on to say that "this type of irony may be seen as consisting, none the less, of a contrasting reality and appearance" (*I*, p. 31).

20. Maurice Merleau-Ponty, "A Prospectus of His Work," trans. Arleen B. Dallery, in *The Primacy of Perception*, ed. James M. Edie (Evanston, Ill.: Northwestern University Press, 1964), p. 6. The book will be referred to hereafter as *PP*.

21. Maurice Merleau-Ponty, *Phenomenology of Perception*, trans. Colin Smith (London: Routledge & Kegan Paul, 1962), pp. xvi-xvii. Hereafter the book will be cited in the text as *PhP*.

22. I am referring, of course, to Booth's *A Rhetoric of Irony*. I have commented at greater length on the book in my review of it in the *Journal of Modern Literature* 4 (1975 Supplement): 942-43.

23. Alexander Pope, *An Essay on Man*, 4.371-72.

24. Ford Madox Ford, *The Good Soldier: A Tale of Passion* (New York: Vintage Books, 1960), p. 245.

25. Julio Cortázar, *Hopscotch*, trans. Gregory Rabassa (New York: Avon Books, 1966), p. 27.

26. Paul Valéry, quoted by Gerald L. Bruns in his book *Modern Poetry and the Idea of Language* (New Haven: Yale University Press, 1974), p. 81.

27. Søren Kierkegaard, *The Concept of Irony*, trans. Lee M. Capel (New York: Harper & Row, 1965), p. 221.

28. Virginia Woolf, "Monday or Tuesday," in *A Haunted House and Other Short Stories*, new ed. (London: Hogarth Press, 1953), p. 12. Since the whole of the brief piece appears on pp. 12-13, I have not documented my further references to it.

29. Virginia Woolf, "How It Strikes a Contemporary," in *Collected Essays*, ed. Leonard Woolf, 4 vols. (New York: Harcourt, Brace & World, 1967), 2:156.

30. William Troy, "Virginia Woolf: The Novel of Sensibility," in *Virginia Woolf: A Collection of Critical Essays*, ed. Claire Sprague (Englewood Cliffs, N.J.: Prentice-Hall, 1971), p. 28.

31. Alan Friedman, *The Turn of the Novel* (New York: Oxford University Press, 1966), p. 16. See pp. xv-xvi for Friedman's distinction between his own approach and that of Robert M. Adams in *Strains of Discord: Studies in Literary Openness* (Ithaca, N.Y.: Cornell University Press, 1958).

32. *The Collected Poems of W. B. Yeats* (New York: Macmillan Co., 1951), p. 234.

33. I am arguing here not only against Friedman's interpretation but also in opposition to my own earlier reading of the novel in *Art and Order: A Study of E. M. Forster* (New York: New York University Press, 1964). See especially pp. 155-58.

34. Barbara Herrnstein Smith, *Poetic Closure: A Study of How Poems End* (Chicago: University of Chicago Press, 1970). See especially chapter 4.

35. *The Portable James Joyce*, ed. Harry Levin (New York: Viking Press, 1948), p. 481.

36. Wayne C. Booth, *The Rhetoric of Fiction* (Chicago: University of Chicago Press, 1961), pp. 327-28.

37. Samuel Beckett, *Molloy*, in *Three Novels by Samuel Beckett* (New York: Grove Press, 1965), pp. 85 and 176.

38. *The English Auden*, pp. 243-44. Unless otherwise indicated, subsequent references to Auden's poems, preceded by *EA*, as well as to *Paid on Both Sides*, will, as noted earlier, be to this edition.

39. W. H. Auden and Christopher Isherwood, *The Dog Beneath the Skin*, in *Two Great Plays* (New York: Random House-Modern Library, 1959), p. 97. The other "great play" is *The Ascent of F 6*. This volume will be referred to as *TGP*.

40. For a fuller discussion of these problems, see chapter 3.

41. The last two references are to Jerome Klinkowitz's *Literary Disruptions: The Making of a Post-Contemporary American Fiction* (Urbana: University of Illinois Press, 1975), and Erich Kahler's *The Disintegration of Form in the Arts* (New York: George Braziller, 1968).

42. See Jacques Derrida, *Positions* (Paris: Editions de Minuit, 1972), p. 17.

43. See chapter 6.

44. Christopher Isherwood, *Down There on a Visit* (New York: Simon & Schuster, 1962), p. 162.

45. Virginia Woolf, *Between the Acts* (London: Hogarth Press, 1953), p. 32.

46. Max Apple, *The Oranging of America and Other Stories* (New York: Grossman Publishers-Viking Press, 1976), p. 45.

Chapter Two

1. Betsy Draine, "An Interview with Angus Wilson," *Contemporary Literature* 21 (Winter 1980): 13.

2. Lionel Trilling, "George Orwell and the Politics of Truth," *The Opposing Self: Nine Essays in Criticism* (London: Secker & Warburg, 1955), p. 156. The quotation in the next sentence appears on the same page.

3. P. N. Furbank, "The Personality of E. M. Forster," *Encounter* 35 (November 1970): 65. Furbank deals with Forster's moralizing throughout his biography, *E. M. Forster: A Life*, 2 vols. (London: Secker & Warburg, 1977-78). The essay will be referred to hereafter as *TPF*.

4. E. M. Forster, *Goldsworthy Lowes Dickinson*, p. 97. Wherever possible my references to Forster's works derive from the Abinger Edition, edited by Oliver Stallybrass (London: Edward Arnold). The dates that follow are those of original publication and of the Abinger volumes: *Where Angels Fear to Tread* (1905; 1975); *A Room with a View* (1908; 1977); *Howards End* (1910; 1973), referred to as *HE*; *A Passage to India* (1924; 1978) referred to as *PI*; *Aspects of the Novel* (1927; 1974), referred to as *AN*; *Goldsworthy Lowes Dickinson* (1934; 1973); *Two Cheers for Democracy* (1951; 1972), referred to as *TC*; *The Life to Come and Other Stories* (1972). Other references are to *The Longest Journey* (New York: Vintage Books, n.d.) and *Maurice* (New York: Norton, 1971).

5. Leonard Woolf, *Sowing* (London: Hogarth Press, 1967), p. 161.

6. Pierre Francastel, *Peinture et Société* (Paris: Gallimard, 1965), pp. 199 and 212.

7. C. S. Lewis, "A Note on Jane Austen," in *Discussions of Jane Austen*, ed. William Heath (Boston: Heath, 1961), p. 60.

8. Alan Wilde, *Art and Order: A Study of E. M. Forster* (New York: New York University Press, 1964), p. 11 and chapter 2, passim.

9. Fielding, as we now know, was originally to have had the vision in the cave. See June Perry Levine, *Creation and Criticism: A Passage to India* (Lincoln: University of Nebraska Press, 1971), pp. 85-86.

10. J. Hillis Miller, *Poets of Reality* (Cambridge: Harvard University Press, 1965), p. 3.

11. See *The Collected Letters of D. H. Lawrence*, ed. Harry T. Moore, 2 vols. (New York: Viking Press, 1962), 2:316-20.

12. Levine, *Creation and Criticism*, p. 119.

13. Frederick P. W. McDowell, "By and About Forster: A Review Essay," *English Literature in Transition* 15 (1972): 321.

14. See Wilde, *Art and Order*, p. 151, n. 8.

15. See Forster's terminal note to *Maurice*, p. 250.

16. See my book *Christopher Isherwood* (New York: Twayne Publishers, 1971), part 1.

17. Wylie Sypher, *Literature and Technology* (New York: Random House, 1968), pp. 106-107.

18. W. H. Auden, "We Too Had Known Golden Hours," in *Collected Shorter Poems, 1927-1957* (New York: Random House, 1967), p. 318.

19. Paul Valéry, "Aurore," *Poésies* (Paris: Gallimard, 1942), p. 86.

20. For a discussion of Pan and Priapus and the recurrence of ideated desire in Forster's work, see my essay, "The Naturalisation of Eden," in *E. M. Forster: A Human Exporation*, ed. G. K. Das and John Beer (London: Macmillan Press, 1979), pp. 196-207.

21. See, especially, the books already referred to by Miller and Sypher and Alain Robbe-Grillet's *Pour un nouveau roman*, translated by Richard Howard as *For a New Novel* (New York: Grove Press, 1965). Also relevant to much of what I've tried to say in this essay is Wilhelm Worringer's seminal work *Abstraction and Empathy*, trans. Michael Bullock (Cleveland: Meridian Books, 1967).

22. Sypher, *Literature and Technology*, p. 239.

23. From an interview with Robert Bechtle, *Art in America* 60 (November-December 1972): 74.

24. Robbe-Grillet, *For a New Novel*, p. 72.

25. Virginia Woolf, *The Years* (London: Hogarth Press, 1951), p. 379.

26. Quoted by Elizabeth Ellem, in "E. M. Forster: The Lucy and New Lucy Novels," *Times Literary Supplement*, 28 May 1971, p. 623. Stallybrass, in his edition of *Where Angels Fear to Tread*, provides a slightly different version of the passage, which includes commas after the words "mine" and "oh" (p. 158).

27. However important the distinction is in the case of many, perhaps most, other modern writers, there seems to me little reason to distinguish between Forster's narrators and the implied authors of the novels. See Francis Gillen's *"Howards End* and the Neglected Narrator," *Novel* 3 (Winter 1970): 139-52. Gillen's argument is subtle but, for me, ultimately unconvincing.

28. The phrase is used by one of Angus Wilson's characters in *As If by Magic* (London: Secker & Warburg, 1973), p. 415.

29. See Elizabeth Ellem's fascinating study of the manuscripts of the novel, "E. M. Forster's *Arctic Summer*," *Times Literary Supplement*, 21 September 1973, pp. 1087-89.

30. See the discussion of Forster's tales in my book *Art and Order*, chapter 3.

31. There is, however, the problem of Forster's "unliberated" attitudes toward homosexuality. See Samuel Hynes, "Forster's Cramp," in *Edwardian Occasions* (New York: Oxford University Press, 1972), p. 121; Frederick P. W. McDowell, "Second Thoughts on E. M. Forster's *Maurice*," *Virginia Woolf Quarterly* 1 (Fall 1972): 47; and George Steiner, "Under the Greenwood Tree," *The New Yorker*, 9 October 1971, p. 165.

32. See Jeffrey Meyers, "'Vacant Heart and Hand and Eye': The Homosexual Theme in *A Room with a View*," *English Literature in Transition* 13 (1970): 181-92. The essay has been reprinted in Meyers's book, *Homosexuality in Literature, 1870-1930* (London: Athlone Press, 1977), pp. 90-99.

33. Noel Annan, "Love Story," *New York Review of Books*, 21 October 1971, p. 15. The quotation later in the paragraph is from p. 17 of the review.

34. In *E. M. Forster: A Life*, Furbank places Forster's "first full physical encounter" in 1916 (2:35). See also 2:40.

35. D. H. Lawrence, *Women in Love* (New York: Viking Press, 1962), p. 35.

36. See Strachey's letter to Forster (12 March 1915) in *E. M. Forster: The Critical Heritage*, ed. Philip Gardner (London: Routledge & Kegan Paul, 1973), p. 430.

37. The phrase appears in a manuscript version of the passage quoted immediately below. See Oliver Stallybrass's *The Manuscripts of Howards End*, Abinger ed. (London: Edward Arnold, 1973), p. 235.

38. This and the quotation later in the paragraph are from "A Dialogue of Self and Soul," in *The Collected Poems of W. B. Yeats* (New York: Macmillan Co., 1951), pp. 230 and 231.

39. E. M. Forster, "The Mission of Hinduism," in *Albergo Empedocle and Other Writings*, ed. George H. Thomson (New York: Liveright, 1971), p. 227.

40. John Fraser, *Violence in the Arts* (Cambridge: At the University Press, 1974), p. 39.

41. Stallybrass is quoting from two of Forster's letters. See his introduction to *The Life to Come*, p. xvi.

42. Forster, quoted by Meyers, in his essay "Vacant Heart," from *Letters to T. E. Lawrence*, ed. A. W. Lawrence (London: Jonathan Cape, 1962), p. 72.

43. Sypher, *Literature and Technology*, pp. 102 and 240.

Chapter Three

1. In an introductory statement to the Penguin edition of *Goodbye to Berlin* (Harmondsworth, Middlesex, 1962), Isherwood writes: "'Christopher Isherwood' is a convenient ventriloquist's dummy, nothing more" (p. 6). Isherwood's full name is Christopher William Bradshaw-Isherwood.

2. Christopher Isherwood, "To the Reader," in *Lions and Shadows* (Norfolk, Conn.: New Directions, 1947), p. 7.

3. Virginia Woolf, "The Leaning Tower," in *Collected Essays*, ed. Leonard Woolf, 4 vols. (New York: Harcourt, Brace & World, 1967), 2:177. Subsequent references to Woolf in this chapter are to this essay.

4. Michael Roberts, *New Country* (London: Hogarth Press, 1933), p. 20.

5. The term is Robin Skelton's. See the introduction to his admirable edition, *Poetry of the Thirties* (Harmondsworth, Middlesex: Penguin Books, 1964), p. 32.

6. The sources of the three quotations are as follows: Stephen Spender, "In railway halls, on pavements near the traffic," in *Collected Poems, 1928-1953* (New York: Random House, 1955), p. 44; Louis MacNeice, "Autumn Journal," in *Collected Poems, 1925-1948* (London: Faber & Faber, 1954), p. 151; and Wyndham Lewis, *One-Way Song* (London: Methuen & Co., 1960), p. 132.

7. Robert Graves and Alan Hodge, *The Reader over Your Shoulder: A Handbook for Writers of English Prose*, 2d ed., rev. and abr. (London: Jonathan Cape, 1947), p. 39. The book was first published in 1943.

8. Michael Roberts, *Critique of Poetry* (London: Jonathan Cape, 1934), p. 86.

9. "August for the people and their favourite islands," *EA*, p. 157.

10. Christopher Isherwood, *The Berlin Stories* (New York: New Directions, 1954), pp. 86-87. Further references are to this edition. To avoid possible confusion (the volume preserves the separate pagination of each novel), page references in the text will be preceded by N (*The Last of Mr. Norris*) or G (*Goodbye to Berlin*).

11. For a more detailed discussion of Isherwood's style, see my book *Christopher Isherwood* (New York: Twayne Publishers, 1971), especially pp. 14-18. Chapters 4 and 5 of the book present analyses of *Mr. Norris* and *Goodbye to Berlin*, respectively.

12. See Richard Ohmann's two essays, "Speech, Literature, and the Space Between," *New Literary History* 4 (Autumn 1972): 50, and "Speech, Action, and Style," in *Literary Style: A Symposium*, ed. Seymour Chatman (London: Oxford University Press, 1971), p. 252.

13. Edward Upward, *The Railway Accident and Other Stories* (London: Heinemann, 1969), p. 58.

14. W. H. Auden and Christopher Isherwood, *The Dog Beneath the Skin*, in *TGP*, pp. 16-17. Hereafter the play will be referred to in the text as *Dog*.

15. See David P. Thomas, "*Goodbye to Berlin*: Refocusing Isherwood's Camera," *Contemporary Literature* 13 (Winter 1972): 44-52, and the fifth chapter of my book *Christopher Isherwood*, especially pp. 66-68.

16. Henry Malcolm, *Generation of Narcissus* (Boston: Little, Brown & Co., 1971), p. 145.

17. "Why I Write," in *The Collected Essays, Journalism and Letters of George Orwell*, ed. Sonia Orwell and Ian Angus, 4 vols. (New York: Harcourt, Brace & World, 1968), 1:7.

18. *Paid on Both Sides, EA*, p. 12.

19. Keith Aldritt, *The Making of George Orwell* (London: Edward Arnold, 1969), p. 55.

20. See, in particular, Norman Friedman, "Point of View in Fiction: The Development of a Critical Concept," *PMLA* 70 (December 1955): 1178-79.

21. Stephen Spender, *The Destructive Element: A Study of Modern Writers and Beliefs* (Boston: Houghton Mifflin, 1936), p. 205.

22. C. Day Lewis, "Learning to Talk," in *Collected Poems* (London: Jonathan Cape with Hogarth Press, 1954), p. 125.

23. See George Orwell, "Inside the Whale," in *Collected Essays*, 1:510-19.

24. W. H. Auden, "We Too Had Known Golden Hours," in *Collected Shorter Poems, 1927-1957* (New York: Random House, 1967), p. 318.

25. George Orwell, "Looking Back on the Spanish War," in *Collected Essays*, 2:249.

26. "Not All the Candidates Pass," in *The Collected Poetry of W. H. Auden* (New York: Random House, 1945), pp. 84-85. These lines (and many others) were dropped in the *Collected Shorter Poems*, where the poem is called "The Watchers." The word "dishonest" was originally "personal." See *EA*, p. 116.

27. Both quotations are from MacNeice's "Snow," in *Collected Poems*, p. 86.

28. Christopher Isherwood, *Christopher and His Kind, 1929-1939* (New York: Farrar, Straus & Giroux, 1976), p. 2. For a fuller discussion of this book see my review of it in the *Journal of Modern Literature* 6 (1977 Supplement): 484-86.

Chapter Four

1. Forster's letter, in which this remark appears, is quoted by Isherwood, in *Christopher and His Kind, 1929-1939* (New York: Farrar, Straus & Giroux, 1976), pp. 203-4. It can also be found in P. N. Furbank's *E. M. Forster: A Life*, 2 vols. (London: Secker & Warburg, 1977-78), 2:209, where an additional sentence is included.

2. Raymond Federman, "Surfiction—Four Propositions in Form of an Introduction," in *Surfiction: Fiction Now . . . and Tomorrow*, ed. Raymond Federman (Chicago: Swallow Press, 1975), pp. 12-13.

3. Virginia Woolf, "Mr. Bennett and Mrs. Brown," in *Collected Essays*, ed. Leonard Woolf, 4 vols. (New York: Harcourt, Brace & World, 1967), 1:320.

4. Virginia Woolf, *Jacob's Room*, new ed. (London: Hogarth Press, 1954), p. 29.

5. See, for example, the following critics: Charles Burkhart, *I. Compton-Burnett* (London: Victor Gollancz, 1965), p. 115; Pamela Hansford Johnson, *I. Compton-Burnett* (London: Longmans, Green for the British Council and the National Book League, 1951), p. 33; and William York Tindall, *Forces in Modern British Literature, 1885-1956* (New York: Vintage Books, 1956), p. 108.

6. R. Glynn Grylls, *I. Compton-Burnett* (London: Longman Group for the British Council, 1971), p. 3.

7. Ivy Compton-Burnett, *Manservant and Maidservant* (London: Victor Gollancz, 1959), p. 5. The novel was first published in 1947. It was published in America as *Bullivant and the Lambs*.

8. For John Gardner's recent attack on the concern with texture in postmodern writing, see *On Moral Fiction* (New York: Basic Books, 1978), pp. 65-72.

9. Jacques Rivière, *The Ideal Reader*, ed. and trans. Blanche A. Price (New York: Meridian Books, 1960), p. 248. The essay was written between 1919 and 1925.

10. Greater strains are put on the reader in the still less verisimilar later novels, which, it seems to me, make even more completely the argument for reading Compton-Burnett's characters in terms of surface.

11. So Burkhart is able to speak, somewhat oddly, of Compton-Burnett's characters as "conceived vitally, complexly, fully" and to describe the novels as "full of round characters" (p. 65), whereas Wolfgang Iser writes, much more persuasively, in *The Implied Reader* (Baltimore: Johns Hopkins University Press, 1974), of "the apparently inexplicable inconsistencies of the characters" (p. 163).

12. It is worth recording Burkhart's comment on the novel: "The author here has essayed *the unusual subject, for her,* of showing a change in character" (p. 115; my italics).

13. Compton-Burnett was born in 1884, that is, a year before D. H. Lawrence, and two years later than Joyce and Virginia Woolf.

14. There is a description of Bullivant, who "returned with a face that might have been a mask, and was one, if a mask is a cover for what is behind" (p. 107), which neatly makes the distinction between secrets and depths.

15. But compare Iser's remark: "Once the self as the point of reference has gone, characters become characterless" (p. 251). See, too, note 11, above.

16. "The novels of Miss Compton-Burnett," Pamela Hansford Johnson writes, "break the most rigid convention of all literature: that in some manner or other, however oblique, retribution must fall upon the unjust. . . . She is the most amoral of living writers" (p. 11).

17. Nathalie Sarraute, "Conversation et sous-conversation," in *L'Ere du soupçon* (Paris: Gallimard, 1956), p. 123.

18. William Gass, *On Being Blue* (Boston: David R. Godine, [1975]), p. 58. The book will be referred to hereafter as *OBB.*

19. Ronald Sukenick, *The Death of the Novel and Other Stories* (New York: Dial Press, 1969), p. 41.

20. Muriel Spark, *The Takeover* (Harmondsworth, Middlesex: Penguin Books, 1978), p. 72.

21. For a recent and relevant discussion of character and the novel, see "Character as a Lost Cause," ed. Mark Spilka, *Novel* 11 (Spring 1978): 197-217.

Chapter Five

1. The phrase is, of course, from Joyce's *Ulysses* (New York: Random House, 1934), p. 682.

2. T. S. Eliot, *The Complete Poems and Plays, 1909-1950* (New York: Harcourt, Brace & Co., 1952), p. 13.

3. Virginia Woolf, *To the Lighthouse*, new ed. (London: Hogarth Press, 1967), p. 99.

4. Raymond Olderman in *Beyond the Waste Land: A Study of the American Novel in the Nineteen-Sixties* (New Haven: Yale University Press, 1972) relates two of Elkin's earlier novels to Eliot's work. See chapters 2 and 6 of his book.

5. Stanley Elkin, *The Bailbondsman*, in *Searches and Seizures* (Boston: David R. Godine-Nonpareil Books, n.d.), p. 107. The book was first published in 1973.

6. The image is derived from William V. Spanos's essay, "The Detective and the Boundary: Some Notes on the Postmodern Literary Imagination," *boundary 2* 1 (Fall 1972). The whole of the essay is relevant to the point I'm making.

7. For the distinction between order and orderliness (Louis Kahn's), see Robert Venturi, *Complexity and Contradiction in Architecture* (New York: Museum of Modern Art, 1968), pp. 46-47. The passage is quoted in part at the beginning of the second section of my first chapter.

8. Stanley Sultan in *Ulysses, The Waste Land, and Modernism* (Port Washington, N.Y.: Kennikat Press, 1977) uses the term "suspended (or inconclusive) ending" to characterize modernist literature, but the endings of modernist works (indeed such works in general) seem to me, it must be clear by now, less suspended or suspensive than equivocal, as I've suggested in my description of absolute irony. See chapter 6 of Sultan's study, especially pp. 59-60.

9. Max Apple, "Free Agents," *Iowa Review* 8 (Fall 1977): 44.

10. Donald Barthelme, *Great Days* (New York: Farrar, Straus & Giroux, 1979), p. 95. The book will be referred to hereafter as *GD*.

11. (1) Raymond Federman, *Take It or Leave It* (New York: Fiction Collective, 1976), n. pag.; (2) Venturi, *Complexity and Contradiction in Architecture*, p. 22; (3) Campbell Tatham, "Mythotherapy and Postmodern Fictions: Magic Is Afoot," in *Performance in Postmodern Culture*, ed. Michel Benamou and Charles Caramello (Madison, Wis.: Coda Press, 1977), p. 137; (4) Ronald Sukenick, *98.6* (New York: Fiction Collective, 1975), p. 167; (5) J. Hillis Miller, "Stevens' Rock and Criticism as Cure, II," *Georgia Review* 30 (Summer 1976): 337 and 341; (6) Ralph Goings, quoted in "The Photo-Realists: 12 Interviews," *Art in America* 60 (November-December 1972): 88; (7) Kurt Vonnegut, Jr., *Breakfast of Champions* (New York: Dell Publishing Co., 1975), p. 210; (8) Robert Coover, "J's Marriage," in *Pricksongs and Descants* (New York: New American Library, 1970), p. 117; (9) Renata Adler, *Speedboat* (New York: Random House, 1976), pp. 134-35; (10) Barthelme, "The Crisis," *GD*, p. 8; (11) T. Coraghessan Boyle, "Drowning," in *Descent of Man* (Boston: Little, Brown & Co., 1979), p. 219; (12) Don DeLillo, *Players* (New York: Alfred A. Knopf, 1977), p. 32; (13) Joan Didion, *Play It as It Lays* (New York: Farrar, Straus & Giroux, 1970), p. 214.

12. Raymond Federman, "Fiction Today or the Pursuit of Non-Knowledge," *Humanities in Society* 1 (Spring 1978): 122.

13. Gerald Graff, *Literature Against Itself: Literary Ideas in Modern Society* (Chicago: University of Chicago Press, 1979), p. 172.

14. Gabriel Josipovici, *The Lessons of Modernism and Other Essays* (Totowa, N.J.: Rowman & Littlefield, 1977), p. 111.

15. From a letter by Sukenick, quoted as an epigraph to Raymond Federman's "Surfiction—Four Propositions in Form of an Introduction," in *Surfiction: Fiction Now . . . and Tomorrow* (Chicago: Swallow Press, 1975), p. 5. I haven't reproduced Federman's italics, which I assume are a typographical convenience.

16. Ronald Sukenick, "The Death of the Novel," in *The Death of the Novel and Other Stories* (New York: Dial Press, 1969), p. 41. The first quoted phrase in the sentence that follows is from the same page.

17. Robert Scholes, "Toward a Semiotics of Literature," *Critical Inquiry* 4 (Autumn 1977): 111.

18. Robert Alter, *Partial Magic: The Novel as a Self-Conscious Genre* (Berkeley and Los Angeles: University of California Press, 1978), p. x.

19. Larry McCaffery, "The Fiction Collective," *Contemporary Literature* 19 (Winter 1978): 109.

20. The novel is unpaginated, and so there can be no references to the text.

21. Donald Barthelme, "The Great Hug," in *Amateurs* (New York: Farrar, Straus & Giroux, 1976), p. 46. The book will be referred to hereafter as *Am*.

22. Allan Rodway, "There's a Hole in Your Beckett," *Encounter* 42 (February 1974): 50 and 53. The essay is a review of A. Alvarez's *Beckett*.

23. William Gass, "In Terms of the Toenail: Fiction and the Figures of Life," *Fiction and the Figures of Life* (New York: Alfred A. Knopf, 1970), p. 57.

24. William Gass, "Three Photos of Colette," in *The World Within the Word* (New York: Alfred A. Knopf, 1978), pp. 144-45. The book will be referred to hereafter as *WWW*.

25. Clive Bell, *Art* (New York: Capricorn Books, 1958), p. 31.

26. Maurice Merleau-Ponty, *The Visible and the Invisible*, ed. Claude Lefort, trans. Alphonso Lingis (Evanston, Ill.: Northwestern University Press, 1968), p. 136.

27. Thomas Pynchon, *The Crying of Lot 49* (New York: Bantam Books, 1967), p. 59.

28. For Scott Sanders, in "Pynchon's Paranoid History," *Twentieth Century Literature* 21 (May 1975): 177-92, Pynchon is, in effect, as paranoid as his characters. But see Tony Tanner's more subtle and ambiguous reading of *Lot 49* in *City of Words: American Fiction, 1950-1970* (New York: Harper & Row, 1971), pp. 173-80.

29. Lawrence Alloway, *Topics in American Art Since 1945* (New York: Norton & Co., 1975), p. 132.

30. Robert Venturi, Denise Scott Brown, and Steven Izenour, *Learning from Las Vegas: The Forgotten Symbolism of Architectural Form*, rev. ed. (Cambridge, Mass.: MIT Press, 1977), pp. 161-62.

31. Robert Indiana, quoted from an interview by John Russell, "Persistent Pop," *New York Times Magazine*, 21 July 1974, p. 27.

32. For a fuller discussion of the connection, see chapter 6.

33. For discussions of ordinariness in *The Origin of the Brunists* and *The Universal Baseball Association, Inc.*, see Margaret Heckard, "Robert Coover, Metafiction, and Freedom," *Twentieth Century Literature* 22 (May 1976): 222-26; and Kathryn Hume, "Robert Coover's Fiction: The Naked and the Mythic," *Novel* 12 (Winter 1979): 134-36.

34. See, for example, Jerome Klinkowitz, *Literary Disruptions: The Making of a Post-Contemporary American Fiction* (Urbana: University of Illinois Press, 1975), pp. 17-18; but also Neil Schmitz's attack on Coover's reflexiveness, "Robert Coover and the Hazards of Metafiction," *Novel* 7 (Spring 1974): 210-19.

35. Lawrence Alloway uses the phrase in *American Pop Art* (New York: Collier Books, 1974), p. 21.

36. Virginia Woolf, "The Mark on the Wall," in *A Haunted House and Other Short Stories*, new ed. (London: Hogarth Press, 1953), p. 42.

37. Paul Ricoeur, *Interpretation Theory: Discourse and the Surplus of Meaning* (Fort Worth: Texas Christian University Press, 1976), p. 88. And see also pp. 19-22.

38. Stanley Elkin, *The Living End* (New York: Dutton, 1979), p. 136.

39. Max Apple, "The Oranging of America," in *The Oranging of America and Other Stories* (New York: Grossman Publishers-Viking Press, 1976), pp. 11 and 5. All of my references are to this volume, except for those to the uncollected "Disneyad," which was published in the final issue of *American Review* 26 (November 1977): 195-212.

Chapter Six

1. Richard Gilman, in *The Confusion of Realms* (New York: Vintage Books, 1970), accurately describes the "new reality" he sees Barthelme articulating as characterized "by horizontal impulses rather than vertical ones" (p. 43).

2. Virginia Woolf, *A Writer's Diary*, ed. Leonard Woolf (New York: Harcourt, Brace & Co., 1954), p. 27.

3. References to Barthelme's works will be given in the text and are to the following editions (the abbreviations used are indicated): *CB: Come Back, Dr. Caligari* (Boston: Little, Brown & Co., 1964); *SW: Snow White* (New York: Bantam Books, 1971); *UP: Unspeakable Practices, Unnatural Acts* (New York: Bantam Books, 1969); *CL: City Life* (New York:

Bantam Books, 1971); *S: Sadness* (New York: Bantam Books, 1974); *GP: Guilty Pleasures* (New York: Farrar, Straus & Giroux, 1974); *Am: Amateurs* (New York: Farrar, Straus & Giroux, 1976). The original publication dates of the books are, respectively, 1964, 1967, 1968, 1970, 1972, 1974, and 1976. The story referred to in the text appears in *Sadness*.

4. Philip Stevick, ed., *Anti-Story: An Anthology of Experimental Fiction* (New York: Free Press, 1971), p. xx.

5. Ronald Sukenick, "The New Tradition in Fiction," in *Surfiction: Fiction Now . . . and Tomorrow*, ed. Raymond Federman (Chicago: Swallow Press, 1975), pp. 43-44.

6. The Donald Barthelme interview (with Jerome Klinkowitz) appears in Joe David Bellamy, ed., *The New Fiction: Interviews with Innovative American Writers* (Urbana: University of Illinois Press, 1974), p. 52. The interview will be referred to hereafter as *TNF*.

7. On collage, see Richard Schickel, "Freaked Out on Barthelme," *New York Times Magazine*, 16 August 1970, p. 42, and Barthelme's remarks in his interview (*TNF*, pp. 51-52). In the same interview (*TNF*, p. 53), Barthelme denies that the statement "Fragments are the only forms I trust" (*UP*, p. 164), is "a statement of [his] aesthetic." It is worth reading the fantastic "recantation" he then goes on to make.

8. Edmund Carpenter, *They Became What They Beheld* (New York: Ballantine Books, 1970), n. pag.

9. Clement Greenberg, "Modernist Painting," in *The New Art: A Critical Anthology*, ed. Gregory Battcock, rev. ed. (New York: Dutton & Co., 1973), pp. 68-69.

10. Virginia Woolf, "Mr. Bennett and Mrs. Brown," in *Collected Essays*, ed. Leonard Woolf, 4 vols. (New York: Harcourt, Brace & World, 1967), 1:327.

11. Maurice Merleau-Ponty, "Indirect Language and the Voices of Silence," in *Signs*, trans. Richard C. McCleary (Evanston, Ill.: Northwestern University Press, 1964), p. 54. Further references to Merleau-Ponty are to texts I've already cited: *PhP: Phenomenology of Perception; PP: The Primacy of Perception*.

12. Lawrence Alloway, *American Pop Art* (New York: Collier Books, 1974), p. 7.

13. Clive Bell, *Art* (New York: Capricorn Books, 1958), p. 54.

14. Tony Tanner, *City of Words: American Fiction, 1950-1970* (New York: Harper & Row, 1971), p. 402.

15. Pierre Thévenaz, *What Is Phenomenology? and Other Essays*, ed. James M. Edie (Chicago: Quadrangle Books, 1962), p. 50.

16. The phrase is the title of a collection of essays on the thought of Merleau-Ponty edited by Garth Gillan (Carbondale: Southern Illinois University Press, 1973).

INDEX